The New
CAMBRIDGE
English Course

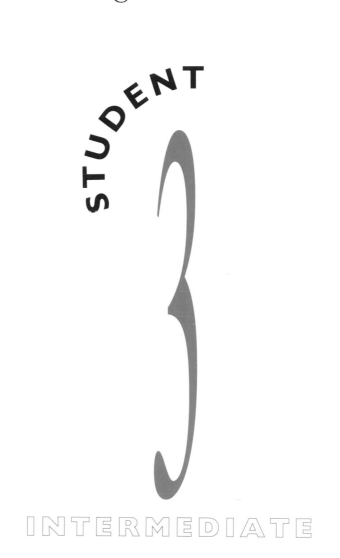

STUDENT

3

INTERMEDIATE

MICHAEL SWAN
CATHERINE WALTER

CAMBRIDGE
UNIVERSITY PRESS

Contents

3

Map of Book 3

	Grammar	Phonology
	Students learn or revise these grammar points	**Students work on these aspects of pronunciation**
Block A	Present and past tenses: terminology, formation and use; non-progressive verbs; infinitives and -ing forms after verbs; -ing forms after prepositions; -ing forms as subjects; verb + object + infinitive; modal auxiliaries; distancing use of past tenses; reported statements and questions.	Problems with sound/spelling relationships; perception and pronunciation of unstressed syllables; stress and rhythm; decoding rapid speech; /əʊ/ and /ɒ/.
Block B	Present Perfect for reporting 'news'; can with verbs of sensation; tenses of there is; use of -ing forms for activities; imperatives; comparative structures: worse and worst; question tags; position of prepositions in questions and relative structures; leaving out object relative pronouns; building sentences with conjunctions and -ing forms; adverbials of degree; so do I, neither do I etc.	Stress and rhythm; /ə/ in unstressed syllables; vowel and consonant linking; intonation of question tags; /ð/ and /θ/.
Block C	Simple Past and Past Progressive; Simple Past tenses with as; Present Perfect Progressive; passives; hypothetical if-clauses with Simple Past and would; modal verbs, including will have to; should(n't) and must(n't); won't for refusals; infinitive of purpose; how to ...; imperative; by ...ing; two-word verbs.	Stress and rhythm; perception and pronunciation of unstressed syllables; stress for emphasis and contrast; weak and strong forms; initial consonant groups; final consonant groups; difficult pronunciation/spelling relationships.
Block D	Present Perfect Simple and Progressive; have to and modal verbs; modal verbs with perfect infinitives; past conditionals; reporting with infinitives; would you rather ...?; frequency adverbs; connecting adverbs and conjunctions; prepositions of movement.	Stress and rhythm; word stress; perception and pronunciation of unstressed syllables; assimilation of consonants and linking; vowel linking with /r/, /j/ and /w/; /ɪ/ and /iː/; /ɜː/ and /eə/; pronunciations of the letter o.
Block E	Past Progressive: use and pronunciation; will-future; it'll and there'll; passive infinitives after modal verbs; contractions; reported speech with would and had; position of frequency adverbs; use of noun, verb or adjective to express the same idea; word order: verb, object and adverb; verbs with two objects; punctuation.	Stress and rhythm; pronunciation of contractions; /h/; typical pronunciations of vowel letters; weak forms.

Functions and specific skills

Students learn or revise ways of doing these things

Topics and notions

Students learn to talk about

Vocabulary

In addition to revising vocabulary taught at earlier levels, students will learn 900 or more new words and expressions during their work on Level 3 of the course.

Grammar Revision

A *Grammar Revision Section* on pages 116–129 gives further practice on elementary grammar points which were covered at earlier levels.

Requesting and giving personal information; making and replying to requests and offers; making corrections; reporting; asking to be reminded; asking about English; expressing degrees of formality; seeing a text as a whole; skimming; reading and listening for specific information; guessing unknown words; using dictionaries; managing discussion; predicting.

Physical appearance; food and drink; weather; animals; wishes, hopes and ambitions; language and language learning; sports, games and leisure; proportion (e.g. *three out of twelve*); various time relations.

Giving advice and instructions; giving news; asking for personal information; asking for confirmation and agreement; expressing opinions; indicating shared and divergent opinions; evaluating; agreeing and disagreeing; asking for things without knowing the exact words; defining, describing and identifying; comparing; greeting and welcoming; operating mealtime conventions; leave-taking; reporting; building up and shaping narratives; dividing text into paragraphs; listening for gist and for specific information.

Likes and dislikes; news; emergencies; parts of a car; honesty; manipulations of objects and materials; processes; condition; obligation; purpose; method; degree; time relations: simultaneous and successive events.

Discussing problems and giving advice; giving instructions; dealing with misunderstandings; making and accepting formal and emphatic apologies; expressing opinions; making complaints; studying text structure; constructing narrative; guessing unknown words; using dictionaries; listening and note-taking.

Work and time-structuring; electrical appliances; household tips; families; boy- and girlfriends; problems with relationships; politics and authority; rules and regulations; driving and traffic regulations; obligation; purpose; method; processes; changes; various time relations.

Speculating about the past; criticising past behaviour; reporting instructions and advice; asking for and giving directions; asking about and expressing preferences; persuading; discussing illness; extracting the main ideas from a text; reading and listening for detail; guessing meaning from context; writing simple reports; writing personal letters.

Places and landscape; buildings and rooms; families; family relationships; games-playing; illness; crime; rules and regulations; obligation; frequency; spatial relations; movement; various time relations; driving.

Making and replying to requests and offers; predicting; reporting; asking for things without knowing the exact words; inviting and replying to invitations; expressing degrees of formality; scanning; listening for detail.

Weather; everyday objects; uses of objects; horoscopes; clothes and accessories; parts of the body; wildlife and conservation; the future; simultaneous past actions.

A1 Something in common

Requesting and giving personal information; asking for help; correcting misunderstandings; writing skills: description; listening skills: listening for gist; spelling and pronunciation.

1 Labels:

1. Write three words on a piece of paper that say something about you. Add a drawing if you want. Example:

engineer
skiing
cooking

2. Put the paper on yourself and look round you, reading labels and trying to find someone whose label has something in common with yours (if you can't, just find someone who looks nice!).
3. Interview the person, asking as many questions as you can – at least five questions about each word on the label. Make notes to help you remember the answers.

2 Find another pair of students, or report to a group. You and your partner should say everything you have learnt about each other from Exercise 1. You can ask your partner for help if you want. You can stop your partner if some of the information he or she gives is not correct. Useful expressions:

Asking for help:
I can't remember – what did you …?
Can you remind me: why did you leave …?
Where did you go …?

Correcting your partner:
Er, that's not quite right.
Well, I didn't exactly …
Excuse me, I didn't mean …

3 Vocabulary: people's appearance. Add as many words to each category as you can.

1. *Weight*: thin, ...
2. *Height*: tall, ...
3. *Eyes*: big, brown, ...
4. *Hair*: short, red, curly, ...
5. *Other*: pretty, ...

4 🔲 Look at these words. Many of them come in this lesson. In each group, do all four words have the same vowel sound or is one word different? Decide, check your answers with the recording, and practise saying the words.

1. hair	wear	learnt	where	5. said	weight	paper	say
2. curly	word	learnt	heard	6. big	pretty	thin	teach
3. eyes	height	right	weight	7. red	ate	went	said
4. tall	short	draw	talk				

5 Write a short report about the person you interviewed in Exercise 1. Start with a physical description. Then give the information you learnt about the person. Pass your description to another student or let your teacher put it up for students to read.

6 🔲 Song. Look at the picture. Which people are being described in the song?

Learn/revise: hair; eyes; height; weight; remember; remind; (hair:) grey, fair, red, black, brown, curly, wavy, straight, long, short; (eyes:) big, small, brown, blue, green, grey; short; tall; of medium height; thin; slim; overweight; pretty; plain; handsome; attractive; good-looking; general; I can't remember – what ...?; Can you remind me: why ...?; Er, that's not quite right; Well, I didn't exactly ...; Excuse me, I didn't mean ...

A2 Focus on systems

A choice of exercises: rules for the use of tenses; pronunciation of unstressed syllables; word-families.

GRAMMAR: USE OF TENSES

1 Do you know the names of the English present and past verb tenses? Try to match the examples with the names (there is more than one example of some tenses).

1. It *rains* nearly every day in winter.
2. When we were children, we usually *went* to the seaside for our summer holidays.
3. I *have* often *thought* of changing my job.
4. She was tired, because she *had been travelling* all day.
5. I *asked* her to come out for a drink, but she *was working*, so she couldn't.
6. Do you know that Phil *has written* a novel?
7. 'You look hot.' 'I've *been playing* tennis.'
8. It's *raining* again.
9. I *live* in Manchester, but I'm *staying* with my sister in Glasgow at the moment.
10. When he *spoke* to me, I realised that I *had seen* him before.
11. He's *been* to East Africa several times, so he speaks quite good Swahili.
12. Who *were* you *talking* to when I came in?
13. I'm *seeing* a lot of Mary these days.

A Simple Present
B Present Progressive
C Simple Past
D Past Progressive
E (Simple) Present Perfect
F Present Perfect Progressive
G (Simple) Past Perfect
H Past Perfect Progressive

… every day in winter.

2 Look at diagram A. It shows three different uses of the Simple Present Perfect tense. Which sentences from Exercise 1 are illustrated in the three parts of the diagram?
Look at diagram B. Which tense does it illustrate? Can you make a similar diagram for one of the other tenses?

A

PAST — ×— ×— ×— ×— ×— ×— ×— ×— ×— ×— NOW
events repeated up to now

PAST — × ——————— RESULT ————→ NOW
past events with a result now

PAST ————— × ——— NEWS ————→ NOW
past events that are still 'news'

B

PAST — × ——————————————— × ————— NOW
'second', earlier past

3 Which tenses would you choose for the following situations?

1. to talk about one of your habits
2. to talk about one of your childhood habits
3. to give news of a success in an examination
4. to answer a question about your movements at midday yesterday
5. to explain that you are tired because of a game of football
6. to explain that you were tired yesterday evening because of a game of football
7. to say that you can't go dancing because of an accident

4 Can you explain these two exceptions?

1. I **want** to go home.
   (~~I'm wanting to go home.~~)
2. How long **have** you **known** Debbie?
   (~~How long have you been knowing Debbie?~~)

When we were children …

5 Test yourself. Choose the right tenses for the following sentences. If you have problems, you may need to do some of the grammar revision exercises from pages 116–129.

1. 'Cigarette?' 'No, thanks. I *don't smoke / I'm not smoking*.'
2. What *do you do / are you doing* in my room?
3. I've had a postcard from Ann. She says they *have / are having* a great time in Canada.
4. He told me *he gets married / he's getting married* next year, but *I don't think / I'm not thinking* it's true.
5. '*Have you been / Were you* here before?' 'No, it's my first visit.'
6. I *am waiting / have been waiting* for Jill to phone since six o'clock.
7. 'Why is your hair all wet?' 'I *swam / have swum / have been swimming*.'
8. *Did you hear? / Have you heard?* John *had / has had* an accident yesterday.
9. He *drove / was driving* down High Street when the car in front of him *suddenly stopped / was suddenly stopping*.
10. When she came in I asked her where she *was / has been / had been*, but she wouldn't tell me.

PRONUNCIATION: HEARING UNSTRESSED SYLLABLES

6 🔲 Listen to the recording. How many words do you hear in each sentence? (Contractions like *don't* count as two words.)

VOCABULARY: WORD-FAMILIES

7 Can you divide these words into four groups, and give each group a name?

bear	butter	camel	carrot	cheek
chin	chop	cloud	elephant	flour
fog	hail	hip	horse	lemon	lettuce
lightning	mouse	moustache
orange juice	pineapple	rabbit	rat
snow	squirrel	stomach	sunshine
thumb	thunder	toe	tongue	wind

8 Choose one of the groups. Work with other students, and see how many words you can add. (Time limit five minutes.)

Learn/revise: *the vocabulary in Exercise 7.*

A3 Would you like to have ...?

Expressing wishes and hopes; spoken and written reports; verbs with infinitives and *-ing* forms; reported speech; pronunciation of /əʊ/ and /ɒ/; looking at vocabulary learning.

1 Work in small groups. Without using a dictionary, see how many names of jobs you can think of in English. Use a dictionary to add ten more useful words to your list. Exchange lists with another group. Do you know all their words?

2 🔲 Read the text and try to guess what words might go in the blanks. Then listen to the recording and see if you were right.

Twenty five-year-old children from a British primary school class were asked what they wanted to be when they grew up. The answers were varied and interesting. Seven of the children had medical ambitions – there were four future ......1......, one ......2......, one ......3...... and one 'air force doctor'. Two children wanted to be ......4...... – not very surprising, as the school is in a small country village. Two of the children obviously liked school: they wanted to be ......5....... One child said he would like to be an ......6......, one hoped to be a ......7...... driver and one had decided to become a fisherman. Of the rest, two did not know what they wanted to be, and four gave rather unexpected answers.

3 What do/did you want to be or do in life? Write three or more sentences (using some of the following structures) and give them to the teacher. Then try to guess whose sentences the teacher is reading.

I want(ed) to be ...
I want(ed) to study ...
I want(ed) to ...
I hope to ...
I would like/love/hate to ...
I would like to start / stop / keep on ...ing
I expect to ...
My parents/teachers want(ed) me to ...
and I still want to
but I changed my mind
My parents don't/didn't mind what I do/did.
I think I have a good chance (of ...ing)
I don't think I have much chance.
When I leave school, I'll ...
I think/hope I'll ...
When I retire, I'm going to ...

4 📼 Put the words into the two groups and practise pronouncing them. One word does not belong in either of the groups.

GROUP 1 /əʊ/	GROUP 2 /ɒ/
no	not
open	often
…	…

don't	go	gone	got	grow	hope
job	know	lost	most	on	one
over	road	stop	want	what	won't

5 Survey. Choose three of the things in the box (or think of three other things) and ask some other students if they would like them. Examples:

'Would you like to have a silver Rolls-Royce?'
'Yes, I would.'

'Would you like to be famous?'
'No, I certainly wouldn't.'

'Would you like to stay in bed all day?'
'I'd love/hate to.'

to have:	more money a different job
	more free time a better love-life
	(more) children more patience
	your picture in a magazine
	political power a different house/flat
	more friends a private plane
	a silver Rolls-Royce a big motorbike
	two wives/husbands
to be:	famous an artist three years old
	more sensible
to:	stay in bed all day live to be 100
	speak a lot of languages travel a lot
	own a museum

6 Write a short report giving the results of your survey. Use some words and expressions from Exercise 2. Other useful structures:

> Three people out of six want …
> One person would like …
> Everybody/Nobody would like / wants …
> (Almost) everybody
> Hardly anybody
> The only exception was …, who would like …
> Most people said they would like / wanted …
> Nobody said they wanted …
> One person said he/she would like …

When you have finished your report, show it to other people in the class.

7 Learning vocabulary. How do you usually like to a) note and b) learn new words? Work with two or three other students and see how many ways you can think of.

Reported speech. Compare:
– Three people **want** to be doctors.
  Three people **said** they **wanted** to be doctors.
  (~~… said they want to be doctors.~~)
– I **hope** to go to university.
  Annette **said** she **hoped** to go to university.
– What **do you want** to be?
  Twenty children **were asked what they wanted** to be. (~~… what did they want to be.~~)
– Phil **would like** to be a painter.
  Phil **said** he **would like** to be a painter.

Learn/revise: actor; artist; dentist; driver; farmer; husband; job; nurse; chance; country; exception; free time; magazine; motorbike; parents; patience; power; primary school; village; wife (wives); change one's mind; expect; grow up (grew, grown); keep on …ing (kept, kept); leave school (left, left); (don't) mind; own; retire; famous; unexpected; varied; rather.

A4 Who should be paid most?

Reading and guessing unknown words; discussion.

1 Read the following text carefully, and try to get a general idea of what it says. Think about the meaning of the words and expressions that you don't know, but DO NOT use a dictionary or ask questions.

WORK AND PAY IN FANTASIA

I had a thought-provoking dream last night. In it, I was living in Fantasia – a place where people are paid according to their real value to society. There are some striking mismatches with what happens in other countries.

In Fantasia, doctors are paid for keeping people alive. A doctor is well rewarded as long as his or her patients stay healthy. But when a patient falls ill, the doctor's pay is reduced by half; and if a patient dies, the doctor has to pay massive compensation to the surviving spouse or relatives. Average life expectancy in Fantasia is 132, although doctors tend to die young.

Soldiers are paid on the same lines as doctors. In peacetime they get a reasonable wage, but as soon as war breaks out the government stops paying them. Officers earn far less than ordinary soldiers, and generals get least of all. This is because of the Fantasian principle that power is its own reward: people can have either money or power, but Fantasians avoid giving them both. Members of the House of Long Sentences (the Fantasian Parliament) get expenses payments, but no salary; the Prime Minister gets the least generous expenses.

Teachers' pay is worked out according to their teaching ability (pupils vote), their pupils' test results and the level at which they teach. On average, primary school teachers get double the pay of secondary school teachers, who in turn are wealthy by comparison with university teachers.

Housewives or househusbands receive a basic salary from the state, plus an extra 16,500 Fantasian Grotniks (about $4,500 US) annually for each small child in the family.

People who do dirty, strenuous, dull or distasteful work (e.g. rubbish collectors, coal miners, factory workers or sewage workers) are at the top of the Fantasian wages scale. Other highly-paid workers include gardeners (Fantasians like looking at flowers), hospital nurses and librarians. Among the poorest-paid workers are advertising agents, TV weather forecasters, traffic wardens and bank managers. Pop singers, who are all employed by the state, are paid starvation wages and allowed to give one concert a year (Fantasians don't like listening to loud noises).

The best-paid people in Fantasia are writers.

Guess what I do for a living.

3 Now choose ten more of the highlighted words or expressions from the text. (Don't choose words or expressions that you already know.) Write down what you think they might mean. Discuss your guesses with other students. What things in the text helped you to guess the meanings?

4 Work with two or three other students. Discuss which of the following should be paid most, which should be next best paid, and so on. You must produce an agreed group answer, listing the jobs in order of pay.

army general
rubbish collector
government minister
head of large factory
hospital nurse
policeman/policewoman
primary school teacher

2 Look at the way these words and expressions are used in the text: *thought-provoking, striking mismatches, rewarded, healthy*. Then decide which of the following explanations is most probably correct.

1. *a thought-provoking dream*
   a. an intelligent dream
   b. a dream that made me think
   c. a frightening dream
   d. a dream that was full of thoughts

2. *there are some striking mismatches*
   a. people don't strike so often
   b. there are frequent contacts
   c. there are some very interesting differences
   d. there are some important things that are the same

3. *a doctor is well rewarded*
   a. doctors get plenty of money
   b. people think doctors are important
   c. plenty of people go to see doctors
   d. doctors are well trained

4. *healthy*
   a. satisfied with the way the doctor treats them
   b. well
   c. ill
   d. well paid

5 Choose a job, and talk for two minutes giving reasons why your job should be the best paid one in the country.

Learn/revise: ability; coal miner; concert; dream; expenses; factory; gardener; head (= boss); level; minister; nurse; peace; policeman (policemen); policewoman (policewomen); power; primary school; rubbish; salary; society; soldier; value; wage; war; work; earn; guess; tend; vote; average; extra; full; generous; healthy; reasonable; annually; double; according to; (far) less; least.

13

A5 Language: what matters most

Speaking and writing skills practice; thinking about language and language learning; asking about English.

1 Find out something new about English. Ask at least one question, using one of the following structures.

What does ... mean?
What's this?
What are these?
What's this called in English?
Is this a pen or a pencil?
How do you say ... in English?
What's the English for ...?
What do you say when ...?
Can you explain this word/expression/sentence?
How do you pronounce ...?
How do you spell ...?
Is this correct: ...?

2 Language learning – what is important to you? Write your answers to the two following questions and give your answers to the teacher.

1. What is your main reason for learning English (in one sentence)?
2. How important is each of the following to you? Give each activity a number from 1 (unimportant) to 5 (extremely important).

   speaking
   understanding spoken English
   writing
   reading

3 Read quickly through the questionnaire. Then do section A, B, C or D.

LANGUAGE PRIORITIES QUESTIONNAIRE

A SPEAKING

Interview a student for whom speaking is important. Find out:

1. How important (1–5) each of the following is: a) natural speed b) a correct accent c) good grammar d) a wide vocabulary.
2. In which countries he/she expects to speak English, and with what kinds of people.
3. If he/she expects to speak English mostly with native speakers (e.g. British, Australian or American people) or mostly with non-native speakers.
4. If he/she expects to use English mostly for business or professional purposes, for travel, for social contacts, or for other reasons (what?).
5. If he/she expects to use English: a) in ordinary conversation b) on the telephone c) in meetings d) to give lectures or demonstrations.
6. What subjects he/she wants to be able to talk about in English.
7. If he/she needs to know the specialist vocabulary of any subjects (which?).
8. If he/she finds it especially difficult to speak English (and if so, why).
9. If he/she has any other information to give you.

B UNDERSTANDING SPOKEN ENGLISH

Interview a student for whom understanding spoken English is important. Find out:

1. How important (1–5) it is to understand each of the following: a) conversations b) phone calls c) TV/radio d) songs e) lectures f) other things (what?).
2. What accents he/she needs to understand.
3. If he/she needs to know the specialist vocabulary of any subjects (which?).
4. If he/she finds it especially difficult to understand spoken English (and if so, why).
5. If he/she has any other information to give you.

C WRITING

Interview a student for whom writing is important. Find out:

1. How important (1–5) each of the following is: a) correct spelling b) correct grammar c) a wide vocabulary.
2. What he/she wants to be able to write in English (business letters, personal letters, examination answers, academic essays, professional papers/reports, ...?).
3. What subjects he/she wants to be able to write about.
4. If he/she needs to know the specialist vocabulary of any subjects (which?).
5. If he/she finds it especially difficult to write English (and if so, why).
6. If he/she has any other information to give you.

D READING

Interview a student for whom reading is important. Find out:

1. How important (1–5) each of the following is: a) fast reading b) exact understanding of every word c) a wide vocabulary.
2. What kind of things he/she expects to read in English (newspapers, novels, letters, reports, technical manuals, ...?).
3. What subjects he/she expects to read about.
4. If he/she finds it especially difficult to read English (and if so, why).
5. If he/she needs to know the specialist vocabulary of any subjects (which?).
6. If he/she has any other information to give you.

4 Write a short report about the student you interviewed, and give it to the teacher. This will help him/her to plan a suitable English course for the class.

5 Work in groups of three or four. In each group, choose one of the activities (speaking, understanding spoken English, writing or reading). Discuss good ways of learning to do this activity better, and write some suggestions for the teacher. Ask for help if necessary.

6 If you speak a language that the other students don't know, prepare and give a short lesson to the class. Discuss the lesson afterwards: did you find out anything about language learning and teaching?

Learn/revise: accent; business; contact; conversation; demonstration; essay; examination; grammar; information; lecture; meeting; novel; purpose; reason (for sth); report; sentence; song; speed; spelling; subject; suggestion; technical manual; travel; vocabulary; choose (chose, chosen); discuss; plan; correct; difficult; exact; important; main; natural; professional; social; specialist; suitable; wide; especially; extremely; mostly; for ... reason; *the questions in Exercise 1.*

A6 Focus on systems

A choice of exercises: word-families; infinitives and *-ing* forms; pronunciation of /əʊ/.

VOCABULARY: SPORTS, GAMES AND LEISURE

1 Do you know the names of these sports, games and leisure activities? How many more can you think of?

GRAMMAR: INFINITIVES AND *-ING* FORMS

2 Some of the sentences in the box have infinitives and the others have *-ing* forms. Look at the rules, and decide which one gives the best explanation.

> I would love **to learn** judo.
> We expect **to win** the basketball championship.
> If you want **to camp** here, you have to register at the office.
> I like **dancing**.
> When did you start **playing** the piano?
> I'm going to stop **boxing** – I'm getting too old.

Rules
1. We use infinitives to say what people do, and *-ing* forms to say what happens to people.
2. We use *-ing* forms to talk about the present and past, and infinitives to talk about the future.
3. We use *-ing* forms after most verbs.
4. We use infinitives after most verbs.
5. We use infinitives after some verbs and *-ing* forms after others.

3 Do we normally use infinitives or *-ing* forms after these verbs?

be able   enjoy   expect   hope   keep on
learn   need   would like

4 Do we normally use infinitives or *-ing* forms as subjects of sentences? Which of the following sentences seem most natural?

1. Skiing is my favourite sport.
   To ski is my favourite sport.
2. Learning a language is a lot of work.
   To learn a language is a lot of work.
3. Running makes me tired.
   To run makes me tired.

Give examples of: your favourite activities; things that are hard work; things that make you happy or tired.

5 Look at the following sentences. Can you make a rule?

In Fantasia, doctors are paid **for keeping** people
  alive.
He is thinking **of taking up** water-skiing.
What's your main reason **for learning** English?
I've got a good chance **of getting** into university.
Thank you **for helping** me.
I'm not very good **at swimming**.
It's difficult to make money **without working**.

Now complete these sentences:

1. I'm (not) very interested in ...ing.
2. I'm thinking of ...ing next weekend / next week /
   next year.
3. Do you think I've got a good chance of ...ing ...?
4 I'm (not) very good at ...ing.
5. I couldn't live without ...ing.

6 Look at the pictures. In one of them, a woman wants some people to sign a
paper. (NOT ~~A woman wants that some people sign a paper.~~) Which picture is it?
Can you make sentences yourself for the other pictures?

PRONUNCIATION: /əʊ/

7 🔲 Listen to the words and try to pronounce them correctly.

no   go   so   hope   know   broke   spoke   over   don't   won't
open   closed   Rome   phone

8 🔲 Now listen to the definitions and say which words the speaker is talking
about.

9 Practise the sentences. Then answer the teacher's
questions, and make up similar questions for other
students.

I think so.	I don't think so.	I hope so.
I hope not.	I don't know.	No.
No, I don't.	No, I won't.	

Learn/revise: *some of the vocabulary from
Exercise 1.*

17

A7 Could you do me a favour?

Conversation skills (requests, offers and replies; formal and informal language);
listening skills (stress and rhythm); modal auxiliary verbs.

1 🔲 Complete the conversation with the words and expressions in the box.
Then listen to the recording and check your answers.

PAUL: Hey, John.
JOHN: Yeah?
PAUL: ....?
JOHN: Sure. What is it?
PAUL: Well, ..., I'm .... until Friday.
        ...., do you think?
JOHN: Yes, OK.
PAUL: ...., John. Thanks ....
JOHN: ....

> the thing is   a lot
> Could you do me a favour
> That's all right
> That's very nice of you
> short of money
> Could you lend me £10

2 🔲 Read the following conversation. Which words or parts of words do you
think are stressed? Mark the stresses, listen to the recording and check your
answers. Then practise the conversation in pairs.

ANNIE: Excuse me. I'm s̲orry to t̲rouble you.
            We've got a problem.
MR OLIVER: Oh, yes? What's the matter?
ANNIE: Well, you see, it's like this. We're cycling,
            and we haven't got anywhere to sleep
            tonight.
MR OLIVER: I see. Have you tried the Crown Hotel?
ANNIE: Yes, but it's much too expensive. So we
            wondered if we could sleep in your barn.
MR OLIVER: Yes, all right. I don't mind. You don't
            smoke, do you?
ANNIE: Oh, no. Neither of us do. Well, thank you
            very much.
MR OLIVER: Not at all. Would you like to come into
            the house for a wash?
ANNIE: Oh, that's very kind of you.
MR OLIVER: This way.

3 📼 Close your books, listen to the recording and write the words and expressions that you hear.

4 Can you find some examples of informal and formal language in the two conversations?

INFORMAL
Hey
Yeah?
...

FORMAL
Excuse me
Oh, yes?
...

5 Can you make these conversations more formal? The expressions in the box will help. Example:

INFORMAL: *'Give me your coat.'* *'Here.'*
FORMAL: *'Shall I take your coat?'*
'Oh, thank you. Here you are.'

1. 'Have some coffee.' 'Yeah, thanks.'
2. 'Can I use your phone?' 'Sure.'
3. 'Do you want to dance?' 'OK.'
4. 'Pass the salt.' 'Here.'
5. 'I'll open it for you.' 'Thanks.'
6. 'More bread?' 'No.'
7. 'Want a drink?' 'Yes, OK.'
8. 'Orange juice?' 'No, water.'

> Shall I ...?
> Would you like ...?
> Could I/you (possibly) ...?
> I wonder(ed) if I/you could ...?
> Would you mind ...ing?
> I'd love one/some.
> I'd love to.
> I'd prefer ...
> That would be very nice.
> Of course.
> Here you are.

6 Do one of the following activities.

EITHER: Prepare a conversation with another student. One of you offers something or asks for something, and the other answers. First act out the conversation *without speaking*. The other students will try to decide what the words are. Then act your conversation again with the words.

OR: Prepare a conversation with one or two other students. The conversation must begin *'I'm/We're sorry to trouble you'* or *'Could you do me/us a favour?'*. Use plenty of words and expressions from the lesson. You must also bring into your conversation at least two of the things in the pictures, and at least two of the sentences in the box.

> We've got a problem.
> It makes too much noise.
> We need at least six.
> It's a funny green colour.
> You are so beautiful.
> I don't like children.
> You see, it's Thursday.

> **Learn/revise:** barn; favour; problem; wash (*noun*); cycle; lend (lent, lent); offer; prepare; wonder; expensive; *expressions from Exercises 1, 2 and 5.*

A8 I told you a bit of a lie

Reading skills: reading for gist, for main ideas, predicting, dictionary skills; listening for gist; oral fluency.

1 Read the article. Don't take more than five minutes. You can use a dictionary or ask the teacher for help (but try to guess the meaning of a word first).

Parachutist, 81, wins place of honour at jump

Even experts were a little surprised when a man of 62 turned up at a parachute training school and said he was interested in learning to become a parachutist.

They agreed to put him through the course, but only after giving him a series of tests to prove that he was fit enough.

Mr Archie Macfarlane completed the course successfully, surprising everyone with his agility and toughness.

A few weeks later, when he was ready for his first jump, he confessed to the chief instructor: "I told you a bit of a lie. I'm really 75."

That was six years ago and yesterday Archie Macfarlane made his 18th jump. He was given the place of honour – first out of the plane – at a weekend meeting for parachutists over 40 years old.

Archie's interest in parachuting is just one of the hobbies that his wife has to worry about. He also enjoys motorcycling and mountaineering.

Last year he fell while climbing on Snowdon, and had to be rescued by helicopter.

His daughter said: "Sometimes I think he ought to give it all up. But as my mother says, so long as he's happy, it's better than being miserable. He tried hang-gliding once and said he thought it was a bit too easy."

Now Archie is thinking of taking up water-skiing.

(adapted from a press report)

2 Here are some dictionary definitions of words from the article. Each word has more than one definition. Choose the definition that fits each of the words in the article best. Do you know what the abbreviations in the definitions mean?

fit /fɪt/ **1** *v* to be the right size or shape (for): *This dress doesn't fit me.* **2** *n* the way in which something fits: *This coat's a beautiful fit.* **3** *n* a short attack (of a slight illness or violent feeling): *a fit of coughing | She hit him in a fit of anger.* **4** *adj* in good health or bodily condition: *She runs three miles every morning; that's why she's so fit.*

take sbdy./sthg. **up** /teɪk ˈʌp/ *v adv* [T] **1** to begin to do; interest oneself in: *John took up writing poetry while at school.* **2** to fill; use: *The work took up the whole of Sunday.* **3** to continue: *I'll take up the story where I left off.*

tough /tʌf/ *adj* **1** strong; not easily weakened: *These mountain sheep are very tough.* **2** difficult to cut or eat: *tough meat –* opposite **tender 3** difficult to do; demanding effort: *a tough job*

4 rough; hard: *The government will get tough with people who avoid paying taxes.* **5** *infml* too bad; unfortunate: *Tough luck!* – **toughly** *adv* – **toughness** *n* (U)

turn up /ˈtɜːn ˈʌp/ *v adv* **1** [T] (**turn** sthg. **up**) to find: *to turn up new information* **2** [I] to be found: *The missing bag turned up, completely empty, in the river.* **3** [T] (**turn** sthg. **up**) to shorten (a piece of clothing) – compare TURN-UP **4** [I] to arrive: *He turns up late for everything.* | *Don't worry, something will turn up.* (= happen) **5** [T] (**turn** sthg. **up**) to increase the force, strength, loudness, etc., of (a radio, heating system, etc.) by using controls

(adapted from *Longman Active Study Dictionary of English*)

3 Re-read the article, using a dictionary where necessary. Then read these three summaries of the article. Which one is the best summary? Why are the other two not so good?

1. Archie Macfarlane started parachuting when he was 75 (although he said he was younger), and he has done 18 parachute jumps over the last six years. Recently he was given the place of honour at a parachutists' meeting. His wife and daughter are worried about him.
2. Archie Macfarlane is an unusual person. Although he is an old man, he is interested in very tough sporting activities like parachuting, mountaineering and water-skiing. His wife and daughter are worried, but think it's best for him to do things that make him happy.
3. When Archie Macfarlane first learnt parachute jumping, he pretended that he was only 62. In fact, he is much older than that, and he is really becoming too old to take part in outdoor sporting activities. His wife and daughter wish that he would stop motorcycling, mountaineering and hang-gliding.

4 Choose at least seven words and expressions to learn from the article in Exercise 1. Work with another student and compare your lists. Talk about the reasons for your choices. Useful expressions:

I think this word is important.
This is a useful expression.
This is a very common word.
I like the sound of this word.
I'm interested in parachuting.

5 Look at this picture, and read the beginning of the article about Janice Burton. How do you think the report will continue?

Blind swimming champion to ride dressage in Greece

Janice Burton, former Special Olympic swimming champion, has been training hard for another sport.

6 🔲 Make sure you know the meanings of the words in the box. Then read the questions below and listen to the interview with Janice Burton. You will only hear her answers, not the interviewer's questions. Match the questions to the answers and write down the correct order for the questions. Then listen to the complete interview to check.

> analyse   attract   compete   competent
> competition   competitive   cross country
> disabled   feel   hips   precise   skating

a. How did you learn that?
b. How often do you work with your horse?
c. What do you enjoy most about the dressage?
d. What first attracted you to this sport?
e. What has been your most exciting moment in dressage?
f. What is dressage exactly?
g. What's the most difficult thing about dressage for you?
h. You've been in quite a few competitions?

7 Work in pairs. Do one of the following tasks. Report to the class if there is time.

1. What sorts of sports (besides swimming and dressage!) could blind people participate in? Choose a sport that you both know about, and discuss how you could help a blind person take part in it. If the sport has rules, would you have to change any of them? Report what you decide to another pair.
2. Think of a shopping area in the town or city where you are studying. What could be done to make it easier for blind people to shop there? Talk with one another, trying to think of as many things as you can. Then report to another pair.

Learn/revise: area; article; champion; city; competition; expert; hips; hobby; lie; rescue; rule; town; training; skating; agree (to do sth); attract; compete; enjoy; feel (felt, felt); ride (rode, ridden); switch; take part in (took, taken); take (sth) up; turn up; blind; competent; competitive; disabled; fit; precise; tough; unusual; worried; outside; preferably; successfully.

Summary A

Rules for the use of present and past tenses

(See also diagrams in Lesson A2)

Simple Present

> repeated or permanent events: past, present and future

It **rains** nearly every day in winter.
I **live** in Manchester, but I'm staying with my sister in Glasgow at the moment.

Present Progressive

> temporary events happening just now, or just around now

It'**s raining** again.
I'**m seeing** a lot of Mary these days.

(Simple) Present Perfect

> events repeated up to now

I have often thought of changing my job.

> past events with a result now

He's been to East Africa several times, so he speaks quite good Swahili.

> past events that are still 'news'

Do you know that Phil **has written** a novel?

Present Perfect Progressive

> events repeated or continuing up to now, or up to a few moments ago

'You look hot.' 'I'**ve been playing** tennis.'

Simple Past

> events that happened one or more times in the past; no connection with now

I **asked** her to come out for a drink.
When we were children, we usually **went** to the seaside for our summer holidays.

Past Progressive

> events continuing around a particular time in the past

What **were** you **doing** this time yesterday?

> events already happening when something else happened

I asked her to come out for a drink, but she **was working**, so she couldn't.
The phone rang while I **was having** a bath.

(Simple) Past Perfect

> 'second', earlier past

When he spoke to me, I realised that I **had seen** him before.

Past Perfect Progressive

> events repeated or continuing 'up to then'

She was tired, because she **had been travelling** all day.

Non-progressive verbs

I **want** to go home. (~~I'm wanting to go home.~~)
How long **have you known** Debbie?
(~~How long have you been knowing Debbie?~~)

> Some other common non-progressive verbs: *like, see, love, hate, prefer, mean, remember, understand, hear, smell, sound, taste, seem*; some uses of *think* and *feel*.

Infinitives and *-ing* forms after verbs

> We use infinitives after some verbs and *-ing* forms after others.

> Examples of verbs usually followed by infinitives: *agree, be able, expect, have, hope, learn, need, want, would like, would love.*

She **agreed to help** me.
I **expect to do** badly in the exams.
I **would love to learn** Japanese.
If you **want to go** to China you **have to get** a visa.

> Examples of verbs usually followed by *-ing* forms: *enjoy, keep on, like, start, stop.*

I **like being** with you.
When did you **start playing** the piano?
When will you **stop smoking**?

Verb + object + infinitive

My parents **wanted me to study** medicine.
(~~My parents wanted that I study medicine.~~)
She **wants him to help** her.
(~~She wants that he helps her.~~)

-ing forms as subjects

Skiing is my favourite sport. (~~To ski is ...~~)
Learning a language is a lot of work.
Running makes me tired.

-ing forms after prepositions

> We use *-ing* forms after all prepositions.

In Fantasia, doctors are paid **for keeping** people alive.
He is thinking **of taking up** water-skiing.
I'm not very good **at swimming**.
It's difficult to make money **without working**.

Reported statements and questions

- Three people **want** to be doctors.
  Three people said they **wanted** to be doctors.
  (~~... said they want to be doctors.~~)
- What **do you want** to be?
  Twenty children were asked **what they wanted** to be. (~~... what did they want to be.~~)
- How important **is** each of the following?
  Find out how important each of the following **is**. (~~... how important is each of the following.~~)

Modal auxiliary verbs

Can I **use** your phone? (~~Can I to use ...?~~)
Could you **lend** me £10? (~~Could you lending ...?~~)
Could you do me a favour?
Shall I take your coat?
I'll open it for you.
Would you like ...?

Irregular verbs in Lessons A1–A8

INFINITIVE	PAST	PAST PARTICIPLE
choose	chose	chosen
feel	felt	felt
grow	grew	grown
keep	kept	kept
leave	left	left
lose	lost	lost
mean	meant	meant
say	said	said
spell	spelt	spelt
wear	wore	worn

Asking about English

What does ... mean?
What's this?
What are these?
What's this called in English?
Is this a pen or a pencil?
How do you say ... in English?
What's the English for ...?
What do you say when ...?
Can you explain this word/expression/sentence?
How do you pronounce ...?
How do you spell ...?
Is this correct: ...?

Asking for help

I can't remember. What ...?
Can you remind me? Why ...?

Correcting

Er, that's not quite right.
Well, I didn't exactly say ...
Excuse me, I didn't mean ...

Reporting surveys

Three people out of twelve ...
Most people want ...
Everybody wants ... (~~Everybody want ...~~)
Nobody wants ... (~~Nobody want ...~~)
almost everybody
hardly anybody
The only exception was ...

Requests, offers and replies

Formal
'Shall I take your coat?' 'Oh, thank you.'
'Would you like ...?' 'I'd love one/some.'
                      'I'd love to.'
                      'I'd prefer ...'
                      'That would be very nice.'
'Excuse me. I'm sorry to trouble you.'
'Could I/you (possibly) ...?' 'Of course.'
                              'Here you are.'
'I wonder(ed) if I/you could ...?' 'Yes, all right. I don't mind.'
'Would you mind ...ing?' 'Not at all.'
'That's very kind of you.' 'Not at all.'
'Well, thank you very much.' 'Not at all.'

Informal
'Have some coffee.' 'Yeah, thanks.'
'Can I use your phone?' 'Sure.'
'Do you want to dance?' 'OK.'
'Pass the salt.' 'Here.'
'More bread?' 'No.'
'Want a drink?' 'Yes, OK.'
'Orange juice?' 'No, water.'
'I'll open it for you.' 'Thanks.'
'Could you do me a favour?'

Vocabulary

> Look through the 'Learn/revise' boxes at the ends of Lessons A1–A8.

Revision and fluency practice A

A choice of activities.

1 Story in sound. Listen to the recorded sounds. Then try to write down everything you heard in the correct order.

2 Half-dictation. The teacher will dictate the first half of each sentence; you decide how to continue and write the rest.

3 Exchanging photos. Work in groups; show the other students photos of your family and friends. Talk about your own photos and ask questions about the others.

4 Follow-up questions. Prepare questions using *Are you ...?*, *Can you ...?* and *Have you got ...?* Talk to at least two students and ask your questions. After each question has been answered, ask two or more 'follow-up questions'. Examples:

'Have you got a car?' *'Yes, I have.'*
'What sort of car? What colour is it?'

5 Which one is different? Can you find a reason why each one of the words in the box is different from all the others? Examples:

'A cow is the only one that has horns.'
'A lion is the only one that is dangerous to people.'

| horse   cat   mouse   camel   lion   cow |

Now do the same for one of these boxes.

| India   China   the USA   France   Egypt   Israel |

| apple   orange   strawberry   banana
grape   peach |

| fridge   piano   armchair   car   bus   table |

| nose   ear   arm   hand   mouth   foot |

| London   Paris   Copenhagen   Beijing   Rio |

6 Look at the advertisements. Do you believe what they say? Possible answers:

'I'm sure it's true.'   *'It might be true.'*
'It's probably true.'   *'It's probably not true.'*
'It may be true.'   *'It can't be true.'*

Make up similar advertisements yourselves in groups.

223052.
WHITE MAGIC MAKES IT HAPPEN! For help with love, money etc, send date of birth, lock of hair, £10 and stamped addressed envelope

SPEAK A NEW LANGUAGE IN ONLY THREE WEEKS! *Have you ever wished you could*

MAKE $1,000,000 FAST! For details, send $8 to

Your hands hold the key to your future! To know about your love life, call 071-276 4530

BUCKETS OF MONEY
FROM MR GLO'S SLOT MACHINES
IT'S TRUE - you will collect your slot machine takings in strong buckets! 'Mr Glo' puts slot machines in your own town ... **For you to collect cash!** Start P/time - 2-3 hrs/wk gives a remarkable income. Add machines gradually to become Full-time (10 hrs will be enough)
NO OVERHEADS, NO PREMISES, NO WORRIES.
MIN INVEST £7,000 AV INVEST £10,000
Phone for brochure
(0742) 723666 24 HOURS
GLO-LEISURE LTD
Glo-Leisure Ltd., Glomel House, 58-64 Penistone Road, Sheffield S6 3AE
Mr. GLO

The lazy way to a great body!
Would you like to make your body beautiful with no exercise or dieting?

College degrees by mail!
Legal, fast, inexpensive.
Bachelors, Masters, Doctorates. Free brochure from The University of

24

7 Are you a good detective?

1. The police stop a car. There are three people in the car: John, Ann and Mary. On the back seat there is a pistol. John says 'It's mine.' Ann says 'It's hers.' Mary says 'It's his.' Nobody is telling the truth. Whose is the pistol?
2. In the car, the police find a diamond necklace, a valuable painting and a fur coat. The police find out that they belong to a film star, a businessman and a doctor. The diamonds don't belong to the doctor. The coat doesn't belong to the businessman. The painting belongs to a woman. The film star never wears fur coats. Who does the painting belong to?

8 Question box. Each student writes three questions on separate pieces of paper. One of the questions must begin *Have you ever ...*, and one must begin *Do you ...* The questions are folded up and put in a box. Students take turns to draw out questions and answer them.

9 Discussion. Look at the following statements. Try to find two with which you agree strongly, and two with which you disagree strongly. Find somebody who has a different opinion from you about one of your four statements, and spend five minutes trying to change his/her view.

Everybody should know how to cook.
The speed limit should be lower.
Education should be more practical.
Everybody in the world should learn English.
Children over 14 should be free to do what they like.
It is always wrong to tell lies.
Smoking should be banned in all public places.
Censorship is always wrong.
Divorce should be easier.
It is always wrong to smack a child.
You should fight for your country if you are asked to.

10 Mime. Work in groups of three. Each group must prepare and act out (without words) a scene in which they are having trouble with a large object. The others must decide what the object is.

11 Sketches. Work in small groups. Prepare and practise a conversation which takes place in one of the following situations: at an airport, in a clothes shop, at dinner, at a hotel reception desk, in a garage. The conversation must include the following: a problem, a misunderstanding, an interruption. When you are ready, act out your conversation for the rest of the class.

12 Look at the cartoons. Tell other students what you think about them. Find out which are the most and least popular cartoons. Useful expressions:

I don't see the joke.
What do you think of this one?
This one's really funny.
It isn't funny at all.
I think it's wonderful/stupid.
It makes / doesn't make me laugh.

"Now if the passengers on the left hand side will put their left arms through the windows and do this – while those on the right hand side ..."

"Your bath's ready, dear."

Test A

LISTENING

1 📼 **Make sure you know what the words and expressions in this box mean. Then listen to the recording. Who does each speaker think should be paid most?**

> army general   rubbish collector
> government minister   head of large factory
> hospital nurse   policeman/policewoman
> primary school teacher

Now make sure you know what these expressions mean. Listen to the recording again. Which jobs are they used to talk about? Can you write down at least two other things that the speakers say about the jobs?

a. demanding job
b. long hours
c. not be paid at all if …
d. one of the most important jobs
e. paid a very good wage
f. taken very seriously
g. thankless job
h. very poorly paid

GRAMMAR

2 **Choose the right tense for each verb.**

Last night I (1) *have seen / saw* an interesting programme on television. It (2) *has been / was* about a new way of teaching science subjects to schoolchildren. For three years now a school in London (3) *has been teaching / is teaching* science in this way to some of its students, and these students (4) *have done / did* significantly better in examinations than the students in ordinary classes. It (5) *is working / works* like this: students (6) *are not only learning / not only learn* about science, but are taught to think about their own way of thinking. One of the teachers on the programme said, 'Older good teaching methods (7) *have made / made* people think, but it (8) *has been / was* in a sense unconscious. When a child (9) *is having / has* to explain to somebody else how they have solved a problem, that really makes them think about their own thinking.'
Researchers (10) *are not fully understanding / do not fully understand* how the methods (11) *are working / work*. But marks in examinations (12) *have increased / increased* dramatically. Unfortunately, nothing (13) *is being done / is done* at the moment to train other teachers in the new methods.

3 **Infinitive or -*ing* form?**

1. I would like (*travel*) all over the world.
2. I think Mary has a good chance of (*win*) the election on Sunday.
3. We expect (*arrive*) at the station at 4.30 on Saturday.
4. Do you think Ann will agree (*have*) the meeting in her office?
5. If the phone doesn't stop (*ring*), I am going to throw it out of the window.
6. When did you start (*learn*) Chinese?
7. They hope (*go*) to the meeting in Helsinki next year.
8. Doesn't your brother want (*learn*) (*drive*)?
9. My sister likes (*swim*), but she doesn't like swimming pools.
10. My cousin doesn't really need (*work*), but he enjoys (*be*) around people and (*do*) something useful.
11. (*Eat*) fatty foods, (*drink*) alcohol and (*smoke*) are all bad for your heart.
12. After (*work*) all day, I don't really feel like going out again in the evening.

LANGUAGE IN USE

4 **In this dialogue, A is speaking formally and B is speaking informally. Change the dialogue to make it *either* all formal *or* all informal.**

A: Excuse me, Barbara. I'm sorry to trouble you, but I'm afraid I have a problem.
B: Yeah?
A: The thing is, I need to go to the doctor's and my car won't start. I wonder if I could possibly borrow yours?
B: Yeah, OK.
A: Thank you very much. That's really very kind of you.
B: Or do you want me to drive you?
A: Oh, yes, please. That would be very nice. Thank you so much.
B: OK. Want to leave now?
A: Well, yes, if it's not too much trouble. My appointment's at ten.
B: OK, give me my keys off that shelf and we can go.
A: Thank you so much, Barbara. Here you are.

5 **Write one sentence or question for each situation.**

1. Say something about what you want(ed) to do or be in life.
2. Say something about your parents' hopes for you.
3. What do you say to someone if you forget what they've told you?
4. What can you say to correct someone politely if they report something you haven't said?

26

PRONUNCIATION

6 In each group, have all the words got the same vowel sound or has one got a different sound? Write *S* for 'the same' or write the word that is different.

1. fair   where   wear   earn   *earn*
2. nurse   shirt   learn   word
3. eyes   weight   mind   height
4. tall   course   talk   draw
5. grey   red   plain   steak
6. don't   grow   hope   one
7. road   over   know   won't
8. want   lost   most   stop
9. not   what   often   gone

VOCABULARY

7 Match each word in column A with one or more words in column B.

A	B
artist	accent
grammar	earn
hair	painting
height	riding
horse	sentence
pronounce	sing
minister	tall
music	vote
soldier	war
wage	wavy

WRITING

8 Choose one of these tasks; write 100 words or more.

1. Describe a real or imaginary friend (what they look like, what kind of a person they are, what they do, what they enjoy doing, …).
2. Write about some things that you really wanted to do when you were younger, and some things that you would really like to do sometime in the next ten years.
3. What should be the best paid job(s) in your country? Why?

READING

9 Read the text and answer the questions.

An intriguing book, *World paychecks: who makes what, where and why*, makes some interesting international comparisons. In Japan, for example, teachers earn far less than factory workers, but in Denmark they are near the top of the wages scale. A New York rubbish collector makes three times as much as an Indian army general. A German bus driver gets double the pay packet of a British bus driver. In China some university teachers earn as much as government ministers, but Chinese newspaper and television journalists are the most poorly paid ones in the world. And so on.

In part, says the writer, this is because of the law of supply and demand. New York rubbish collectors are well paid because it is hard to find enough people who want to do the job, and in India generals do badly because everyone (well, almost everyone) wants to be a general. But other facts – whether having a certain job makes you famous, for example – also make a difference.

It may interest you to know that the President of the United States earns three times what the Prime Minister of Britain does, but that the Prime Ministers of India and China get only about £40 a week. I leave you to draw your own conclusions.

One of the other interesting bits of information in the book is that Britain pays its civil servants (the people who are paid to help the government run things like the tax system and the post office) more than America and most of Europe. Don't ask me who decides these things; no one asked for my opinion.

(from an article by William Davis in *Punch*)

1. True or false: in Denmark, factory workers earn more than teachers.
2. Who earns more, an Indian army general or a New York rubbish collector?
3. If a British bus driver earns £500 a month, how much does a German bus driver earn?
4. Who earns more in China, university teachers or journalists?
5. Which is true:
   a. A lot of people want to be New York rubbish collectors.
   b. Not many people want to be New York rubbish collectors.
6. Do civil servants earn more in America or in Britain?

SPEAKING

10 Work with another student. Each of you must tell the other about someone in your family. Speak for about two minutes while your partner listens carefully. Then the partner must tell the teacher as much as she or he remembers.

B1 Emergency

Reporting and responding to emergencies; giving advice; Present Perfect for reporting 'news'; *can* with verbs of sensation; *there has been*; imperatives; /ð/ and /θ/; listening for gist; listening for specific information.

1 📼 Listen to the recording, and match the sentences with the pictures. Then turn to page 130 and fill in the missing words in the sentences.

2 Look at these pictures. Imagine you are in these situations, and make sentences like the ones in Exercise 1.

3 Work in small groups. Suppose friends phone you to announce the emergencies in Exercises 1 and 2. What do you say to them? You can ask your teacher for help with words. Examples:

'My baby has just eaten some aspirins.' *'Take her to hospital immediately.'*
'I can't turn the water off in the bathroom.' *'Turn it off at the mains.'*

4 Practise saying these after your teacher or the recording.

There's a   There's a fire   There's a fire in my kitchen.

There's been   There's been an accident.   There's been a burglary.

there   right there   We'll be right there.

through   put you through   I'll put you through.

think   I think   I think his leg is broken.

5 Phoning about an emergency. Here are some instructions from a British phone box.

Fill in the blanks in the conversation; then listen to the recording. Have you thought of some good words and expressions that are not on the recording?

OPERATOR: Emergency. .... service, please?
FATHER: Ambulance.
OPERATOR: ....?
FATHER: 744-6972.
OPERATOR: .... I'll put you through.
OFFICER: Ambulance Service. ....?
FATHER: .... wall, and .... broken.
OFFICER: ....?
FATHER: Colin Jackson, 7 Latton Close.
OFFICER: ...., Mr Jackson, we'll be right
there. .... warm, but don't move
him.
FATHER: ....

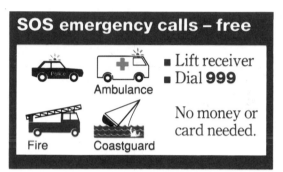

(reproduced by kind permission of BT)

6 Role play: work in groups.
Emergency service workers (fire, police and ambulance): you are going to answer the telephone. First spend some time thinking of what sort of emergencies people may ring about, and what you will say to the people who ring.
People with emergencies: you are going to phone the emergency services. First make a list of five emergencies to phone about.

Present Perfect for announcing 'news'
There's been an accident.
   (~~There was an accident.~~)
My baby has just eaten some aspirins.

Can* with *see, hear, smell, feel
I can smell gas.   (~~I am smelling gas.~~)
I can hear terrible screaming.   (~~I am hearing ...~~)

Imperatives
Keep him warm, but **don't move** him.

Learn/revise: accident; ambulance; aspirin; burglary; corridor; emergency; fire; flat; gas; help; hospital; leg; officer; operator; service; smoke; bleed (bled, bled); break (broke, broken); drive (drove, driven); fall (fell, fallen); move; scream; steal (stole, stolen); turn off; terrible; warm; immediately; upstairs; (We'll be) right there.

B2 Focus on systems

A choice of exercises: pronunciation of /ð/ and /θ/; tenses of *there is*; building sentences with conjunctions and *-ing* forms; vocabulary expansion.

PRONUNCIATION

1 🔲 The same or different? You will hear twelve pairs of words. If the two words in a pair are the same, write *S*. If they are different, write *D*.

2 🔲 Can you hear a *th*? Write the numbers of the pairs; then listen to the recording, and write ✔ if you hear *th* and ✘ if you hear something else.

/ð/ or /d/	/ð/ or /z/	/θ/ or /s/	/θ/ or /t/
1. there / dare	6. then / Zen	11. think / sink	16. three / tree
2. than / Dan	7. with / whizz	12. thought / sort	17. through / true
3. they / day	8. writhe / rise	13. thing / sing	18. thank / tank
4. other / udder	9. bathe / bays	14. youthful / useful	19. path / part
5. those / doze	10. thee / zee	15. path / pass	20. fourth / fought

GRAMMAR: *THERE IS*

3 Can you use the different forms of *there is*? Look at the expressions in the box and then complete the sentences. You will need to use questions or negative forms in some of them.

there is/are	there was/were
there has/have been	there had been
there will be	there would be

1. .... an accident! Come at once!
2. I don't think .... another world war.
3. Do you think .... people like us on other planets?
4. She came screaming out of the bathroom because .... a spider in the bath.
5. When I got to the hotel she told me .... a mistake, and they had given my room to somebody else.
6. If people drove more slowly, ... fewer accidents.
7. .... many people who speak three languages perfectly.
8. .... anybody at home if I come round to your place tomorrow?
9. .... any letters for me, have there?
10. .... policemen in the 18th century?

4 Think of three things that were different when you were a small child, or when your parents were children. Begin *There was(n't)* ... or *There were(n't)* ... Think of three things that will be different in 100 years. Begin *There will/won't be* ...

GRAMMAR: BUILDING SENTENCES

5 Look at the examples.

*Walk round the room **reading** everybody else's label.*
*Interview the person, **asking** as many questions as you can.*
*Mr Archie Macfarlane completed the course successfully, **surprising** everyone.*
*I sat in the garden **wondering** what to do next.*

Now rewrite these sentences using *-ing* forms.

1. She sat in the corner and cried.
2. Walk round the room and ask people questions.
3. She played cards all night, and lost a lot of money.
4. I lived in France for a year, and worked as an English teacher.
5. He drove round the corner on the wrong side of the road, and nearly killed an old lady.
6. We had a nice evening together; we talked and listened to music.
7. Two metres of snow fell; it completely blocked the road.
8. He slept peacefully, and dreamt that he was back at home.
9. He ran out of the house; he was screaming.
10. I took Lucy's car; I knew that she would understand.

6 Look at the examples of how to use conjunctions. Do you know all the conjunctions?

The phone always rings **when** I'm cooking supper. / **When** I'm cooking supper, the phone always rings.

I didn't say anything **when** he asked my name. / **When** he asked my name, I didn't say anything.

He joined the army **after** he left school. / **After** he left school, he joined the army.

My bicycle was stolen **while** I was shopping. / **While** I was shopping, my bicycle was stolen.

Come and see us **before** you go to America. / **Before** you go to America, come and see us.

I'll give you a ring **as soon as** I arrive. / **As soon as** I arrive, I'll give you a ring.

I never travelled abroad **until** I was 18. / **Until** I was 18, I never travelled abroad.

She passed her exams **because** she worked hard. / **Because** she worked hard, she passed her exams.

She passed her exams **although** she had a bad teacher. / **Although** she had a bad teacher, she passed her exams.

There wasn't any beer, **so** I had a glass of fruit juice.

Now use the conjunctions to join some of these sentences together.

They fell in love.
She got very angry.
The train arrived.
Nobody spoke.
It was raining.
Mary failed all her exams.
She hated her teacher.
He ate too much.
She got up.
He started work.
The police were looking for him.
This job is finished.
Ann walked out of the house.
Jake fell off his bicycle.
He went to Scotland.
He wasn't very good-looking.
I'll stay here.
She telephoned the police.
There was nothing in the fridge.
I walked and walked.
I was really tired.
There was nothing to do.
We danced all night.
You answer my question.
The cat ran away.
He couldn't drive.
It was a warm day.
There was water all over the floor.
We went to a restaurant.
He lost his job.
I'll be very happy.

Learn/revise: *vocabulary from Exercise 7.*

TWO VOCABULARY AREAS

7 Choose one of these exercises.
1. Study picture A and learn as many of the words as you want to. Then go and look at a car. See how many of the words you can remember without looking at your book.
2. Study picture B. How many of the objects do you know the names of? Use your dictionary to find out the names of the others. Close your book and try to write down the names of all the objects in the picture from memory. Test yourself tomorrow – how many of the words do you still know?

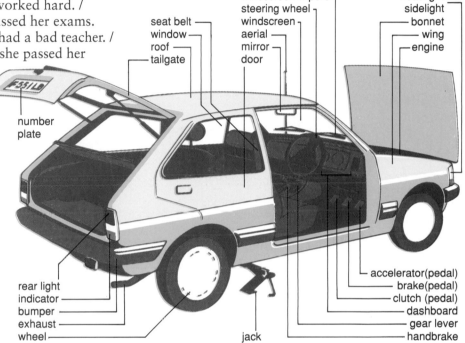

A

windscreen wipers
steering wheel
windscreen
aerial
mirror
door

seat belt
window
roof
tailgate

headlight/ sidelight
bonnet
wing
engine

number plate

rear light
indicator
bumper
exhaust
wheel

jack

accelerator(pedal)
brake(pedal)
clutch (pedal)
dashboard
gear lever
handbrake

B

1
2
3
4
5
6
7
8
9
10
11
12
13
14
15

31

B3 How honest are you?

Vocabulary expansion; revision of comparatives; linking vowels and consonants; general skills practice.

1 Read the questions and note your answers.

1 You find a wallet containing £1,000. There are no papers inside to show who it belongs to. Do you hand it to the police or keep it?
   a Hand it to the police.
   b Keep it.
   c Not sure.

2 You have an expensive meal in a restaurant. When you check the bill, you see that the waiter has forgotten to charge you for the drinks. Do you tell him or keep quiet?
   a Tell him.
   b Keep quiet.
   c Not sure.

3 Do you think it is all right to hide some of your earnings from the tax inspector?
   a Yes.
   b No.
   c Not sure.

4 Have you ever pretended to be ill to get off work or school?
   a Often.
   b Once or twice / occasionally.
   c Never.

5 You are staying in a hotel, and you see that they have very nice towels. Do you take any home with you?
   a All of them.
   b Just one.
   c None.
   d Not sure.

6 You advertise your house for sale. Somebody offers you a good price, and you agree to sell to her. Before you sign the contract, somebody else offers you another £5,000. Do you stay with the first buyer or sell to the second?
   a Stay with the first.
   b Sell to the second.
   c Go back to the first and ask for £5,000 more.
   d Not sure.

7 One of your family (mother, father, wife, husband, child) has some very strange friends. One day you find a letter from one of these people lying around the house. Do you read it?
   a Yes.
   b Certainly not.
   c Perhaps.

8 In your opinion, how serious is shoplifting?
   a Not at all serious – most people do it at one time or another.
   b You might do it if you really needed something and hadn't got enough money.
   c You would never do it.

9 You are playing cards (not for money) and you see that somebody is cheating. What do you think about it?
   a It doesn't matter.
   b It's annoying, but not too serious.
   c You refuse to go on playing unless they stop.
   d You stop the game, because you won't play with people who cheat.

10 Travelling in a taxi, you find a torch lying on the seat – it must have been dropped by the last passenger. What do you do?
   a Put it in your pocket.
   b Give it to the taxi driver.
   c Just leave it.
   d Not sure.

11 Have you ever cheated in an exam?
   a Often.
   b More than once.
   c Once.
   d Never.

12 What do you think about travelling without a ticket on public transport?
   a OK.
   b Not really OK, but you might do it.
   c Completely wrong – you would never do it.

13 Is it ever right to tell lies about yourself to impress other people?
   a It can be.
   b Never.
   c Not sure.

14 Is it all right to take stationery from the place where you work?
   a Yes.
   b No.
   c Not sure.

15 Have you answered all the questions completely honestly?
   a Yes.
   b No.
   c Well, nearly.

Check your score at the bottom of the next page.

2 Vocabulary. Choose some words and expressions to learn from the questionnaire. Compare notes with another student and talk about the reasons for your choices.

3 You probably feel that some of these things are worse than others. Make sentences. Examples:

'I think shoplifting is worse than cheating at cards.'
'I don't think reading other people's letters is as bad as cheating in exams.'
'I think telling lies is the worst thing.'

shoplifting
reading other people's letters
cheating at cards
cheating in exams
travelling without a ticket
avoiding income tax
stealing towels from a hotel
telling lies about yourself

4 📼 Pronunciation: joining words together. Choose the group(s) that you find difficult and practise saying the expressions.

consonant + vowel
you find a wallet
hand it to the police
some of your earnings
tax inspector
one of your family
lying around
not at all serious
put it in your pocket

r + vowel
in your opinion
at one time or another
your earnings

joining two vowels
to impress other people
who it belongs to
somebody else offers you another £5,000
you agree

joining two consonants
a wallet containing £1,000
who it belongs to
hand it to the police
when you get the bill
you see that the waiter has forgotten
lying around the house
it doesn't matter

vowel + h
in a hotel
do you take any home?
you have an expensive meal
to hide some of your earnings
you advertise your house for sale
lying around the house

5 Work with two or three other students. Make up a questionnaire for the class (you choose the subject). Some ideas: 'How sociable are you?' 'How generous are you?' 'How hard-working are you?'

"Don't lie to me—you've been to the pub again."

Learn/revise: bill; meal; pocket; price; public transport; score; shoplifting; tax; ticket; torch; towel; wallet; advertise; avoid; belong (to); cheat; check; contain; drop; find (found, found); hide (hid, hidden); impress; keep (kept, kept); leave (left, left); lie (lying, lay, lain); lose (lost, lost); need; offer; play cards; sign; steal (stole, stolen); tell lies (told, told); expensive; generous; hard-working; honest; quiet; serious; sociable; strange; sure; valuable; wrong; all right; for sale; keep quiet; it doesn't matter; nearly.

terrible!
60: You even give dishonest answers to questionnaires – that's
you're kind to children and animals.
46–59: You seem to be a rather dishonest person. But perhaps
others.
31–45: You're honest about some things and dishonest about
23–30: You're more honest than average.
16–22: You're a very honest person.
15: Are you sure you answered Question 15 honestly?
RESULTS

12: a4, b3, c1   13: a3, b1, c2   14: a3, b1, c2   15: a1, b3, c2
9: a3, b3, c2, d1   10: a3, b1, c1, d2   11: a4, b3, c2, d1
5: a6, b4, c1, d3   6: a1, b4, c3, d2   7: a4, b1, c3   8: a5, b3, c1
1: a1, b6, c3   2: a1, b4, c3   3: a4, b1, c3   4: a4, b2, c1
CHECK YOUR SCORE

33

B4 No trousers

FOLE

Writing skills: predicting a story line, shaping narratives, connecting sentences, dividing texts into paragraphs, expanding stories; speaking skills: storytelling.

1 Your teacher will read or play you a story sentence by sentence. Try and guess how the story continues.

2 Now turn to page 130 and look at the story. Then work in pairs to answer the following questions.

1. What are the words or expressions in the story that tell you about time? For example, *Last week* or *While he was putting the first pair of trousers on.*
2. The word *and* is used to join ideas in the story, as in *He chose two suits to try on **and** went to the changing rooms.* How many other ways can you find of joining ideas?
3. Why do you think the paragraph divisions come where they do?

3 Here is the first sentence of the story with two new pieces of information added in different ways. Which ways do you think are most successful?

1. Last week my next-door neighbour Steve went to a department store to buy a new suit. *The department store is in the middle of town. Steve needed the suit for a job interview.*
2. Last week my next-door neighbour Steve went to a department store *which is in the middle of town* to buy a new suit, *which he needed for a job interview.*
3. Last week my next-door neighbour Steve went to a department store *in the middle of town* to buy a new suit, *which he needed for a job interview.*
4. Last week my next-door neighbour Steve went to a department store *which is in the middle of town* to buy a new suit *for a job interview.*
5. Last week my next-door neighbour Steve went to a department store *in the middle of town* to buy a new suit *for a job interview.*
6. Last week my next-door neighbour Steve went to a department store *in the middle of town* to buy a new suit, *because he had a job interview.*
7. Last week my next-door neighbour Steve, *needing a new suit for a job interview*, went to a department store *in the middle of town.*
8. Last week my next-door neighbour Steve needed a new suit *for a job interview*, so he went to a department store *in the middle of town.*

34

4 Now choose two or more of these pieces of information, and add them to the story. Make any other changes that are necessary, and write out the part of the story that has the new information.

1. I was at my office when Steve phoned.
2. The man who phoned Steve said that Steve's driving licence was in the wallet (but no money).
3. The store is about half an hour's drive from Steve's home.
4. When we got to the store we went straight to the security department.
5. The security department phoned several other departments. Nobody knew who had called Steve.

5 Work on your own. Look at the pictures. Your task is to write the story. Imagine you are one of the characters – the mother, the father, the daughter or the son. Then decide who you will write to – a friend, a relative … Imagine what happens in the blank frames; add any other imaginative details you want to. When you have finished, exchange stories with another student and read each other's stories.

6 Have you ever been tricked (like Steve in the first story)? Or has someone you know been tricked? Or do you know a good story about this kind of trick? Work in groups of three to five, and tell each other your stories. If there is time, each group should choose one of the stories to tell to the whole class.

Learn/revise: credit card; department; department store; driving licence; hand; key; middle; money; neighbour; pair; phone call; security; story; suit; thief (thieves); town; trick (*noun and verb*); trousers; wallet; catch (caught, caught); choose (chose, chosen); drive (drove, driven); find (found, found); get (got, got); happen; leave (left, left); manage (to); phone; rescue; reach; run after (ran, run); shout; wonder; try on; nobody; stuck; as well; last (week, *etc.*); later that (afternoon, day, *etc.*); next door.

B5 Small talk (1)

Greeting and welcoming; asking for confirmation; asking for personal information; mealtime conventions; question tags; intonation; listening skills: listening for specific information.

1 📼 Listen to the dialogue, and write the numbers and letters of the expressions you hear.

1. a. I go.
   b. I'm going.
   c. I'll go.

2. a. Nice to see you.
   b. It's nice to see you.
   c. Nice seeing you.

3. a. Are we late?
   b. We're late.
   c. Aren't we late?

4. a. You're first.
   b. You're the first.
   c. You're not first.

5. a. Who is coming?
   b. Who ever's coming?
   c. Who else is coming?

6. a. Can I take your coat?
   b. Let me take your coat.
   c. Shall I take your coat?

7. a. You know Lucy, do you?
   b. You know Lucy, don't you?
   c. You don't know Lucy, do you?

8. a. I think we've met her once.
   b. I think we met her once.
   c. I think we'll meet her one day.

9. a. What can I get you to drink?
   b. What can I give you to drink?
   c. What would you like to drink?

10. a. The room doesn't look nice, John.
    b. Does the room look nice, John?
    c. Doesn't the room look nice, John?

11. a. You've changed it about.
    b. You've changed it round.
    c. You've changed it over.

2 📼 Listen again. Which of these do you hear?

a. don't you?
b. do you?
c. isn't it?
d. wasn't it?
e. aren't we?
f. haven't you?

3 📼 Real questions or not? Listen to the sentences. Does the voice go up or down at the end? Examples:

The piano was over by the window, wasn't it?

You know Lucy, don't you?

1. It's a lovely day, isn't it?
2. You're French, aren't you?
3. She's got fatter, hasn't she?
4. The train leaves at 4.13, doesn't it?
5. Children always like cartoon films, don't they?
6. It's your birthday next week, isn't it?
7. Hotels are expensive here, aren't they?
8. Ann said she'd phone, didn't she?

4 Work with two or three other students. Act out a 'greeting' scene like the one in Exercise 1.

5 Listen to the dialogue. Then look at the following sentences. Are they true or false? Write T (true), F (false), or DK (don't know).

1. Lucy works in a pub.
2. She likes her work.
3. She doesn't meet many interesting people.
4. Lucy's job is always hard work.
5. There is only one barman in her pub.
6. John works in a bank.
7. He likes his job very much.
8. He has just been made manager.
9. He's going to move to another town soon.
10. Lucy wouldn't like to move to another town.
11. John has lived in the same place for six years.

6 Listen again. Can you write down some sentences from the dialogue?

7 Real questions. Listen and repeat.

1. That's hard work, isn't it?
2. You're an accountant, aren't you?
3. You have to move round, don't you?
4. It'll be in another town, won't it?

8 Asking for agreement. Listen and repeat.

1. It's a nice day, isn't it?
2. She's very pretty, isn't she?
3. Good clothes are expensive, aren't they?
4. You're tired, aren't you?

9 Listen to the dialogue. Write down all the words you hear for things that you can eat or drink.

10 Turn to pages 130 and 131 and look over the tapescripts of the dialogues. Choose seven to ten words or expressions to learn. Show your list to another student and say why you have chosen two of the words/expressions.

11 Work with four or five other students. You are all in the same compartment on a long train journey. Act out a conversation in which you get to know one another.

Learn/revise: bean; beef; bread; butcher; carrot; (a) change; coat; food; ground; job; manager; meat; mustard; piece; potato; pub; salt; weekday; wine; ask for; look for; move; boring; cheap; delicious; lovely; ready; stupid; worse; hard work; actually; else; somewhere else; Who else?; over there; probably; Come in and have a drink; Could you pass me …; Have a drink; Here you are; How do you mean?; How stupid of me!; I beg your pardon?; I'm so glad you could come; I should think; I've had enough; It depends; It doesn't matter (at all); Lovely/Nice to see you; That's right; What can I get you to drink?; You know Lucy, don't you?

B6 Focus on systems

A choice of exercises: question tags; position of prepositions in questions; /ə/ in unstressed syllables; verbs for everyday actions involving objects and materials.

GRAMMAR: POSITION OF PREPOSITIONS IN QUESTIONS

1 Can you complete these questions?

What are you looking ....?
What are John and Lucy talking ....?

Now read the following answers and write the questions.

1. They're talking about politics.
2. I went with Henry.
3. I'm looking for Alice.
4. I bought it for you.
5. I'm thinking about holidays.
6. I'm listening to Radio 2.
7. I'm looking at your ear-rings.
8. The letter was from Andy.
9. She's in love with me.
10. She comes from Iceland.

GRAMMAR: QUESTION TAGS

2 Study the examples and then complete the sentences.

Your father **is** a doctor, **isn't** he?
The film **was** pretty boring, **wasn't** it?
We **were** right, **weren't** we?
The Lewises **have** gone on holiday, **haven't** they?
Ann **will** be pleased to see us, **won't** she?
Peter **would** like to be a doctor, **wouldn't** he?
Rita **can** speak seven languages, **can't** she?

There **are** tigers in Siberia, **aren't there**?

I'm late, **aren't** I? (...amn't I?)

You **drink** coffee, **don't** you?
She **arrived** late, **didn't** she?

1. It's cold, ...?
2. Anne was ill last week, ...?
3. You've met Sally, ...?
4. Your children were all at the same school, ...?
5. You'll be home before midnight, ...?
6. Maurice looks very like his father, ...?
7. It would be nice to go and see Chris, ...
8. Your father came from Canada, ...?
9. These cars use a lot of petrol, ...?
10. You're working next weekend, ...?
11. There's somebody at the door, ...?
12. I'm cooking supper tonight, ...?

3 Study the examples and then complete the sentences.

She **isn't** happy, **is** she?
You **haven't** seen my brother anywhere, **have** you?
The film **wasn't** much good, **was** it?
You **can't** swim, **can** you?
Your mother **wouldn't** like to come, **would** she?
Cats **don't** eat cornflakes, **do** they?
The postman **didn't** come this morning, **did** he?
There **isn't** any milk in the fridge, **is** there?

1. It isn't raining, ...?
2. You weren't there this morning, ...?
3. Kate can't speak Spanish, ...?
4. The meat doesn't look very nice, ...?
5. You wouldn't like to help me, ...?
6. Penny hasn't phoned, ...?
7. You won't get married before you leave school, ...?
8. They didn't tell you to work at the weekend, ...?
9. John wasn't happy in his last job, ...?
10. There weren't any messages for me, ...?
11. You don't mind if I open the window, ...?
12. This isn't your coat, ...?

4 🔲 Asking for agreement. Listen and say the question tags. Example:

'It's a nice day,...' *'...isn't it?'*

PRONUNCIATION: /ə/ IN UNSTRESSED SYLLABLES

5 🔲 The vowel /ə/ comes one or more times in each of the following words (the number of times is shown in brackets). Decide which vowels are pronounced /ə/. Listen to the recording and check your answers; then practise the words.

barman (1) autumn (1) breakfast (1)
compare (1) continue (1) concert (1)
Britain (1) England (1) foreign (1)
London (1) tomato (1) usually (1)
photograph (1) excellent (2) America (2)
accountant (2) agreement (2) dangerous (2)
policeman (2) photographer (3)

6 🔲 Listen to the recording and decide how many words there are in each sentence. (Contractions like *don't* count as two words.)

VOCABULARY: DOING THINGS TO THINGS

7 Match the verbs and the pictures.

bend   break   catch   cut   drop   hit   kick   lift   mend
pick up   polish   pour   pull   push   put down   roll   scratch
sharpen   slice   swing   switch off   switch on   tear   throw
tie   touch   turn

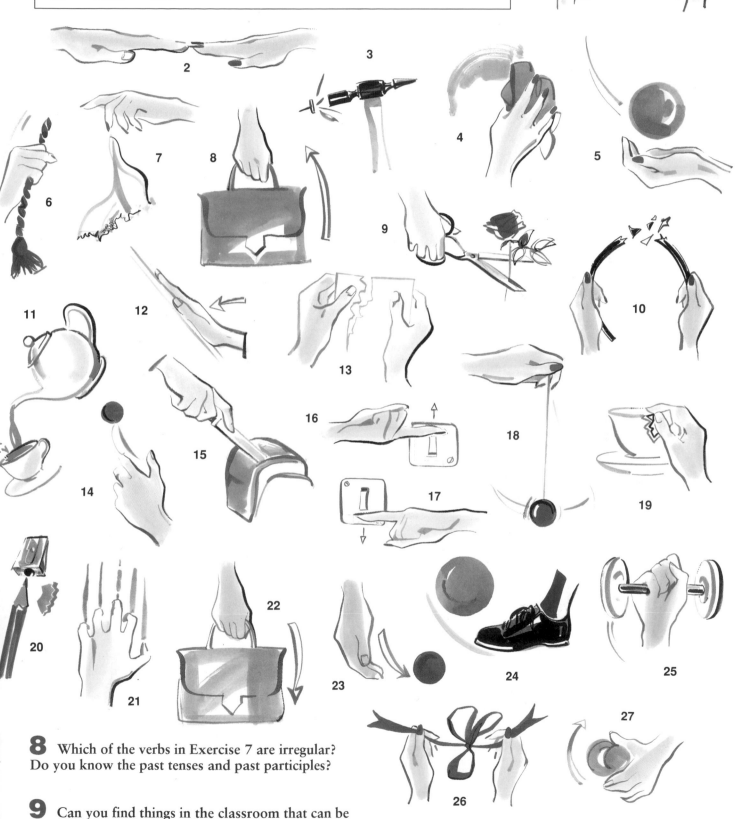

8 Which of the verbs in Exercise 7 are irregular? Do you know the past tenses and past participles?

9 Can you find things in the classroom that can be bent, broken, cut, dropped *etc.*? Try to find one thing for each verb.

Learn/revise: *the verbs in Exercise 7.*

39

B7 Small talk (2)

Expressing opinions; agreeing and disagreeing; *So/Neither (do) I*; leave-taking;
listening skills: listening for gist and for specific information; speaking;
pronunciation: fluency practice.

1 Listen to the dialogue. What do you think they were talking about? Can you remember any of the things they said?

2 Which of these words and expressions come in the dialogue? Write down your answers; then listen again and see if you were right.

I liked it all   lovely   nonsense
I didn't think much of it   I cried
I couldn't help it   It made him laugh
It didn't say anything to me
I may be very old-fashioned   So am I
I like violence   Why did you like it?
It was really really boring   three old men
Who wrote it?   I've never heard of him

3 Write down the names of a food, a sport, an animal and a person (singer, actor, writer, ...) that you like. Tell another student, and listen to his or her answers.

I like ...
I quite like ...
I really like ...
I like ... very much.
I love ...

So do I.
I don't.
I quite like him/her/it/them.
I've never heard of him/her/it/them.

Write down the names of a food, a sport, an animal and a person (singer, actor, writer, ...) that you don't like. Tell another student, and listen to his or her answers.

I don't like ...
I don't much like ...
I really don't like ...
I don't like ... at all.

Neither/Nor do I.
I do.
I don't mind him/her/it/them.
I've never heard of him/her/it/them.

4 Write down the names of three books / films / television programmes / plays *etc.* that you liked and three that you didn't. Tell another student, and listen to his or her answers.

> I liked …
> I really liked …
> *etc.*

> So did I.
> I didn't.
> I didn't think much of it.
> I haven't seen it.
> I've never heard of it.
> *etc.*

> I didn't like …
> I didn't much like …
> *etc.*

> Neither/Nor did I.
> I did.
> I quite liked it.
> I haven't read it.
> *etc.*

5 Talk some more about books / films / television programmes / plays *etc.* that you have read or seen.

6 Look at these sentences. They are like sentences in Dialogue 5, but they are not quite the same. Listen to the dialogue and write the exact sentences.

It's late.
We've got to go a long way.
We'd better go, too.
Thank you very much, Ann.
I really enjoyed myself.
Thanks for coming.
You must come and see us soon.
I'll phone you.
This isn't mine.
Well, whose is that, then?
It's old and dirty.

7 Turn to page 134 and look over the tapescripts of Dialogues 4 and 5. Choose seven to ten words or expressions to learn. Show your list to another student and say why you have chosen two of the words/expressions.

8 Turn to pages 130 and 131, and then to page 134. Listen again to Dialogues 1 to 5 as you read the tapescripts. Then choose a sentence and try to say it with a good pronunciation. The teacher will say it for you correctly.

9 Improvisation. Work in groups of six to eight. Act out a dinner party. See how long you can go on for.

> **Learn/revise:** beginning; coffee; end; middle; nonsense; ring (telephone); rubbish; sex; violence; enjoy (yourself); hear of (heard, heard); move (house); awful; boring; dirty; lovely; old; old-fashioned; quite (= rather); whose; mine; I couldn't help it; I didn't think much of it; It didn't say anything to me; Thank you for coming; We ought to be on our way; We'd better be going.

41

B8 What's a hamburger?

SKILLS FOCUS
SKILLS FOCUS
SKILLS FOCUS
SKILLS FOCUS
SKILLS FOCUS
SKILLS FOCUS

Listening for overall meaning; giving spoken descriptions and definitions;
asking for things when you don't know the exact words; reading and interpreting;
guessing unknown words; summarising.

1 🔲 Listen to the descriptions. Can you do better?

2 How quickly can you match the words and the descriptions? (There is one word too many.)

bill	boat	bus	crash	cup	cupboard
dancing	envelope	hairbrush	hotel		
ice cream	microphone	office	perfume		
rabbit	salt	sing	sleep	soap	
station	suitcase	trees	window	wrist	

1. Something that makes you cool in hot weather.
2. The thing that joins your hand to your arm.
3. A thing that is useful when you travel.
4. A liquid that makes you smell nice.
5. Stuff (that) you put on food.
6. A thing (that) you tidy your hair with.
7. Something (that) you put a letter in.
8. A thing (that) you speak into.
9. Stuff for washing with.
10. A thing for drinking out of.
11. A place where you can stay overnight.
12. A place where you go to catch a train.
13. A room that has a desk, typewriter, telephone *etc*.
14. A big vehicle with seats.
15. A way of moving to music.
16. A kind of box on the wall: you keep things in it.
17. You can travel across water in it.
18. Very big plants; birds and animals live in them.
19. You have to pay it.
20. When you do this, it may sound nice.
21. It can happen if you drive too fast.
22. You do it at night when you are tired.
23. You can see through it.

3 Now describe one of the things in the pictures. You must not use its name (if you know it), and you must not use your hands to help you explain. The other students will try to decide which thing you are talking about. Useful structures:

something (that) ...
a thing (that) ...
something / a thing that you wear when ...
something / a thing that you use to ... / for ...ing
a thing for ...ing
a thing with ...
a thing that has ...
stuff that ...
stuff for ...
liquid that/for ...
you use it to ... / for ...ing
you use it when you ...
you can ... it
a kind/sort of ...
it happens when you ...
you do it ...

42

4 Read the text carefully, but without using a dictionary. Then answer the questions.

ELEPHANTS ARE DIFFERENT TO DIFFERENT PEOPLE

Wilson and Pilcer and Snack stood before the zoo elephant.

Wilson said 'What is its name? Is it from Asia or Africa? Who feeds it? Is it a he or a she? How old is it? Do they have twins? How much does it cost to feed? If it dies, how much will another one cost? If it dies, what will they use the bones, the fat and the hide for? What use is it besides to look at?'

Pilcer didn't have any questions; he was murmuring to himself, 'It's a house by itself, walls and windows, the ears came from tall cornfields, by God; the architect of those legs was a workman, by God; he stands like a bridge out across deep water; the face is sad and the eyes are kind; I know elephants are good to babies.'

Snack looked up and down and at last said to himself, 'He's a tough son-of-a-gun outside and I'll bet he's got a strong heart, I'll bet he's strong as a copper-riveted boiler inside.'

They didn't put up any arguments.
They didn't throw anything in each other's faces.
The three men saw the elephant three ways.
And let it go at that.
They didn't spoil a sunny Sunday afternoon.
'Sunday comes only once a week,' they told each other.

from *Home Front Memo* by Carl Sandburg

1. Whose way of looking at the elephant do you like best – Wilson's, Pilcer's or Snack's?
2. Find out what *tusk* means. Then decide which of the three men might have said each of these sentences.
   a. Those tusks could break down a house.
   b. Those tusks are curved like the sky.
   c. How much do those tusks weigh?
3. Look at how these words are used in the text: *feed, twins, hide, murmuring, arguments, spoil.* Write down what you think each one might mean (in English or in your own language). Then check in a dictionary and see if you were right.
4. Here are three summaries of the text. Which do you think is the best?
   a. Elephants are complicated animals and you can see them in different ways.
   b. Different people see the world in different ways; that is no reason to fight.
   c. People should agree with each other on Sundays.

5 🔲 Listen to the song. Each of the four verses describes one of the following things: a TV, a motorbike, a telephone, a car, a fire extinguisher, a washing machine, a camera. Can you decide which? (The text is on page 131.)

Leaving out object relative pronouns
a liquid (that) people put on
a thing (that) you tidy your hair with
stuff (that) you put on food

End-position of prepositions
a thing you tidy your hair with
something you put a letter in
a thing you speak into
stuff for washing with
a thing for drinking out of

Learn/revise: argument; arm; bill; boat; bone; box; bridge; desk; envelope; hairbrush; hand; hotel; ice cream; kind (*noun*); microphone; office; perfume; rabbit; sort; stuff; suitcase; thing; twins; typewriter; window; wrist; bet (bet, bet); cost (cost, cost); describe; die; feed (fed, fed); join; keep (kept, kept); put on (put, put); smell (smelt, smelt); spoil; taste; tidy; travel (travelled); use; alive; cool; deep; kind (*adjective*); tired; tough; besides; I'll bet.

Summary B

Present Perfect for giving 'news'

My baby **has** just **eaten** some aspirins.
There **has been** an accident. (~~There was an accident.~~)

can with verbs of sensation

I **can** smell gas. (~~I am smelling gas.~~)
I **can** hear terrible screaming.

Tenses of there is

Do you think **there are** people on other planets?
There has been an accident.
She screamed because **there was** a spider in the bath.
The hotel receptionist told me **there had been** a
    mistake: they had given my room to somebody
    else.
I don't think **there will be** another world war.
If people drove more slowly **there would be** fewer
    accidents.

Irregular verbs in Lessons B1–B8

INFINITIVE	PAST	PAST PARTICIPLE
bend	bent	bent
bet	bet	bet
bleed	bled	bled
break	broke	broken
catch	caught	caught
choose	chose	chosen
cost	cost	cost
cut	cut	cut
drive	drove	driven
fall	fell	fallen
feed	fed	fed
feel	felt	felt
find	found	found
hear	heard	heard
hide	hid	hidden
hit	hit	hit
keep	kept	kept
leave	left	left
lie	lay	lain
lose	lost	lost
put	put	put
read /riːd/	read /red/	read /red/
run	ran	run
see	saw	seen
smell	smelt	smelt
steal	stole	stolen
swing	swung	swung
take	took	taken
tear	tore	torn
tell	told	told
throw	threw	thrown

-ing forms for activities

reading other people's letters   **telling** lies
shoplifting   **cheating** at cards   **stealing** towels

Giving advice and instructions: imperatives

Take her to hospital immediately.
Keep him warm, but **don't move** him.

Comparative structures; worse and worst

Travelling without a ticket isn't **as bad as** shoplifting.
I think shoplifting is **worse than** cheating at cards.
I think telling lies is **the worst** thing.

Question tags after affirmative sentences

Your father **is** a doctor, **isn't** he?
The Lewises **have** gone on holiday, **haven't** they?
Ann **will** be pleased to see us, **won't** she?
Peter **would** like to be a doctor, **wouldn't** he?
Rita **can** speak seven languages, **can't** she?
There are tigers in Siberia, **aren't there?**
    (~~... aren't they?~~)
I'm late, **aren't** I? (~~... amn't I?~~)

You **drink** coffee, **don't** you?
She **arrived** late, **didn't** she?

Question tags after negative sentences

She **isn't** happy, **is** she?
You **haven't** seen my brother anywhere, **have** you?
The film **wasn't** much good, **was** it?
You **can't** swim, **can** you?
Ann **wouldn't** like to help us, **would** she?
Cats **don't** eat cornflakes, **do** they?
The postman **didn't** come this morning, **did** he?
There isn't any milk in the fridge, **is there?**

Intonation of question tags

Real questions

Your father **is** a doctor, **isn't** he?
You **haven't** seen my brother anywhere, **have you?**

Asking for agreement

The film **was** pretty boring, **wasn't it?**
She **isn't** happy, **is she?**

Position of prepositions in questions

What are you looking **at**?
What are John and Lucy talking **about**?
Who did you go **with**?

Position of prepositions in relative structures

a thing you tidy your hair **with**
something you put a letter **in**

Building sentences with conjunctions

The phone always rings **when** I'm cooking supper.
When I'm cooking supper, the phone always rings.
He joined the army **after** he left school.
While I was shopping my bicycle was stolen.
Come and see us **before** you go to America.
As soon as I arrive, I'll give you a ring.
I never travelled abroad **until** I was 18.
Because she worked hard, she passed her exams.
She passed her exams **although** she had a bad teacher.
There wasn't any beer, **so** I had a glass of fruit juice.
… a new suit, **which** he needed for a job interview.

Leaving out object relative pronouns

a thing (that) you tidy your hair with
stuff (that) you put on food

Building sentences with *-ing* forms

Walk round the room **reading** everybody else's label.
Interview them, **asking** as many questions as you can.
Mr Archie Macfarlane completed the course
   successfully, **surprising** everyone.
I sat in the garden **wondering** what to do next.

Indicating time in stories

Last week Steve went to a department store.
While he was putting the trousers on, he saw …
Now he was stuck in the department store.
Later that afternoon he got a phone call.
When we got to the store nobody knew …

Uses of *get*

He **got** the new trousers on.
He **got** a phone call.
We think we have **got** your keys as well.
Would you like to come and **get** them?
When we **got** to the store …
They had used Steve's keys to **get** into his house.
What can I **get** you to drink?

Expressing opinions; adverbials of degree

I like …	I don't like …
I quite like …	I don't much like …
I really like …	I really don't like …
I like … very much	I don't like … at all
I love …	
I don't mind …	

Sharing and not sharing opinions

'I like …'	'So do I.' / 'I don't.'
'I liked …'	'So did I.' / 'I didn't.'
'I don't like …'	'Neither/Nor do I.' / 'I do.'
'I didn't like …'	'Neither/Nor did I.' / 'I did.'

I quite liked it.   I didn't think much of it.
I've never heard of it.   I haven't read/seen it.

Greeting and welcoming

Nice to see you.
Let me take your coat.
You know Lucy, don't you?
I think we've met her once.
Lovely to see you.
I'm so glad you could come.
What can I get you to drink?

Mealtimes

'Could you pass me …?' 'Here you are.'
This is delicious.
Would you like some more?
Have another potato.
No, thanks. That was lovely, but I've had enough.
'I *am* sorry.' 'That's all right. It doesn't matter at all.'

Time to go

We'd better be going.
We ought to be on our way.
Thank you so much.
We really enjoyed ourselves.
Thank you for coming.
You must come and see us soon.
I'll give you a ring.

Describing

something / a thing (that) …
something / a thing that you wear when …
something / a thing that you use to … / for …ing
a thing for …ing / with … / that has …
stuff / liquid that … / for …
you use it to … / for …ing / when you …
you can … it
a kind / sort of …
it happens when you …
you do it when … / to …

Vocabulary

Look through the 'Learn/revise' boxes at the ends
of Lessons B1–B8.

Revision and fluency practice **B**

A choice of activities.

1 📼 Listen to the story about the lift, and see if you can answer the question at the end.

2 Reading report. Talk to the class about what you have been reading recently in English.

3 Three wishes. Imagine that your fairy godmother appears and gives you three wishes. You can wish for anything you like (except for more wishes). Write your wishes. Now work with someone else. Write down what you think he/she has wished for. Then exchange wishes and see if you were right. Useful structures:

I want ...
I would like ...
I wish I was/had/could ...
I thought you would wish for ...
I'm surprised you want ...

4 Happy memories. Work in groups of three or four. Tell each other about a happy memory that you have.

5 Make up a class story. One person starts, the next person continues, and so on in turn. Here is a possible beginning:

'Mary was walking home late at night ...'

6 Work with another student and complete the following dialogue. Practise it and act it out to the class.

Hello.
....
Yes, speaking. Who's that?
....
Oh, hello. Didn't recognise your voice.
....
No, I haven't seen her for a long time.
....
No, she hasn't. Not for two or three months.
....
Yes, she probably is.
....
No, I'm afraid I don't.
....
My God! Really? What are you going to do?
....
....
....

Well, let me know if I can help at all. That's terrible. I *am* sorry.
....
I'd love to, but I'm not free on Tuesday. How about Thursday?
....
OK. What time?
....
Right. See you then. Bye.

7 Here are some typical English children's jokes. Read them and say what you think about them. Do you know any better jokes? Useful expressions:

I don't see the joke.
What do you think of this one?
This one's really funny.
It isn't funny at all.
I think it's wonderful/stupid.
It makes / doesn't make me laugh.
I think number 4 is the best/worst.

1. LUCY: How did you get that cut on your forehead?
   MIKE: I bit myself.
   LUCY: But how could you bite yourself on the forehead?
   MIKE: I stood on a chair.

2. A little man asked for a job cutting down trees. 'You don't look very strong,' said the manager. 'What experience have you got?' 'I cut down thousands of trees in the Sahara desert,' said the man. 'But there aren't any trees in the Sahara,' said the manager. 'No,' said the man. 'Not now.'

3. GIRL: You remind me of the sea.
   BOY: You mean I'm wild, restless, romantic?
   GIRL: No, you make me sick.

4. WOMAN: I'm having trouble with my husband. Every morning he washes the car.
   FRIEND: You should be pleased. Most wives wish their husbands would wash the car more often.
   WOMAN: In the bath?

5. A girl took her dog with her to the film of *Alice in Wonderland*. The usherette saw the dog, and was about to throw it out. But then she saw that the dog seemed to be enjoying the film, so she let it stay. After the film she said to the girl 'It certainly surprised me to see your dog enjoying the show.' 'Me too,' said the girl. 'He didn't like the book at all.'

8 Improvisation. Work in groups of four, and act out the following situation.

Mrs Smith is annoyed because her neighbours play loud music late at night. She goes next door to complain, but they won't turn the music down. So she calls the police, and a three-sided argument develops.

9 Are you good at organising? Study the plan and the information. Then work in groups and find a good way of reorganising the zoo.

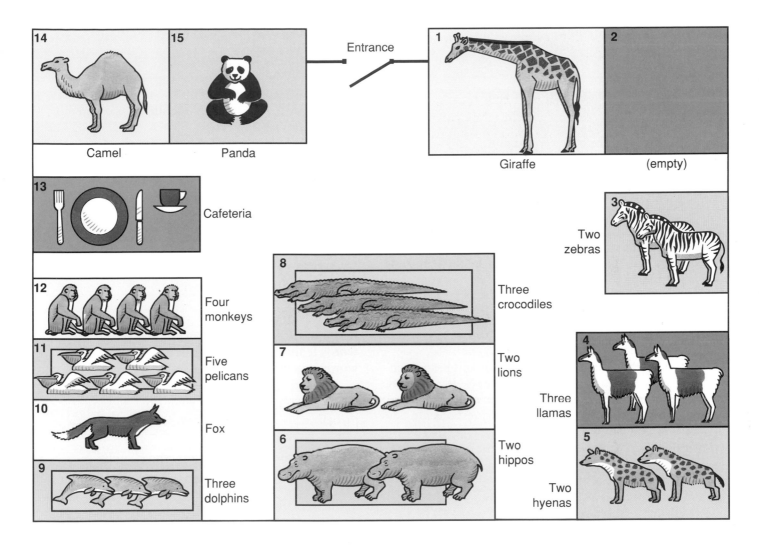

INFORMATION
1. The giraffe is going to have a baby soon, so it must be put somewhere quiet.
2. One of the lions has died; the other should move to a smaller enclosure.
3. Small children are frightened by seeing the crocodiles as they come in.
4. The zoo has been given a new panda.
5. The monkeys are very noisy.
6. The camel is rather smelly.
7. All the enclosures should be filled.
8. Harmless animals should not be put next to predators (animals which are their natural enemies and might frighten them).
9. The zoo has enough money to buy two wolves or four flamingoes or a pair of small deer.

(from *Discussions that Work*, Penny Ur)

Test B

LISTENING

1 📼 **Which of these expressions come in the dialogue? Write S (the same) or D (different).**

1. We'd better be going
2. So have we
3. Thank you so much
4. We've had a wonderful time
5. Will you be in tomorrow
6. That would be lovely
7. Have you left them in your coat
8. They don't seem to be here
9. Those are yours, aren't they
10. Thank you for a lovely evening

2 📼 **Listen to the dialogue again and answer the questions.**

1. Why were the people together?
2. What time of the day was it?
3. What did David lose? Where did he think he had put them? Who found them?

PRONUNCIATION

3 📼 **Real question or not? You will hear seven questions. Listen to each one, and write R if the end of the question goes up and N if the end of the question goes down. The first two questions are done for you as examples.**

1. You're from Jersey, aren't you? ......R......

2. Hilary didn't come, did she? ......N......
3. Your sister's a journalist, isn't she?
4. Helen's had measles, hasn't she?
5. Jeremy hasn't left, has he?
6. You've finished your work, haven't you?
7. You'll be here for a while, won't you?

4 **Circle the vowels which are pronounced /ə/. The first word is done for you as an example.**

adv(e)rtise   bumper   burglary   delicious
department   generous   microphone   mustard
officer   potato

GRAMMAR

5 **Choose the right verb forms.**

1. .... there .... any teachers at the meeting tomorrow? (*be*)
2. There .... a major accident on the M4 near Reading, and motorists are asked to drive very carefully. (*be*)
3. I .... over the bridge yesterday when I .... my pen and it .... into the river. (*walk*; *drop*; *fall*)
4. Gloria .... last night while I .... a shower. (*phone*; *have*)
5. I .... to phone her back, but there .... no answer. (*try*; *be*)
6. You work in Barcelona, ... you?
7. You haven't got a pen I could borrow, ... you?
8. Carolyn won't be here before nine, ... she?
9. 'My sister ran in the Boston Marathon last year.' 'Really? So .... I!'
10. He ran out of the room, ... his briefcase open on the desk. (*leave*)

6 **Join each pair of sentences using one of the words from the box (add or take away any other words you need to).**

after	although	as soon as	because
before	so	until	when

1. She'll arrive. I'll phone you immediately.

   I'll phone you as soon as she arrives.

2. She was only twelve. She was very strong.
3. My father died. Then we stopped going to the mountains.
4. I like coffee, but we didn't have any. I drank tea.
5. I wore a coat. I thought it was going to be cold.
6. He used to travel a lot more. Then his children were born.
7. I can't leave for the moment. I can leave at ten.
8. I was watching television. There was a knock at the door.

7 **Write these questions in the right order.**

1. are at looking what you ?
2. about are talking they who ?
3. buy did for it she who ?

8 **Describe these.**

1. a boat (Begin *A boat is ...*)
2. salt
3. an artist

48

READING AND WRITING

9 Read the newspaper article and answer the questions.

Buried Sisters

TWO ELDERLY SISTERS whose collection of newspapers almost filled their small home are in stable condition in hospital after a tunnel
5 through the papers collapsed, trapping them for several hours Saturday.

Police said Eva Collins, 82, and her sister, Margaret Wentworth, 79, had
10 thousands of papers dating back to the 1960s in the semi-detached home they shared on Roderland Road.

"They were piled nearly to the ceiling," according to Sergeant Alex
15 Dungannon, who said the sisters had apparently devised a series of tunnels through which they could move on hands and knees to various rooms. The women were heading from their living
20 room to the kitchen Saturday when the passage they were using gave way, he said.

The collapse "sounded like an avalanche, like the whole house was coming down," said neighbor Tim
25 Francis, who occupies the other side of the house. Francis rushed next door, but was unable to reach the women. It took fire department and police officials
30 several hours to rescue them, working through precarious piles of newspapers.

"There were tons of them," said Dungannon. "It may sound funny now, but it was a dangerous situation."
35 Neighbors said the sisters seemed friendly and normal when they encountered them outdoors, but they knew of no one who had been invited inside the home.
40 A hospital official said the women suffered a variety of injuries, none of them life-threatening. "They're both pretty tough, I guess," she said.

(from *Family News*, by Joan Barfoot
© copyright Joan Barfoot 1989)

Find words or expressions that mean:

1. ill, but not getting worse (*lines 1–7*)
2. fell down (*lines 1–7*)
3. put on top of one another (*lines 8–15*)
4. invented (*lines 13–22*)
5. going (*lines 13–22*)
6. fell down (*lines 13–22*)
7. unsafe, likely to fall down (*lines 23–31*)
8. met (*lines 35–43*)

10 Choose one of these tasks. Write 150 words or more.

1. Imagine you are Tim Francis, the neighbour in the story. Write a letter to a close friend telling the story from your point of view.
2. Write a story about something that surprised you, or surprised other people. The story does not have to be true.

LANGUAGE IN USE

11 Write appropriate replies to these.

1. Ambulance service. May I help you?
2. Would you like some more wine?
3. Oh, I am sorry. How stupid of me!
4. What can I get you to drink?
5. What did you think of the film?

VOCABULARY

12 Write the past tense and past participle forms of fifteen or more of these verbs.

bend   bleed   break   catch   choose   cut
drive   fall   feel   find   get   hide   keep
leave   lie   lose   put   run   smell   steal
take   tear   tell   throw

13 Write the opposites of these words and expressions.

1. pull *push*
2. hard
3. heavy
4. switch on
5. beginning
6. mend
7. pick up
8. find
9. expensive

14 Two-word expressions. Complete these.

1. driving *licence*
2. credit ....
3. department ....
4. ambulance ....
5. brake ....
6. .... belt
7. steering ....

SPEAKING

15 Work with two other students. Imagine one of you has invited the other two, and your teacher, to your home for a dinner party. Say hello, have drinks, and begin dinner.

C1 I wander round the kitchen

Listening and reading skills; discussion; vocabulary; stress and rhythm.

1 [cassette] Close your books and listen to the recording. What are Tony's two jobs? Can you remember anything about how he spends his day?

2 Read the transcript of Tony's interview, and then see if you can put the pictures in the right order.

INTERVIEWER: How do you organise your work?

TONY: Well, I'm married, so to be alone in the mornings, the first thing is to get rid of my wife, who fortunately has a job, so she gets up in the morning, makes a cup of tea, rouses me, I come downstairs, wander round the kitchen, have my cup of tea, iron her clothes for her that she's put out for me on the first floor landing on top of the ironing board, so I do her ironing – by that stage she's in the bath, so I'm – by that stage it's half past eight, quarter to nine, I'm only half an hour from being on my own – come down and make sure she's got all the lunch in a bag, by that stage I've finished my tea, I've finished the ironing, she's out of the bath, I'm in the bath, she goes upstairs and gets dressed; by the time – if this is all synchronised properly – by the time I get out of the bath and go upstairs she's fully dressed; and then by the time I'm dressed and come downstairs she's just about to hop on her bicycle and go off to work, which makes it about nine o'clock or nine fifteen.

And then I'm on my own. And I fluffle around for half an hour, putting off sitting down, make myself another cup of tea; but I'm usually working by ten o'clock. Then I work till twelve o'clock, half past twelve, then reward myself with some lunch, have a cup of tea, waste another ten minutes, start working about one o'clock again, and work till two o'clock, half past two.

Thereafter I become a househusband, and get the house organised for the evening when my wife comes home, at anywhere between six and seven o'clock, and the house has got to be tidy or I get into trouble. And doing it all myself involves doing most of the housework, most of the ironing, all the washing, a good part of the cooking …

3 Tony is a writer and 'househusband'. He works alone all day. Would you like his kind of life? Why (not)?

4 Complete the text with the words and expressions in the box. You may need to make small changes. You can use a dictionary or ask somebody for help if you like.

> able   all day   anywhere between   careful
> chance   cooking   extremely   get rid of
> grow up   housework   ironing   job
> on business   on one's own   organise
> outdoors   put off   relationships   salary
> shopping   trade union   washing
> waste (time or money)

Bill Radford has a ......1...... in a small factory. He doesn't much like the work, but he enjoys the ......2...... with the other workers, and he gets on well with the boss. He belongs to a ......3...... and helps to ......4...... the work of the local branch. Sometimes he has a ......5...... to travel ......6......, which he enjoys very much.

His wife, Ann, has been unemployed for the last two years. She stays at home and looks after the house. After getting their six-year-old daughter Sally ready and driving her to school, she starts on the housework. Although she likes being ......7......, she finds ......8...... boring, and doesn't like to stay at home ......9....... So she tries to get through the washing up, the ......10......, the ......11......, the ......12...... and so on as quickly as possible. This takes her ......13...... two and three hours; after that she usually has lunch. She doesn't like to ......14...... time, so after lunch she goes off to the public library and reads books on politics or history until it's time to fetch Sally from school. In the evenings Bill and Ann share the ......15......

At weekends they try to spend some time ......16......: they often go walking in the country, or take Sally on trips to places like the zoo or the seaside.

Money is a big problem. Bill doesn't earn a very good ......17......, and their income is hardly enough for three people to live on, so they have to be very ......18...... about what they spend. They can't really afford to keep the car, and will have to ......19...... it soon, but they have decided to ......20...... selling it until Sally is old enough to go to school by bus. They are just not ......21...... to save money, and they're ......22...... worried about their old age. Sally wants to be a teacher or a nurse when she ......23......, but Ann and Bill hope she will do something where she can earn enough money to live a better life than her parents.

5 Choose words and expressions to learn from Exercises 2 and 4. Compare notes with other students, and talk about the reasons for your choices. Do you choose words because they are common, because they are important, because they are useful, because you are interested in the subject, because you like the sound of them, because they are easy to learn …?

6 📼 Pronunciation. The first five stressed syllables are marked. Which other syllables do you think are stressed? Listen to the recording and see if you were right.

Well, I'm married, so to be alone in the mornings, the first thing is to get rid of my wife, who fortunately has a job, so she gets up in the morning, makes a cup of tea, rouses me, I come downstairs, wander round the kitchen, have my cup of tea …

7 Imagine that you can do exactly what work you like. Think about the job, and plan your daily routine. When you are ready, tell the class. You must use at least five of the new words and expressions that you have learnt from this lesson.

'I get up at ten o'clock …'

Learn/revise: bag; branch; chance; cooking; factory; first floor; housework; income; ironing; job; relationship; salary; shopping; TV; washing; fetch; get dressed; get up; grow up (grew, grown); iron; organise; put off …ing (put, put); share; waste (time/money); alone; boring; careful; married; tidy; unemployed; extremely; outdoors; upstairs; by (= not later than); all day; as … as possible; be able to; get into trouble; get on with sbdy; get rid of sbdy/sth; make (a cup of) tea; on business; on my own; on top of.

C2 Focus on systems

A choice of exercises: the names of common electrical appliances; two-word verbs; *should(n't)* and *must(n't)*; pronunciation of final consonant groups; hearing unstressed syllables.

VOCABULARY: ELECTRICAL APPLIANCES

1 Work in groups of three or four and make a list of all the electrical appliances (e.g. *fridge*, *CD player*, *iron*) you can think of. Try to find at least twenty.

2 If you could have just five of the things in your list (plus leads, plugs and sockets), which would you choose? Which five are the least important?

3 📼 Look at the picture below and listen to the recording. Which thing is described in each sentence? Example:

'It's plugged in and switched on. It's black and white.'
'The radio.'

GRAMMAR: TWO-WORD VERBS

4 Look at the examples. Can you make a rule?

Please switch the light off.
Please switch off the light.
Please switch it off.
BUT NOT ~~Please switch off it.~~

Could you pick those papers up?
Could you pick up those papers?
Could you pick them up?
BUT NOT ~~Could you pick up them?~~

5 Look at the sentences and say what you should do. Use these verbs.

switch on	switch off	turn up
turn down	plug in	unplug

Example:
What should you do if you've finished using your calculator? *'Switch it off.'*

What should you do if:
1. the radio isn't loud enough?
2. the CD player's too loud?
3. you see in the newspaper that there's an interesting TV programme just starting?
4. you don't want to watch TV any more?
5. the TV's on fire?
6. the cooker's too hot?
7. you want to use your calculator?
8. the iron isn't getting the creases out of your clothes?
9. the iron's burning your clothes?
10. you've finished with the iron?
11. you've just taken the hoover out of the cupboard and you want to start using it?

GRAMMAR: *SHOULD, SHOULDN'T, MUST* AND *MUSTN'T*

6 Look at the examples. What do you think is the difference between *should* and *must*?

You should switch the light off before you change a bulb.
You must use the right kind of batteries in a calculator.
You shouldn't drive too fast on wet roads.
You mustn't drive at over 30mph in towns.

7 Which word do you feel is best – *should, shouldn't, must* or *mustn't*?

1. You .... always switch electrical appliances off when you are not using them.
2. Small children .... watch violent programmes on TV.
3. In Britain, before you start using a new electrical appliance, you .... put the right kind of plug on.
4. When you put a plug on, you .... be careful to put the wires in the right places.
5. You .... touch electrical appliances when you are in the bath.
6. When you move into a new house or flat, you .... check the electrical wiring.
7. You .... plug too many things into the same socket.
8. You .... wash white and coloured clothes separately.
9. You .... clean out the fridge from time to time.
10. You .... let the iron get too hot if you are ironing silk.
11. You .... turn your radio up loud at night.
12. In Britain, you .... buy a licence every year if you have a TV.

8 Look at the road signs and complete the descriptions. Use *must*, *should* or *must not*.

1. You .... go.
2. You .... stop.
3. You .... stop if the road in front of you is not clear.
4. You .... drive into this street.
5. You .... turn right.
6. People .... walk here.
7. You .... drive carefully – the road is slippery.
8. You .... park here.
9. You .... overtake.
10. You .... look out for fallen rocks.

9 Do one of these tasks.

1. Make up some traffic regulations for Fantasia (a strange country where everything is different). Example:
   '*You must not drive at over 30 mph on Sundays.*'
2. Give some advice to somebody who wants to go on a safari in East Africa. Example:
   '*You must have injections. You should take binoculars.*'
3. Give some advice to a foreigner who is planning to visit your country.

PRONUNCIATION: FINAL CONSONANT GROUPS; UNSTRESSED SYLLABLES

10 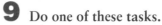 Say these words and expressions. Be careful to pronounce the ends of the words clearly.

lamps   bulbs   lamps and bulbs
plugs   sockets   plugs and sockets

plugged   plugged in   It's not plugged in.
finished   finished it   I finished it.
switched   switched on   It's not switched on.
thanked   thanked him   I thanked him.
asked   asked for   She asked for help.

fridges   They've got two fridges.
switches   Where are the switches?
torches   The torches were in the car.

isn't   She isn't in.
doesn't   It doesn't open.
wasn't   It wasn't switched on.
hasn't   She hasn't arrived yet.
hadn't   She said she hadn't forgotten me.
wouldn't   I wouldn't use it.
couldn't   I couldn't understand him.
shouldn't   You shouldn't ask questions like that.

11 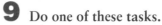 Listen to the recording. How many words do you hear in each sentence? What are they? (Contractions like *that's* count as two words.)

> **Learn/revise:** plug in; unplug; pick up; switch on/off; turn up/down; electric(al); *the names of the electrical appliances in Exercise 1.*

53

C3 How to do it

1 Here are some useful practical tips for everyday life.
Unfortunately, the beginnings and ends have got mixed up.
Can you sort them out?

To make tomatoes easier to peel,	rub them with lemon first and then wash them.
If you want to pick up a rabbit,	you should rub it with liquid brass cleaner.
To get cigarette stains off your fingers,	cover them with very hot water for a minute or two.
If you catch German measles,	put cold water in one and stand the other in hot water.
You can clean dirty saucepans	by packing them with wet newspaper and leaving them overnight.
To get dust out of a guitar,	don't hold its ears.
If two glasses are stuck together,	don't visit anyone who is pregnant unless you're sure she's already had them.
To get small scratches off your watch glass,	you should put rice inside it, shake it and empty it.
You can make tight shoes more comfortable	by filling them with cold water and vinegar and letting them boil for five minutes.

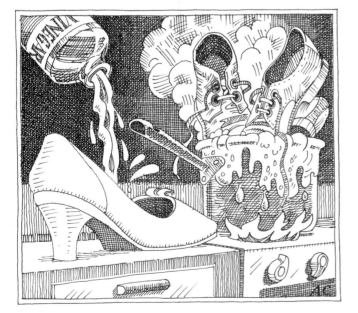

2 Look at the different beginnings and ends from Exercise 1. Which of the following beginnings can go with which ends?

BEGINNINGS: ENDS:
To ...   imperative (e.g. *rub*)
If ...   negative imperative (e.g. *don't hold*)
You can ...   *you should ...*
            by ...ing

Rewrite two of the tips using different beginnings and/or ends. Rewrite one of the tips using *you shouldn't* or *you mustn't*.

3 Can you complete these tips?

The night before an examination, ...
To find out how far away a thunderstorm is, ...
You can get a tight ring off ...
You can keep a mirror from misting up ...
If you're going on a long flight, ...
To keep wasps away from a picnic, ...
To get chewing gum off a piece of clothing, ...

4 🔲 Pronunciation: practise these words. Can you think of any other words that begin with *s* + consonant?

school   scratches   small   smell   smoke
specialist   speed   spelling   sport   stains
stand   stop   stuck   stuff

Now practise these. Can you think of any other words that begin with *ex*?

examination   excuse   explain   extremely

5 Choose the five most useful new words to learn from Exercises 1 and 3. Compare notes with other students – have you chosen the same words?

6 Work in groups. Each group writes four tips (serious or funny). Then copy the tips, with the beginnings and ends out of order, and give them to another group to put in order. Ideas:

How to mend things.
How to clean things.
How to cook things.
How to keep things safe/clean.
How to make cats/dogs/people/children do what you want them to.
How to stop cats/dogs/people/children doing things that you don't want them to do.
How to attract men/women.

7 Prepare a talk about how to do something. (For example, how to make ...; how to mend ...; how to cook ...; how to use ...) When you are ready, give your talk to the other students.

'... then you put the other one on top of the first one and glue them together.'

Infinitive of purpose
To get dust out of a guitar, ...
   (~~For to get dust out of a guitar ...~~)
   (~~For get dust out of a guitar ...~~)

Modal verbs
You **can** clean dirty saucepans ...
   (~~You can to clean ...~~)
You **should** put rice inside it ...
   (~~You should to put ...~~)
You **mustn't** visit anyone ...
   (~~You mustn't to visit ...~~)

Imperative
Rub them with lemon.
Don't hold its ears.

Learn/revise: brass; chewing gum; dust; examination; flight; (German) measles; guitar; lemon; liquid; mirror; newspaper; picnic; rabbit; rice; ring; stain; saucepan; thunderstorm; tip; vinegar; wasp; attract; boil; clean; cover; empty (*verb and adjective*); fill; mend; mix up; pack; peel; rub; shake (shook, shaken); sort out; comfortable; dirty; everyday; practical; pregnant; safe; tight; useful; overnight; unfortunately.

SKILLS FOCUS
SKILLS FOCUS
SKILLS FOCUS
SKILLS FOCUS
SKILLS FOCUS
SKILLS FOCUS

C4 Quick thinkers

Reading and writing skills (studying text structure; past narrative); vocabulary study; Past Progressive.

1 Here are four reports from British newspapers. The sentences have been mixed up. Work in groups of four. Each student should choose a different report and try to put it together, with the sentences in the right order. See if you can do it without looking up any words in the dictionary. When you are ready, read your report to the others in your group.

Policeman saves boy on motorway

Quick-thinking van driver

Firemen catch a man in mid-air

Helicopter pilot saves swimmers

A quick-thinking helicopter pilot saved 3 swimmers from shark attacks yesterday.

A quick-thinking van driver saved 11 people trapped in a blazing house in Birkenhead early today.

After a few minutes they were frightened away, and the swimmers were able to get back safely to the beach.

After shouting for help, the man jumped from a top-floor window with his clothes on fire.

But a policeman had seen him fall.

Firemen who were fighting the fire on a balcony below heard his shouts and realised what was happening.

Four adults and seven children were trapped in the bedroom above.

He brought his helicopter down until he was just over the water, and hovered above the sharks.

He dashed across the motorway and grabbed the five-year-old to safety from under the wheels of a vehicle that was almost upon them.

He was seriously injured and lay helpless in the fast lane with traffic hurtling towards him.

Last night 22-year-old Mr Luke Savage, of Moreton Grove, Chester, was recovering in hospital.

Little John Parker faced death when he fell from a car as it sped down a busy motorway.

Mrs Anne Redman of Newbury was driving past a house in Beaufort Road when she saw the ground floor on fire.

Mrs Redman backed her van across the pavement, smashed through the front fence, and drove up to the front of the house.

Police Constable Peter O'Donnell, careless of his own life, leapt from a moving patrol car.

Swimmer Marion Jacobs said afterwards, 'He saved our lives. If he hadn't come when he did, the sharks would have had us.'

The trapped occupants were able to jump to safety via the roof of the van.

They leaned out and grabbed him by the legs as he hurtled past.

Three firemen caught a man in mid-air yesterday as he leapt from a blazing house.

While he was flying off the Australian coast near Sydney, the pilot saw sharks approaching the swimmers.

Yesterday John, of The Close, Newleigh, Herts, was in hospital with head and leg injuries, but was described as 'satisfactory'.

2 Find the words *blazing*, *grabbed*, *above*, *leapt*, *hurtling* and *sped* in the reports in Exercise 1. Look at how they are used. Can you see what they mean without using a dictionary? Can you find other words in the reports that mean the same as *blazing*, *grabbed*, *above* and *leapt*?

3 Choose some more words to learn from the reports. Ask the teacher, or use a dictionary, to help you find out the exact meanings.

4 Look at the way the Past Progressive tense is used in the example. Can you find more examples of the Past Progressive in the reports?

Mrs Anne Redman of Newbury *was driving* past a house in Beaufort Road when she *saw* the ground floor on fire.

5 Here are the beginning and end of another news report. Can you write the middle? Try to use some vocabulary and structures from Exercises 1–4.

Quick-thinking five-year-old saves cyclist

Cyclist Norman Pratt went out of control as he was coming down a steep cliffside road yesterday, and ended up hanging by his hands from a small bush, with a 200-foot drop below his feet.

23-year-old Pratt, from Harlow, Essex, said 'She was wonderful. I couldn't have held on much longer. If she hadn't come when she did, I would have fallen to my death.'

Simple Past and Past Progressive tenses
Mrs Anne Redman of Newbury *was driving* past a house in Beaufort Road when she *saw* the ground floor on fire.

Learn/revise: adult; death; ground floor; helicopter; motorway; neighbour; pilot; safety; traffic; vehicle; approach; dash; frighten; jump; pull; recover; save; trap; busy; helpless; injured; quick; above; afterwards; almost; away; on fire; over; seriously; via.

C5 It doesn't work

Making and accepting apologies; correcting misunderstandings; making complaints; listening skills: predicting, listening for specific information; reading skills: guessing words from context; pronunciation: stress for emphasis and contrast.

1 Here is a dialogue with most of the words missing. Some blanks need one word; some need several words. See if you can guess what is missing, and listen to the recording to check your guesses.

ASSISTANT: ...., madam. .... help ....?
CUSTOMER: .... manager, ...
A: Furniture, madam? Second floor.
C: .... <u>Ma-na-ger</u>.
A: .... furniture.
C: .... But .... manager, ...?
A: Well, ... busy .... appointment?
C: No, ... complaint.
A: A complaint. .... Well, I'll just see if she's free.

2 Work with a partner, and make up a short conversation which includes a misunderstanding and an apology. You can use one of these sentences if you like.

I thought you said Thursday.
I thought you said goodbye.
I thought you said five pence.
I thought you said five o'clock.
I thought you said steak.
I thought you were talking to me.

3 Close your book, and listen to the second dialogue. How much can you remember?

4 Now read the second dialogue and do the tasks.

MANAGER: Good afternoon, madam. I understand you have a complaint.
C: Yes, I've got a problem with this hair-dryer.
M: I'm sorry to hear that. What's the trouble?
C: Well, first of all, I ordered it two months ago and it only arrived yesterday.
M: Oh, dear. That's very strange.
C: Well, it's probably because you addressed it to Mr Paul Jones at 29 Cannon Street. I'm *Mrs Paula* Jones, and my address is *39* Cannon Street.
M: Well, I'm really sorry about that, madam. We do …
C: And secondly, I'm afraid it's useless. It doesn't work.
M: Doesn't work?
C: No. It doesn't work. It doesn't dry my hair. When I switch it on, it just goes 'bzzzzz', but it doesn't get hot at all.
M: Well, I really am very sorry about this, madam. I do apologise. We'll be happy to replace the dryer for you. Or we'll give you a refund instead, if you prefer.
C: And thirdly, …

1. **Thinking about meaning: match each word or expression in *italics* in the first column with the closest meaning in the second column.**

1. I *ordered it* two months ago …	a. wrote on it the name and address of
2. *That's very strange.*	b. take this and give you money
3. … *addressed it to* …	c. take this and give you another
4. I'm afraid *it's useless.*	d. no one can use it
5. It doesn't *work.*	e. in place of my other suggestion
6. … to *replace the dryer* …	f. I'm surprised
7. … we'll *give you a refund* …	g. do what it should do
8. … give you a refund *instead,* …	h. asked you to send it

2. **Find these expressions in the second dialogue.**

1. Find an expression to use before you say something unpleasant: for example, ... *I've crashed your car.*
2. Find four ways of saying *I'm sorry* and write them down from weakest to strongest.
3. Find a verb to fit in this sentence: *When I touched it, it* .... *'whirr'.*
4. Find a verb to fit in this sentence: *It was warm this morning, but now it has* .... *cooler.*

3. **Listen to the second dialogue again.**

5 📼 Stress. Listen carefully to these questions, and then write answers to them (beginning *No, …*). When you have done that, practise saying the questions and answers.

1. You've got *two* sisters, haven't you?
   No, just one.

2. You've got two *sisters*, haven't you?
   No, two brothers.

3. You work in London, don't you?
4. Is that Mary's father?
5. Did you say you had a new red Lancia?
6. Do you need English for your work?
7. Would you like me to telephone Peter and Anne?
   (*three times, with different answers*)

6 Match the objects with the problems. You can use a dictionary. The first two answers are done for you.

a. It's started going very fast. *2, 4*

b. It won't start. *4*

c. It doesn't work.
d. It makes a funny noise.
e. One of the buttons is stuck.
f. It won't turn off.
g. It's stopped.
h. It won't switch on.

7 Your teacher will tell you to be a customer or a shop manager. Follow the appropriate instructions.

Customers
There is something wrong with your camera/watch/telephone *etc*. Decide what is wrong. Decide whether you want it repaired or replaced, or whether you want a refund. Decide whether you are going to be friendly to the shop manager. You can look back at the dialogues for vocabulary. Then go and complain.

Shop managers
You are the manager of a shop. Decide whether you are feeling friendly or not today. Decide whether your shop gives refunds, or only offers to repair or replace. Decide how long repairs take. You can look back at the dialogues for vocabulary. Then get ready for some complaints.

Learn/revise: appointment; complaint; conversation; customer; furniture (*uncountable*); hair-dryer; manager; problem; refund; complain; dry; get (for changes) (got, got); go (for sounds) (went, gone); order; repair; replace; busy; free (= not busy); funny (= strange); stuck; useless; first of all; instead; probably; secondly; thirdly; whether; I do apologise; I really am very sorry; I thought you said …; if you prefer; It doesn't work; It won't start; That's all right; That's very strange; What's the trouble?

C6 Focus on systems

A choice of exercises: passives; situational language; contrastive stress; weak and strong forms.

GRAMMAR: PASSIVES

1 Choose the correct caption for the cartoon.

'They die if they | don't put | the right way up.'
| aren't put |
| haven't put |

2 Look at the sentences. Do you remember how to make passive verbs? Try to match the tense names with the sentences (there is one name too many).

1. Britain *is governed* from London.
2. Where's the TV? *Is it being repaired*?
3. Some very good comedy films *were made* in Britain in the 1950s.
4. The President started feeling ill while he *was being interviewed*.
5. He *has been taken* into hospital.
6. When do you think the first restaurant *will be opened* on the moon?

```
Past Progressive
Future
Simple Present
Simple Present Perfect
Present Progressive
Present Perfect Progressive
Simple Past
```

3 Active or passive? Choose the best continuation. Can you see why it is best?

1. She lives in a charming old house.
   a. Somebody built it in the 15th century.
   b. It was built in the 15th century.
2. Spanish is a very useful language to learn.
   a. People speak it in a lot of different countries.
   b. It is spoken in a lot of different countries.
3. She bought a new dress, but she didn't like it.
   a. So she gave it to her sister.
   b. So it was given to her sister.
4. My aunt is a very successful writer.
   a. She has just written a new novel.
   b. A new novel has just been written by her.
5. The novel is about a woman who becomes a dictator.
   a. They are publishing it next month.
   b. It is being published next month.
6. I'll tell you what made me so cross.
   a. The way Mary told everybody what to do annoyed me.
   b. I was annoyed by the way Mary told everybody what to do.

4 Imagine that you are in a busy station restaurant at about 10.30 in the morning. Can you think of ten or more things that *are being done*? Examples:

Coffee is being served.
Sandwiches are being made.

Useful vocabulary:	bake	boil	clean
cook	cut up	defrost	fry	make
prepare	pay	roast	serve	wash

5 Imagine that you return to your old school after 20 years. A lot of things *have been done*, and the place looks very different. Can you think of six or more changes? Examples:

A new library has been built.
My old classroom has been turned into a museum.

Useful vocabulary:	build	close down
extend	modernise	open	pull down
rebuild	renovate	repair	turn into

VOCABULARY: SITUATIONAL LANGUAGE

6 What situations do you think the following expressions might be used in? Choose one of the situations and see how many more typical expressions you can think of.

Could I have the bill, please?
I want to send this airmail to Russia.
It's a nice colour, but it's a bit too small.
How many nights?

What time does it leave?
Could you check the oil?
Three pounds of the big ones and two of those, please.
I'm sorry. You've got the wrong number.

PRONUNCIATION: CONTRASTIVE STRESS; WEAK AND STRONG FORMS

7 Contrastive stress. Look at the pictures and listen to the sentences. There are some mistakes in the sentences. Can you correct them? Make sure you use the right stress. Example:

'It's ten past two.'
'No, it isn't. It's ten past three.'

8 Weak and strong forms. Some words have two pronunciations: a 'weak form' and a 'strong form'. Examples:

	WEAK FORM	STRONG FORM
must	/ms, məst/	/mʌst/
can	/kn, kən/	/kæn/
have	/(h)əv/	/hæv/
was	/w(ə)z/	/wɒz/

Which pronunciation do you think *must*, *can*, *have* and *was* have in these sentences? Listen and check your answers.

1. I must go soon.
2. Oh, must you?
3. I really *must* stop smoking soon.
4. Yes, you must.
5. We must get some more milk.
6. I can swim, but not very well.
7. Yes, I can.
8. Nobody can understand what he says.
9. Where have you been?
10. What time do you have breakfast?
11. We've been talking about you.
12. Oh, have you?
13. I was late for work this morning.
14. That *was* nice – thank you very much.
15. Sally was here this afternoon.
16. Oh, was she?

Learn/revise: airmail; bill; wrong number; bake; boil; build (built, built); check; clean; close down; cook; cut up (cut, cut); discover; fry; govern; interview; invent; modernise; pay (paid, paid); prepare; publish; pull down; record; repair; rebuild; roast; send (sent, sent); serve; speak (spoke, spoken); turn into; wash.

C7 Love and other problems

Discussion, reading and writing; *should*; Present Perfect Progressive; conditionals.

1 The following texts are typical of letters and replies which are published in British teenagers' magazines. Read them carefully, but don't use your dictionary unless it is absolutely necessary. Are you surprised by anything in the letters or the answers? Do you agree or disagree strongly with anything that is said? Which reply do you agree with more? Why?

Should I lie to my parents?

Can you help me? I've fallen in love with a really nice boy I know at College. I'm 16, but I don't have a lot of freedom – I'm Asian, and my family have very strict attitudes because of their religion. So I'm not allowed to go out in the evenings, and even if I did go out with this boy during College hours I couldn't tell my parents, because they'd be really upset if they knew I was going out with a white boy. I feel bad about the situation, because I love my parents and they trust me, but this relationship is really important to me. What do you advise?

■ I understand your problem, but I really don't think you should go out with him. It's all right for the two of you to be friends, but you mustn't get yourself into a situation where you have to lie to your parents. Their religious beliefs are an important part of your family life, and it would be a mistake to go against the rules that they have made for you. If you did go out with the boy you would eventually get found out, and then the trust between you and your parents would be destroyed.

If you need to talk it over, you could get in touch with ASHA – a group that gives advice to young Asian women like yourself who are caught between two cultures. Their help is free and confidential. You can phone them on 071 274 8854.

SHOULD I ASK HER OUT?

I'm 16, and I really fancy a girl at my school. For the last few weeks I've been getting more and more attracted to her, and it's turning into a very serious relationship. The trouble is that she's Asian, and I know my parents would object if I asked her out. They are Catholics, and they would be shocked and angry if I got involved with a Muslim girl. I respect their beliefs, and I don't want to go behind their backs, but I have to think of myself. What should I do?

The first thing is to make absolutely sure of your own feelings. You haven't been seeing this girl for very long, and there's no point in upsetting your whole family for a relationship that might not last.

But if you're convinced that this is the real thing, then you must make sure what your parents' attitude is. Do you really know they wouldn't let you go out with the girl? Maybe they will. Talk the situation over with them, calmly and openly – that way you can be certain what they feel instead of just guessing.

If they really do object, you will have to make a decision. You can either respect their beliefs and live the way they want, or you can do what *you* think is right. If you tell your parents firmly that you're going to go out with the girl, then you won't be going behind their backs, and you will be showing them that you have a right to follow your own opinions, even if these are very different from theirs.

2 Which of the following sentences is closest to the answer to the first letter, and which is closest to the answer to the second letter?

1. Your parents may let you go out with your friend, but if they don't you will have to decide between your beliefs and your parents' beliefs.
2. If you talk carefully to your parents they will almost certainly let you go out with your friend.
3. You shouldn't go out with your friend because it is bad to go against your family's religion and culture.
4. You shouldn't go out with your friend because it would make your parents unhappy.

3 Look at these two examples of the Present Perfect Progressive.

*For the last few weeks I've **been getting** more and more attracted to her.*
*You **haven't been seeing** this girl for very long.*

Why is the Present Perfect Progressive used here?
Look out for more examples in the lesson.

4 Here are some expressions that are useful when discussing problems or giving advice. Can you find any others in the letters in Exercise 1? Can you think of any more useful expressions for discussion that you would like to know in English? Ask your teacher if necessary.

I (don't) think you should …
There's nothing wrong in …ing
I would(n't) advise you to …
I (don't) think it's a good idea to …
It's not worth it
It's (not) worth …ing
I'd be surprised if …
You can either … or …
It is important to …
If I were you, I'd …
Why don't you …?
Try …ing

5 Work in groups of three. Choose one of the following questions; say what you think, and find out what the others in the group think. Talk about your own experience, or about people you know, if possible. Use a dictionary or ask for help if necessary. Finish by giving a brief report of your discussion (two or three sentences) to the class.

1. Should children be free to choose their own boy/girlfriends at age 13? At age 16?
2. At what age should children be free to go out with their friends in the evenings?
3. Should there be different rules for boys and girls?
4. What advice would you give to a friend who wanted to marry somebody of a different race?
5. How much should children respect their parents' religious and cultural beliefs?

6 The class should work in groups of three or four, and do one of these three activities.
EITHER: Each group chooses one of the following letters and writes an answer.
OR: Each group writes a problem letter, makes two copies, exchanges problems with two other groups, and writes answers to the problem letters it gets.
OR: Each group writes a problem letter. Four or five students (the 'experts') then come and sit at the front of the class. The others read out their problem letters; the 'experts' give their advice.

CHOCOLATE ADDICT

I'm a chocolate addict. My friends and family cannot believe how much I can eat. I often choose to eat chocolate rather than a proper meal, partly because it's quicker, but also because I prefer it. It seems to give me more energy, though I feel sick if I eat too much.

I've put on a lot of weight, and I hate that, but if I'm feeling fed up about being fat, I just eat some chocolate to cheer myself up.

The people at work treat it as a joke, and often buy me presents of chocolate – they don't realise I've got a real problem. I really do think I'm addicted to chocolate. What can I do?

EXTRA LESSONS

I'm 17, and I've fallen in love with my maths teacher. He's in his first teaching job since he left university, and there's only about ten years' difference in our ages. Recently he's been giving me extra maths lessons after school and yesterday he asked me out for a drink. What should I do?

MUM'S A SLAVE

I have just been spending a week with my parents, who are a happily-married couple in their fifties. What worries me is that my father has a very old-fashioned attitude to housework. He really treats my poor mother like a servant. She has a bad heart, and it makes me angry to see her carrying in heavy loads of shopping, doing all the cooking, cleaning and washing, and so on. Should I speak to my father?

STILL A PRISONER

I'm 25 and have just come out of prison after two years inside. My problem is that I feel very insecure and lonely and I don't know what to do with myself. I have no friends, as in the past I've behaved very badly to people. I'm worried that I won't ever be able to live a normal life again. Can you help?

Learn/revise: advice; attitude; belief; culture; decision; magazine; opinion; parents; problem; race; religion; reply; rule; the right to do sth; advise; agree (with sbdy); allow; ask sbdy out; destroy; disagree; fall in love with (fell, fallen); fancy; find out (found, found); go out with sbdy; guess; lie (lied, lied); object; respect; talk sth over; trust (*verb*); Asian; attracted (to sbdy); confidential; cultural; religious; surprised; worried; eventually; behind sbdy's back; *the 'useful expressions' in Exercise 4.*

C8 Government

1 How much do you know about these governments? Can you fill in any of the blanks?

	Britain	The USA	Your country or another country
consists of	.... countries; each is divided into counties	50 states; each is divided into counties	....
is governed from	London	....	....
Laws are made by	....	....	....
which consists of	House of Commons and House of Lords	....	....
Members are called	...............s of .... ('MPs') (Commons)	....	....
They are elected	every five years or less (Commons)	....	....
Head of government is called	.... Minister ('PM')	....	....
Is head of government separately elected?	No; leader of majority party in House of Commons becomes PM	....	....
Real power is held by	PM and his/her ministers ('cabinet')	....	....
Do local or regional government bodies have any power?	partly responsible for education, health care, police, roads	....	....
How many large political parties are there?	three; Labour (...............-wing), ... (right-wing) and Liberal Democrats (centre)	....	....
Ceremonial head of state?	King or	....	....

2 Dictionary skills: these three words come in Exercise 1. There are two or more definitions for each word. Which definition gives the meaning that the word has in Exercise 1?

cab•i•net /ˈkæbɪnɪt, ˈkæbənət, ˈkæbnɪt, ˈkæbnət/ *n* **1** a piece of furniture, with shelves and doors, or drawers, used for showing or storing things: *a* FILING CABINET | *I put my collection of old glasses in the cabinet.* **2** [+ *sing./pl. v*](in various countries) the most important ministers of the government, who meet as a group to make decisions or to advise the head of the government

coun•try /ˈkʌntri/ *n* -tries **1** [C] a nation or state with its land or population: *Some parts of this country are much warmer than others.* **2** [C] the people of a nation or state: *The country is opposed to war.* **3** [*the* S] the land outside cities or towns; land used for farming or left unused: *We're going to have a day in the country tomorrow.* **4** [U] land with a special nature or character: *good farming country.*

house /haʊs/ *n* houses /ˈhaʊzɪz, ˈhaʊzəz/ **1 a** a building for people to live or work in **b** the people in such a building. **2** a building for a stated purpose: *a hen house* | *a storehouse.* **3** a law-making body, or the building where it meets | *the* **Houses of Parliament** (= both Britain's law-making bodies) | *the* **House of Commons** (= the lower but more powerful law-making body, whose members are elected by the people) | *the* **House of Lords** (= the higher law-making body whose members are not elected). **4** (*cap. in names*) an important family, especially noble or royal: *The House of Windsor is the British royal family.*

(adapted from *Longman Active Study Dictionary of English*)

3 [cassette] You will hear part of a talk on the government of the United States. Before you listen, look at these notes.

US federation 50 states
48 between Canada, Mexico; + Alaska, Hawaii
fed cap Washington, S of N Y, near E coast

4 [cassette] Now listen to the next part of the talk and try to complete these notes.

Washington centre federal govt, but each state has own ....
State govts make own laws, responsible for ....

5 [cassette] Now listen to the rest of the talk and try to make notes yourself. (You will need abbreviations for these words: *Congress, Representatives, Senate/ Senators, Democrats, Republicans, President.*)

6 Look back at Exercise 1. Can you fill in any more of the blanks now?

7 Do one of these activities.

1. Work with one or two other students, or work alone. Write a political speech – serious or funny – to try and get yourself elected president of your English class. Students and teacher each have one vote. You, or one of you, should give your speech to the class. Practise your speech beforehand so that you can look at the class for at least part of the time instead of just reading the speech.
2. Work with one or two other students, or work alone. Write and give a political speech for a serious national political party or a funny one (for example: the anti-television party; the cats for Congress party; the anti-shoe party). Practise your speech beforehand so that you can look at the class for at least part of the time instead of just reading the speech.
3. Is there something you would like to change in another country – the killing of certain animals, or the making or testing of certain types of weapons or chemicals, for example? Work alone or with another student to write a letter to the head of that country in English. Find out where to send the letter by asking the consulate or embassy of that country. Send the letter. Report any answers to the class orally.
4. If you are in a class with students from other countries, choose one student to interview about how her/his country is governed. Make notes and report to a group or the whole class.

Learn/revise some of these: appointment; body; cabinet; capital; Congress; Conservatives; country; county; Democrats; federation; government; head (= person); head of state; health care; House of Commons; House of Lords; King; Labour; law; Liberal Democrats; majority; member; Member of Parliament (MP); minister; minority; parliament; police (*plural*); (political) party; power; President; Prime Minister (PM); Queen; Representative; Republicans; road; Senate; Senator; state; approve; become (became, become); consist (of); divide (into); elect; govern; hold (held, held); centre; federal; left-wing; local; national; political; real; regional; responsible; right-wing; each; every (five years); own (*determiner*); partly; separately; slightly.

Summary C

Simple Past and Past Progressive tenses

Mrs Anne Redman of Newbury **was driving** past a house in Beaufort Road when she **saw** the ground floor on fire.

Simple tenses with *as*

They leaned out and grabbed him by the legs **as** he **hurtled** past.

Three firemen caught a man in mid-air yesterday **as** he **leapt** from a blazing house.

Present Perfect Progressive

For the last few weeks I've **been getting** more and more attracted to her.

You **haven't been seeing** this girl for very long.

Recently he's **been giving** me extra maths lessons after school.

I **have** just **been spending** a week with my parents.

Passives

Simple Present

Britain **is governed** from London.

Paper **is made** from wood.

Present Progressive

Where's the TV? **Is** it **being repaired?**

Be careful what you say – this conversation **is being recorded.**

Simple Past

Some very good comedy films **were made** in Britain in the 1950s.

Our house **was built** in the 15th century.

Past Progressive

The President started feeling ill while he **was being interviewed.**

They knew that they **were being watched.**

Present Perfect

He **has been taken** into hospital.

Oil **has been discovered** under the White House.

Future

When do you think the first restaurant **will be opened** on the moon?

Her new book **will be published** next month.

if with Simple Past and *would*

My parents **would** object if I **asked** her out.

If you **did go** out with the boy you **would** eventually get found out.

Modal verbs

You **can clean** dirty saucepans … (~~You can to clean …~~)

You **should put** rice inside it … (~~You should to put …~~)

You **mustn't visit** anyone … (~~You mustn't to visit …~~)

Should I lie?

Should I go out with him?

will have to

If they really do object you **will have to** make a decision.

should and *must*

You **should** switch the light off before you change a bulb.

You **must** use the right kind of batteries in a calculator.

You **shouldn't** drive too fast on wet roads.

You **mustn't** drive at over 30mph in towns.

Infinitive of purpose

To get dust out of a guitar, put rice inside it, shake it and empty it.
(~~For to get dust out of a guitar …~~)
(~~For get dust out of a guitar …~~)

how to …

how to mend things

how to clean things

Do you know **how to** get to Dover?

Imperative

Rub them with lemon.

Don't hold its ears.

by …*ing*

You can make tight shoes more comfortable **by packing** them with wet newspaper and **leaving** them overnight.

Two-word verbs

Please **switch** the light **off.**

Please **switch off** the light.

Please **switch** it **off.**

BUT NOT ~~Please switch off it.~~

Could you **pick** those papers **up?**

Could you **pick up** those papers?

Could you **pick** them **up?**

BUT NOT ~~Could you pick up them?~~

Irregular verbs in Lessons C1–C8

INFINITIVE	PAST	PAST PARTICIPLE
become	became	become
build	built	built
cut	cut	cut
fall	fell	fallen
find	found	found
grow	grew	grown
hold	held	held
pay	paid	paid
put	put	put
send	sent	sent
speak	spoke	spoken

by (= not later than)

I'm usually working **by** ten o'clock.
By that stage she's in the bath.
By the time (that) I get out of the bath she's fully
    dressed.
By the time (that) I come downstairs she's just about
    to go off to work.

Discussing problems and giving advice

I (don't) think you should …
There's nothing wrong in …ing
I would(n't) advise you to …
I (don't) think it's a good idea to …
It's not worth it
It's (not) worth …ing
I'd be surprised if …
You can either … or …
It is important to …
If I were you, I'd …
Why don't you …?
Try …ing

Misunderstandings

I thought you said Thursday.

Formal apologies

I'm really sorry about that.
I really am very sorry.
I do apologise.

Stress

In a sentence, we usually stress (pronounce more loudly and clearly) the words with most meaning – nouns, ordinary verbs, adjectives and adverbs. Other words (pronouns, auxiliary verbs, prepositions, conjunctions and articles) are more often unstressed – they are pronounced more quickly and quietly.

Well, I'm married, so to be alone in the mornings, the first thing is to get rid of my wife, who fortunately has a job, so she gets up in the morning, makes a cup of tea, rouses me, I come downstairs, wander round the kitchen, have my cup of tea …

Longer words are not stressed on all syllables: one syllable usually carries the stress, and the others are pronounced more quickly and quietly.

married   alone   fortunately

Vocabulary

Look through the 'Learn/revise' boxes at the ends of Lessons C1–C8.

Revision and fluency practice C

A choice of activities.

1 📼 Listen and say how the people sound. You can use some of the adjectives in the box. Example:

'She sounds surprised.'

afraid	amused	angry	cross	pleased
relaxed	unhappy	surprised	upset
worried				

2 📼 Finding differences. Read the text and then listen to the recording. There are eleven significant differences between the two reports. Can you find all of them?

AN UNEMPLOYED man killing time before a date decided to turn to crime to ease his money problems. He wrote out a note reading 'I've got a gun in my pocket and I'll shoot it off unless you hand over the money'.

But David Smith, aged 21, failed to get any cash in spite of going into three shops in London Road, West Croydon.

At a chemist's a girl assistant refused to accept the note, believing that it contained an obscene suggestion. Next door, in a hardware shop, the Asian assistant said that he could not read English.

In desperation Smith, of High Road, Whitelea, Kent, went to a takeaway food shop, but the assistant could not read the note because he did not have his glasses.

Smith told police 'I've been a fool. When the judge hears about this he won't believe anyone could be so stupid. I only pretended to have a gun'.

3 Logic problems.

1. You are trying to win money at roulette, by betting on red or black. Red has come up the last ten times. How do you think you should bet?
   a. Red is obviously 'hot' tonight, so you should bet on red.
   b. It's obviously time for black to come up again, so you should bet on black.
   c. Red and black are equally likely, so it doesn't matter how you bet.
2. A couple have four children. What are the chances that they have two boys and two girls?
   a. 50–50.
   b. More than 50–50.
   c. Less than 50–50.

4 Mystery man. You are detectives working for the missing persons office in a big city police headquarters in Scotland. A man has been found wandering in the streets, suffering from loss of memory. Look at the following pieces of evidence, and then try to make up a theory about the man – what he does, where he comes from, *etc.*

1. The man looks European; he has a dark complexion and black hair. He is about 40, tall and athletic, but rather overweight.
2. He is dressed in pink silk pyjamas, made in Bangkok.
3. When questioned, he only says 'I can't remember', in English but with a strong French accent.
4. His hands are covered with engine oil.
5. He has a bag containing the following:
   - $60,000 in US currency
   - photographs of three beautiful women: two European-looking, one Oriental
   - a photograph of the British Minister of Defence
   - a receipt from a car-hire firm
   - two love letters: one in English, beginning 'My Darling Freddy', and the other in French, beginning 'Serge, mon amour'
   - a gun with the number removed
   - a screwdriver
   - a silver spoon
   - one more thing (you choose)

5 Here are some words from a dialogue. Can you complete it?

ANDY: going/shops/Mike
MIKE: Yes/get/something/you
ANDY: If/mind haven't/toothpaste/left
       Could/me/some
MIKE: OK
ANDY: like/Sanident/if/got
MIKE: OK
ANDY: Oh/run out/soap
MIKE: OK/get/you
ANDY: And/mind/posting/same/time
MIKE: Not at all
ANDY: give/you/money
MIKE: No/wait/come back/simpler
ANDY: All right Thanks/indeed
MIKE: welcome

6 Now practise the dialogue in Exercise 5 with a partner, but imagine that one of you is hard of hearing, tired, very old or bad-tempered. Make whatever changes you like.

7 Improvisation (groups of four). Two of you come home and find two strangers in your house/flat. Act out the scene.

8 Mime: verbs and adverbs. The teacher will give you two cards – one with a verb and one with an adverb. Act out the combination; the class will try to decide what you are doing. Example:

'You're reading unhappily.'

9 What makes a good teacher? Here are four of the qualities needed by a good teacher: *knowledge of the subject, patience, humour, intelligence*. List them in order of importance, and add any others that you think are missing. Then work with two other students and try to draw up an agreed group list, running from most to least important.

10 Look at the cartoons and talk about your reactions. Which ones do you find funny? Which ones don't make you laugh? Are there any that you don't understand? Discuss your reactions with other students.

'Nobody calls me stupid. Meet me outside when the big hand and the little hand are on the 12'

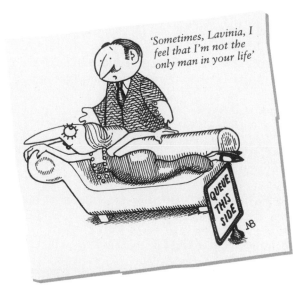

'Sometimes, Lavinia, I feel that I'm not the only man in your life'

QUEUE THIS SIDE

SUPER FAST

'Cheesebur...'

Test C

LISTENING

1 📼 Listen and take notes. The words in the box may help you.

> Dublin   Éire   Fianna Fáil   Fine Gael
> local authorities   national language
> official   Progressive Democrats   province

PRONUNCIATION

2 📼 Stress. Listen carefully to these questions, and write answers beginning *No,...* Examples:

Your sister lives in *Spain*, doesn't she?
No, she lives in Italy.

Your *sister* lives in Spain, doesn't she?
No, my brother does.

1. Has Anne got a red car?
2. Is Mike's aunt a dentist?
3. Did you say that your brother was coming this evening?
4. Didn't the President study mathematics at university?
5. Would you like some wine before dinner?

3 Remember that some words have two pronunciations: a 'weak form' and a 'strong form'. Examples:

	MUST	CAN	HAVE	WAS
WEAK:	/ms, məst/	/kn, kən/	/(h)əv/	/w(ə)z/
STRONG:	/mʌst/	/kæn/	/hæv/	/wɒz/

Which pronunciation do *must, can, have* and *was* have in these sentences? Write *W* (weak) or *S* (strong). Don't worry about negatives – they're always strong.

1. Of course she must.
2. I think I must phone my mother today.
3. I can't come today, but I can tomorrow.
4. When can we leave?
5. I wonder where the twins have gone.
6. We haven't lost Ted, have we?
7. I think I'll have a shower.
8. That *was* a nice dinner. Thank you so much.
9. Yes, she was.

4 Look at these words. In each group, the underlined sounds are the same except in one word. Which word is different?

1. <u>ou</u>t   kn<u>ow</u>   h<u>ow</u>   f<u>ou</u>nd
2. t<u>au</u>ght   w<u>a</u>lk   p<u>a</u>ss   t<u>a</u>ll
3. d<u>e</u>stroy   <u>e</u>ventually   r<u>e</u>spect   h<u>e</u>licopter
4. <u>a</u>fterwards   <u>a</u>dvise   <u>a</u>gree   <u>a</u>llow

GRAMMAR

5 Put the verb in the right form.

1. .... red wine out of clothes, ... white wine on the stain. (*get, pour*)
2. You can .... sunglasses by .... them with washing-up liquid. (*clean, wash*)
3. If you want .... a musical instrument well, you must .... every day. (*play, practise*)
4. Do you know how .... this? (*mend*)
5. Ms Abbott .... home from work when she .... the child fall off the bridge. (*walk, see*)
6. After .... for help, she .... off her shoes and .... in .... him. (*shout, take, jump, save*)
7. A lot of modern medicines .... from plants. (*make*)
8. The music for 'The Marriage of Figaro' .... by Mozart. (*write*)
9. The results .... tomorrow morning at nine o'clock. (*announce*)
10. All the beautiful buildings in our cities .... by exhaust gases from cars – we must .... something to stop this. (*destroy, do*)
11. The statue .... while it .... to another room in the museum. (*break, move*)
12. I don't think it's a good idea .... the children about it. (*tell*)
13. Do you think people should have the right .... what's on their medical records? (*know*)
14. For the last few weeks, I .... extra lessons after school. (*have*)

6 Choose the best word: *should* or *must.*

1. If you are American, you .... have a passport to get into Britain.
2. If you go to Hawaii, you .... take sunglasses.
3. You .... pay tax on most things that you buy in Britain.
4. If you want to become an Irish citizen, you .... learn some Irish – it's the law.
5. If you want to enjoy a holiday in Greece, you .... learn some Greek.

LANGUAGE IN USE

7 Write appropriate replies to these.

1. Oh, I *am* sorry.
2. I'm afraid this personal stereo I bought from you doesn't work.
3. I've got a problem.
4. Hello. Is Kevin there, please?
5. My wallet's just been stolen.

VOCABULARY

8 Two-word expressions: match the two halves.

bus	cleaner
cassette	dryer
chewing	fire
clothes	floor
convector	gum
find	heater
food	machine
ground	mixer
on	office
personal	out
political	party
post	player
vacuum	station
washing	stereo

9 What goes with what?

bad line	boil
cabinet	clean
check the oil	clothes
date	garage
elect	go out with
helicopter	minister
hoover	phone
iron	pilot
saucepan	plug
socket	president
traffic	vehicle

10 Write the opposites.

1. agree
2. break
3. empty
4. get a letter
5. liquid
6. push
7. switch on

11 Write the missing words.

1. I'm not sure how long I'll be out, but I'll be back .... ten.
2. Kevin is really attracted .... Janice, but he's too shy to ask her out.
3. There's nothing wrong .... asking about it.
4. Congress consists .... the Senate and the House of Representatives.
5. Scotland is divided .... counties.
6. My sister has fallen in love .... a much older man, and my parents are really upset.
7. Look, can we talk this problem ....?

READING AND WRITING

12 Here is a letter from a magazine. Read it and do the task.

How do I choose?

Dear Joyce,

1 I have been going out with Tom for two years now, and we are planning to get married. We share a lot of interests, and have enormous fun together. I know that
5 we would have a good and stable marriage.

Last autumn, however, we had a few problems. I was working abroad for a month, and shortly after I left Tom wrote to
10 me saying that he had been out with his ex-girlfriend a few times. He said they were just friends, but I was quite upset. About this time I met Alan, who was working on the same project as me. I was
15 very, very attracted to him, and we began going out together. He is obviously very much in love with me, and I am in love with him too, in a way. I have never been so physically attracted to a man as I am to
20 him – the memory of certain moments with him still makes me go weak with pleasure. But it is not only physical: we have all sorts of things in common. He wants me to marry him. We have continued to write,

25 and have seen each other once since then, when he came to England. If I did marry him, I would have to give up my job and go abroad, which bothers me – my career is important to me. And I am
30 worried that our relationship might not last.

Tom knows that I went out with Alan, but he does not know how powerfully I am attracted to him. Tom and I have talked
35 over the problem of his ex-girlfriend, and I was very impressed with the way that we were able to discuss things. I am still very, very fond of Tom, and I am sure that we would have a good life together. In every
40 way but one, we are probably much better suited to one another than Alan and I are.

What should I do? I feel so mixed up. Should I marry Alan and give up my job? Should I stay with Tom? If I do, I couldn't
45 tell him the whole truth about Alan; but I hate the idea of keeping a secret from my husband.

Please help me.

Linda

Put the events in order.

a. Alan asked Linda to marry him.
b. Linda and Tom began going out together.
c. Linda and Tom talked over their problems.
d. Linda went abroad to work.
e. Linda went out with Alan.
f. Tom had a serious relationship with another woman.
g. Tom went out with his ex-girlfriend.

13 Find words or expressions that mean:

1. strong, lasting (*lines 1–6*)
2. in a foreign country (*lines 7–12*)
3. a big and complicated piece of work (*lines 13–18*)
4. suddenly not feel strong (*lines 18–24*)
5. decide to stop doing (*lines 24–31*)
6. worries (*lines 24–31*)
7. job (over many years) (*lines 24–31*)
8. unsure (*lines 42–47*)

14 Write an answer to Linda's letter.

SPEAKING

15 Work with another student. One of you is a shop manager and the other has come to complain about something he/she bought in the shop. You will have a few minutes to prepare before having a conversation.

D1 Danger – little old ladies!

Reading for gist, for detail; grammar (past conditionals and modals); pronunciation: /iː/ and /ɪ/; speaking practice.

1 Work in pairs. One person in each pair should turn to page 132 and study the newspaper report 'MUGGER MEETS LITTLE OLD LADY'. The other person should prepare questions to find out the information listed below. When both students are ready, they should close their books, and then ask and answer the questions. Finally, both students should look at page 132 and check that the answers were correct.

Find out:
1. the place, day and time of the incident
2. the little old lady's appearance and dress
3. what exactly happened
4. the names of the people involved
5. what the police did
6. how much, if anything, was stolen

2 Now exchange roles and do this in the same way as Exercise 1 (the person who read the text last time should prepare the questions this time, and vice versa). The newspaper report is on page 134, and is entitled 'LITTLE OLD LADY IN KNIFE RAID'. The questioner should find out the same information as in Exercise 1.

3 Grammar. Write answers to the following two questions.

1. If you had been the lady in the first report, what would you have done? (*If I had been the lady, I would have ...*)
2. If you had been the shop assistant in the second report, what would you have done?

Now complete these sentences.

3. If the mugger had known what Lady Tucker was like, he would not have ...
4. If Lady Tucker had not hit the mugger, ...
5. ..., the lorry driver might not have come to help.
6. ..., the mugger would have got back on his bicycle.
7. ... bicycle, he could have got away.
8. ... would not ... if she had not kept screaming.
9. If Lady Tucker had been an ordinary old lady, the mugger might have ...

If ... had (not)	been ..., hit ..., come, *etc.*	... would (not) have ... might (not) have ... could (not) have	attacked ... been ... got ... *etc.*

4 Now write three or more sentences about yourself, using the following structures.

If I had (not) ... when I was younger, I would have ...
If I had ..., I might have ...
If I had had more money/time last year, I could have ...
I should never have ...

5 🔲 Pronunciation.
1. **Listen to each word, and say whether you think it came in one of the stories in Exercises 1 and 2. Examples:** '*eat*' '*No.*' '*is*' '*Yes.*' '*till*' '*Yes.*'

2. **Listen to the recording. Say whether each word is from list A or list B.**
   A deed   ease   eat   heat   teal
   B did   is   it   hit   till

3. **Listen to the recording and say whether the words are the same or different. Examples:** '*hit, hit*' '*the same*' '*hit, heat*' '*different*'

4. **Now say these words.**

   appealing   easy   Georgina's   police   screams   unbelievable
   assistant   business   sandwich   until   with   witnesses

6 Work in groups of three or four. Prepare and act out either a dramatisation of one of the texts in Exercises 1 and 2, or another scene involving a criminal, a victim and a policeman or policewoman (and someone else if you wish).

Learn/revise: appearance; arm; bicycle; business; coat; dress; handbag; help; knife; lorry driver; luck; mugger; note; owner; policeman; policewoman; prisoner; pub; robbery; scream (*noun and verb*); shop assistant; shoulder; till; umbrella; victim; witness; allow (sbdy to do sth); escape; fight (fought, fought); force (sbdy to do sthg); grab; hit (on + part of body with + object) (hit, hit); hold (held, held); involve; keep (...ing) (kept, kept); push; refuse; steal (stole, stolen); threaten; armed (with); experienced; ordinary; beneath; expensively; in business; at the top of her voice; it's over (= finished).

D2 Focus on systems

A choice of exercises: past modal structures; buildings; pronunciation of *o*; word stress.

GRAMMAR: PAST MODAL STRUCTURES

Structure: modal verb + *have* + past participle

I **could have played** football yesterday (but I didn't).

He **should have stopped** the newspapers (but he forgot).

Why did she go out? It **must have been** because ...

Granny **may have had** an accident.

She **can't have gone** to the cinema.

If the mugger had known what she was like, he **would** not **have attacked** her.

If she hadn't screamed, the lorry driver **might** not **have come** to help.

1 Write a sentence to say how you spent last weekend. Then write five sentences to say what you could have done instead. Example:

*I stayed at home and worked. But I **could have played** football. Or I **could have gone** ...*

2 Robert went on holiday for two weeks, but he fell in love with the receptionist in his hotel and stayed away for six weeks. When he got back home he found a number of problems. Look at the illustration and say what he should(n't) have done. Example:

'*He should have stopped the newspapers.*'

3 The teacher will give you a paper with a problem or a piece of advice. Find the person whose paper goes with yours. Example:

'*I felt really ill yesterday.*'   '*You should have gone to the doctor.*'

4 A woman got a phone call and rushed out of the house, saying nothing to her family. They are wondering what can have happened. Look at the clues and see if you can make some of their sentences. Examples:

'It must have been because of the phone call.'
'Granny may have had an accident.'
'She can't have gone to the cinema.'

'It must have been because of the phone call.'

'Granny may have had an accident.'

'She can't have gone to the cinema.'

'It ...'

'She ...'

'She ...'

'She ...'

'She ...'

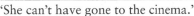
'She ...'

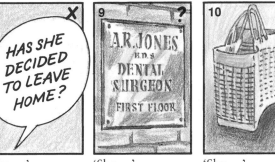
'She ...'

VOCABULARY: BUILDINGS

5 How many words can you add to these three lists? (Time limit ten minutes.)

Rooms: bedroom, office, cellar, ...
Buildings: house, factory, hotel, ...
Parts of buildings: wall, ceiling, roof, ...

6 Read the advertisement and listen to the recording. How many differences can you find between the two descriptions of the house?

Central York
MAGNIFICENT TOWN RESIDENCE
Four double bedrooms, luxury bathroom, upstairs and downstairs cloakrooms, lounge, dining-room, kitchen/breakfast room, double garage, beautiful mature garden, gas-fired central heating.
In first-class condition.
£150,000

7 Write an advertisement for your home, your school, or some well-known building (The Eiffel Tower, The White House, ...).

PRONUNCIATION: THE LETTER O; WORD STRESS

8 Divide these words into two groups, according to the pronunciation of the letter *o*. Listen to the recording and check your answers, and then practise saying the words.

done   gone   got   holiday   lost   lot   love
not   nothing   off   often   one   stop

9 Mark the main stress on these words. Listen to the recording and check your answers, and then practise saying the words.

accident   according   advertisement   advice
cinema   description   difference   divide
example   family   happened   holiday   hotel
illustration   instead   newspaper   nothing
picture   practise   problem   pronunciation
recording   sentence   weekend   yesterday

Learn/revise: accident; advertisement; (piece of) advice; building; ceiling; cellar; description; difference; factory; office; phone call; problem; receptionist; roof; wall; check; divide; rush; spend time (spent, spent); wonder; well-known; according to; because of; on holiday.

D3 Families

Talking about families; asking about and expressing preferences; writing: connecting sentences; *Would you rather ...?*; listening for gist, for detail; pronouncing words together.

1 Work with a partner. Look at the box and try to fill in the blanks. Do you know what all the words mean?

> mother/father/parent
> daughter/ .... /child(ren)
> grand............... / .... / grandparents
> grand............... / .... / grandchild
> wife/...............   aunt/...............
> niece/...............   cousin
> ....-in-law (*several possibilities*)   relative
> single/............... / .... / ....   adopted

Now look at the pictures and talk about what you think the family relationships might be. You can use the words in the box to help you. Example:

'I think this woman is this boy's mother.'
'Perhaps – or perhaps she's his grandmother.'

2 📼 Listen to the recording and try to match the voices and the pictures.

A

B

C

D

E

F

76

3 🔲 Pronouncing words together. Some words change their pronunciation before vowels. Listen to the differences in pronunciation.

1. we   we adopted him
2. who   who is five now
3. Claire   Claire and I

Now pronounce these.

4. our own child
5. May and I are married
6. we enjoy playing
7. Lucy and Emma
8. we often help one another out
9. their aunt and uncle
10. Beth, who is my six-year-old daughter
11. see their father almost every week
12. too ill to live on his own

4 Make sure you know all the words in the box. Then put one word in each of the blanks in the text.

also	although	and	because	besides
but	so			

........1........ there are many different kinds of families in the world, there are some things that are the same everywhere. Not all societies have western-type marriage with one wife and one husband, ...2........ some kind of marriage is universal. And when a person marries, ...3........ the new wife or husband, he or she also gets a complete new family of in-laws. Marriages with close relatives do not always produce healthy children, ...4........ all societies have rules about who can marry who. Each society ....5........ has a division of work based on age and sex. In modern western societies, there is a move to change this last rule ....6........ it can be unfair to women, ...7........ it will be interesting to see if this succeeds.

5 Class survey. Make sure you understand the questions. Then choose one question to ask other people in the class.

a. Would you like to live alone part of the time – say, one week a month?
b. Would you rather have more or fewer brothers and sisters than you have?
c. Would you like to have children? How many? OR: Would you like to have more or fewer children than you have?
d. Would you rather live in the same town as your parents or not?
e. Would you rather spend less time working or studying and more time with your family?
f. If you were very rich, would you rather give your parents the money to have a nice holiday on their own, or take them on holiday with you?
g. What's the best age for having children? Is it better to be young or a bit older?

6 Report the results of your survey to the class or to a group. Example:

'Nine people would rather spend less time working or studying and more time with their families, and six people think they see enough of their families.'

7 🔲 Listen to the recording. Some British people are answering questions from the survey. As you hear their answers, write the letters of the questions they are answering.

8 🔲 Listen to the song. Tell the teacher some of the words you remember. Then turn to page 132: can you write down any of the missing verb forms? Listen to the recording again to check your answers.

G

> **Learn/revise:** age; aunt; bride; cousin; division; family; gold; granddaughter/son/child; grandmother/father/parent; groom; husband; in-laws; marriage; mother/father/brother/sister/daughter/son/parents-in-law; neck; nephew; niece; relative; rule; sex; society; uncle; wife (wives); adopt; continue; dream (dreamt, dreamt); enjoy (...ing); get on (with) (got, got); hope; produce; share (sth with sbdy); spend (time) (spent, spent); succeed; alone; close (*adjective*); divorced; full-time; healthy; ill; married; romantic; separated; single; unfair; fewer; less; together; also; although; besides; so; outside (*preposition*).

SKILLS FOCUS
SKILLS FOCUS
SKILLS FOCUS
SKILLS FOCUS
SKILLS FOCUS
SKILLS FOCUS

D4 Having an amazing time

Writing: personal letters (persuasion); reading: main ideas, guessing words from context, inference; vocabulary work.

Introduction to the lesson
Your teacher will put you in **Group A** (young people) or **Group B** (parents).
Group A (*young people*): Start on Exercise 1. When you have written your letter, go to Exercise 3. If you get a reply to your letter, break off and answer it; then go back to Exercise 3.
Group B (*parents*): Start on Exercise 3. When you get a letter, break off, go to Exercise 2, and answer the letter. When you have done that, go back to Exercise 3 until you get another letter.

1 Group A (young people): You are on a hitchhiking and camping holiday abroad. Write a letter to your parents saying that you would like to stay abroad and work at one of the jobs listed in the box. You need money to be able to do this; try and convince your parents to help you. Ask your teacher for help with any words you don't understand.

> bouncer in nightclub   busker   lion tamer
> photographer   pop singer   private detective
> taxi driver   a job of your choice

When you have written your letter, give it to the teacher and go to Exercise 3. Be ready to stop if you receive an answer from your parent.

2 Group B (parents): Read the letter you receive and answer it. You are not happy with your child's choice of job, will not send him/her any money, and want him/her to return home as soon as possible and begin one of the jobs in the box. Try and convince your child that this is the right thing to do. When you have written an answer to your child's letter, go back to Exercise 3 (but be ready to stop if you receive another letter).

> bank clerk   car salesman/woman   nurse
> policeman/woman   postman/woman
> shop assistant   soldier   teacher
> a job of your choice

3 Here are two letters written on the same day. Read them and answer the questions.

Triton Hotel
Ayia Trias
Greece
28 June 1992

Dear Mum and Dad,

I'm having an amazing time. The sea's lovely, and the weather's been wonderful.

And something else has been wonderful, too: I've met the most marvellous woman. I thought I'd never fall in love again after Angela and I broke up, but this is the real thing. It just knocked me over. Her name's Anastasia, she comes from a family that's lived in the village since time began, and she's beautiful and clever, and, well, just wonderful. She's a year younger than me, but has been running the family grocery business on her own since her parents died four years ago.

I know this is sudden, but I'm sure she's the one for me. I've asked her to marry me, and I hope I'll have your blessing. I'd like to bring her home for you to meet when the tourist season's over, and we'd like to get married here in January.

Meanwhile, I wonder if I could ask you a favour? We'd really like to expand the grocer's shop to meet the growing demand from tourists. Would you consider making us a loan? We could pay you back over five years or so, and pay the same kind of interest as you'd get from a bank account. I hope you'll say yes. And I hope you'll like Anastasia – I can't wait for you to meet her.
Love,

Jonathan

28 June 1992

Dear Jonathan,

We hope you're enjoying yourself. The weather here's lovely at the moment, lots of sun and flowers everywhere – a perfect English summer. Your Mum's recovering well from her operation, and we're all set to go to Wales in the third week of July.

Jonathan, I'm writing to say that I've been talking to my old school friend Peter. You remember him – he's the one who used to bring you chocolates when he came to see us. Well, I've been playing badminton with him from time to time. The other night when we were having a drink after a game he asked how you were doing. He's always been fond of you, you know. Well, when I told him you'd finished school and were a bit undecided about what to do, he offered you a job! You know he works for Scottish Standard, the insurance company. Well, he has a place in his department for a school leaver 'with good maths and an outgoing personality'. You could begin in September, and you'd be in their management trainee programme. So you could end up President of the company, if you kept at it!

I hope you'll consider this seriously. Your mother and I think it's a marvellous opportunity for you.
Much love,

Dad

A. The main ideas. You can work in pairs or small groups, but you may have to stop before the end of the exercise. For each letter: choose the three main points from the list and write them out in the same order as in the letter.

Jonathan's letter
1. The weather has been wonderful.
2. I want to marry her.
3. I would like you to meet Anastasia.
4. Please lend us some money for her business.
5. I am in love with a wonderful woman.

Dad's letter
1. You could begin work in September.
2. Mum and I think you should take the job.
3. My friend Peter has offered you a job.
4. Your Mum is better.
5. You could end up President of the company.

B. Guessing words from context. Find words or expressions in the letters that mean the following (the expressions here are in the same order as the words and expressions in the letters).

Jonathan's letter
1. unbelievably good
2. stopped being together
3. managing, organising
4. fast and surprising
5. make (something) bigger
6. think about
7. money that is earned by letting someone keep your money for a time

Dad's letter
1. getting back to normal health
2. completely ready
3. one night recently
4. liked you
5. someone who's just finished secondary school
6. chance

C. Find things in the text that tell you:

1. Jonathan had probably been very much in love with his girlfriend Angela.
2. The grocer's shop is probably not very busy out of the tourist season.
3. Jonathan is probably on holiday.
4. Jonathan's parents are probably happy being in Britain.
5. Peter probably has quite a good job.
6. Jonathan is probably good at maths.

D. Choose seven or more words or expressions from the letters to learn. If you have time, tell another student why you have chosen those items.

Learn/revise: bank account; business; company; interest; loan; opportunity; personality; policeman/woman (policemen/women); school leaver; break up (with sbdy) (broke, broken); choose (chose, chosen); consider; enjoy; fall in love (with sbdy) (fell, fallen); meet (met, met); pay back (paid, paid); recover (from sth); run (sth) (ran, ran); amazing; clever; fond (of sbdy); marvellous; outgoing; sudden; undecided; wonderful; really; seriously; the other night.

D5 Places

1 Look at the picture. Which word goes with which number?

hill   mountain   valley   wood   stream   waterfall   island
river   lake   bridge   path   road

2 How do you get from A to B? Use the words in
Exercise 1 with these prepositions: *across*, *through*,
along, *up*, *down*. Start:
'You go down the hill ...'.

3  Look at the map and listen to the recording.
Decide whether the sentences are true or false. Example:

There's an island at the south
end of Derwent Water.

False.

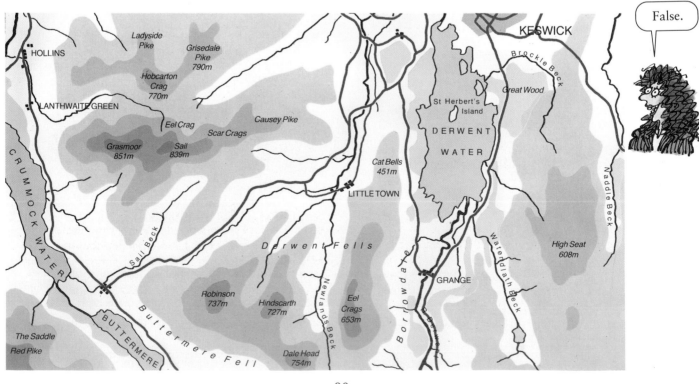

80

4 📼 Pronunciation. Listen to the recording. How many words do you hear in each sentence? What are they? (Contractions like *there's* count as two words.)

5 Look at the town plan. Imagine that somebody asked you how to get from the car park to the post office. What would you say? If you don't know the answer, put these sentences in order.

Then take the first left.
You'll see it on your left.
Then turn right at the big crossroads.
Go straight ahead for about 200 metres.
Keep straight on past the station.

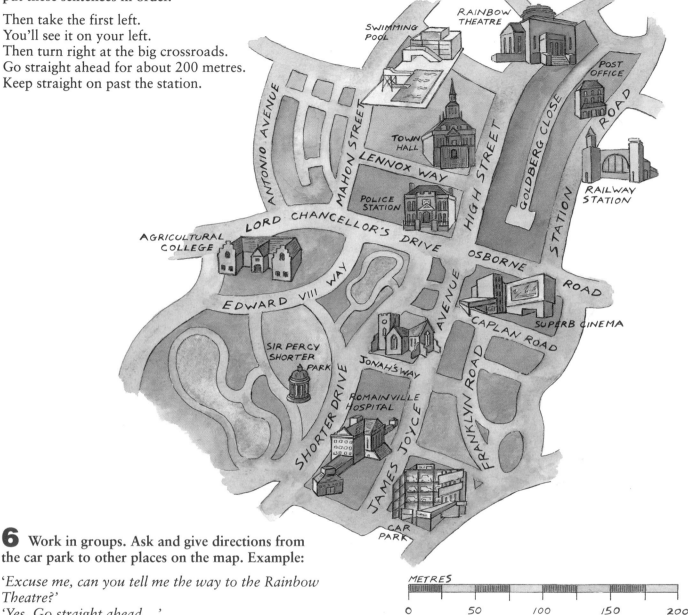

6 Work in groups. Ask and give directions from the car park to other places on the map. Example:

'*Excuse me, can you tell me the way to the Rainbow Theatre?*'
'*Yes. Go straight ahead ...*'

Give directions to the other students, and then ask them where they think they are. Example:

'*You are at the car park. Go straight ahead for two hundred metres, turn left at the crossroads, ..., and take the first right. Where are you?*'

7 Work in groups of three or four.
EITHER: Tell the other students in the group about a place that you like (somewhere in the country, a town, a street, a building, a room, or any other kind of place).
OR: One of you is a stranger visiting the local town. He/she asks the other two for directions. They disagree. Act out the situation.

8 📼 Listen to the song and see how much you can understand. Then look at the words on page 132 and listen again. Sing along if you like.

Learn/revise: bridge; hill; island; lake; mountain; path; river; road; stream; valley; waterfall; wood; car park; college; hospital; park; police station; post office; railway station; swimming pool; theatre; town hall; north; south; west; east; true; false; across; through; along; up; down; past; Can you tell me the way to ...?; take the first left / second right / *etc.*; turn left/right at ...; go/keep straight on/ahead.

D6 Focus on systems

A choice of exercises: Present Perfect Simple and Progressive; *have to*, *don't have to* and *mustn't*; the vocabulary of games-playing; /ɜː/ and /eə/.

GRAMMAR: PRESENT PERFECT SIMPLE AND PROGRESSIVE

1 Which Present Perfect tense (Simple or Progressive) is used to express ideas of *completion* and *change*?

1. Have you *finished / been finishing* that report yet?
2. He thinks he's a great novelist, but he's never *written / been writing* anything worth reading.
3. What's *happened / been happening* to the little shop that used to be here?
4. The children *have been getting / have got* much bigger since I last saw them.

Which tense is used to say 'x times up to now'?

5. He's *changed / been changing* schools three times this year.
6. 'How are you getting on at tennis?' 'I've *won / been winning* every match this summer.'

Which tense is used to talk about *continuation/repetition* up to now?

7. I've *thought / been thinking* about you all day.
8. Jane and I have *seen / been seeing* a lot of each other lately.
9. What have you *done / been doing* since I last saw you?
10. 'You look hot.' 'Yes, I've *played / been playing* tennis.'

Which tense is used to talk about *duration* ('how long?') up to now?

11. Sorry I'm late – have you *waited / been waiting* long?
12. We've *tried / been trying* to find a place to live since Christmas.

Which tense do we use for *very long* or *permanent* states? Compare:

13. I've *stayed / been staying* with Jake for the last few days.
14. My family have always *lived / been living* in York.

2 Present Progressive or Present Perfect Progressive? Why?

1. *I'm working / I've been working* in a bookshop just now.
2. *I'm working / I've been working* there for about six weeks.
3. My parents *are travelling / have been travelling* round America at the moment.
4. They *are travelling / have been travelling* since May.

5. How long *are you studying / have you been studying* English?
6. Recently *I'm getting / I've been getting* more and more interested in a boy in my class.

Present or Present Perfect? Why not Progressive?

7. How long *do you know / have you known* Pete?
8. *I have / I've had* a headache since I got up this morning.

3 Choose the right tense (Present Perfect Simple or Progressive).

1. I .... letters all morning. (*write*)
2. I .... sixteen letters. (*write*)
3. And I still .... them all. (*not finish*)
4. One of the people I've written to ....; I don't know her new address. (*move*)
5. I .... to find out where she is for weeks, but nobody seems to know. (*try*)
6. I'd be sorry to lose touch with her; we .... each other since we were babies. (*know*)
7. I'm a bit worried about her, because she .... more and more depressed recently. (*get*)
8. She .... her job twice this year, and I know she's got problems at home. (*change*)
9. I hope she .... anything stupid. (*not do*)

GRAMMAR: HAVE TO, DON'T HAVE TO AND MUSTN'T

4 Put the beginnings and ends together.

SOME OF THE RULES OF 'SNAKES AND LADDERS'
In order to move,
Before you can start,
If you come to a snake,
If you come to a ladder,
If you throw a six,
If you land on an occupied square,
If you throw three sixes one after another,

you have to throw a dice.
you have to go down it.
you have to go back four squares.
you have to throw a six.
you have to go up it.
you have to miss a turn.
you can have another throw.

5 Match the games and the rules. Then think of a game that the others may not know (or invent a game) and write out the rules for it.

> hockey   chess   football   golf   tennis   baseball

1. You have to hit a ball over a net; it mustn't land outside the white lines.
2. You can kick the ball but you mustn't touch it with your hands.
3. You have to hit a ball and run; you can have three tries.
4. You have to hit a ball into a small hole; you don't have to run.
5. You have to capture a king.
6. You have to hit a ball into a goal with a stick; you mustn't use your hands.

VOCABULARY: PLAYING GAMES

6 Match the words in the box with the pictures.

> ball   baseball bat   chess/draughts board
> chess pieces   dealing   dice   goal   golf club
> kicking   moving   net   playing-cards
> serving   snooker table   tennis racket

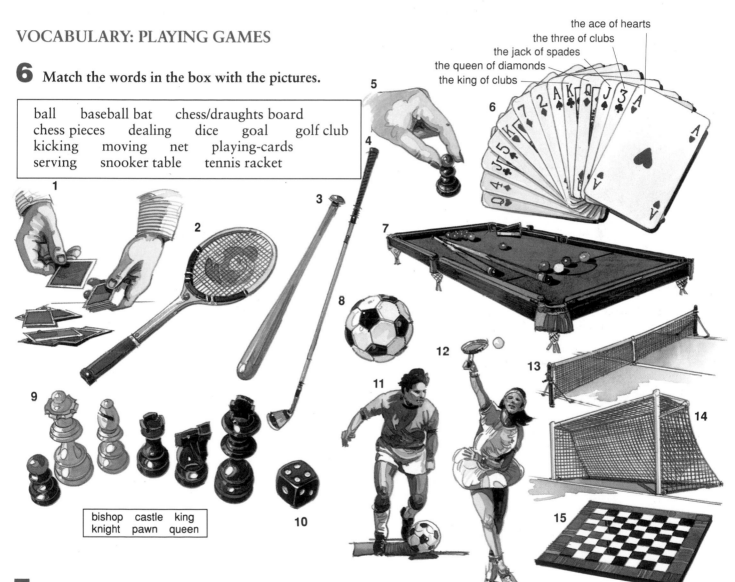

the ace of hearts
the three of clubs
the jack of spades
the queen of diamonds
the king of clubs

> bishop   castle   king
> knight   pawn   queen

7 Work alone or with other students, as you prefer. Choose a game and find out five or more English words connected with it. (Use your dictionary, ask other students or ask the teacher.)

PRONUNCIATION

8 [cassette icon] Two of these words have a different vowel sound from the others. Which are they? Can you pronounce all the words?

air   dirty   early   learn   prefer   serve
square   turn   word   work

> **Learn/revise:** ball; baseball; chess; game; goal; golf; headache; hockey; hole; ladder; match; novelist; report; rule; snake; square; stick; tennis; change schools/jobs *etc.*; go back; hit (hit, hit); kick; miss; move; run (ran, run); stay (with sbdy); think about (sbdy/sth); throw (threw, thrown); touch; travel (travelling, travelled); try (tried); win (won, won); occupied; one after another; all day; worth ...ing.

D7 Where does it hurt?

Talking about illness; giving advice; reporting orders and advice; frequency adverbs; reading and listening for detail; listening for gist; pronunciation: connecting words together.

1 📼 Read the dialogues below while you listen to the recording. Listen for the differences. (D = doctor; P = patient)

A

D: Where does it hurt?
P: Just here, doctor.
D: Mm. And is that all the time?
P: No. Only when I walk, or when I'm going downstairs. Sometimes when I carry things.
D: When you carry things. Big things?
P: Yes.
D: I see. Now I want you to stand up ...

B

D: How often do you get them?
P: Oh, three or four times a week.
D: Three or four times a week. I see. Are they very bad?
P: Oh, yes. They stop me driving. Sometimes I can hardly see, you know.
D: Yes. Do you often get colds?

C

P: It's a really bad cough. It's really bad.
D: Does it hurt when you talk?
P: If I talk a lot, yes.
D: I see. Well, I'll just have a look at your chest. Do you drink?

Now listen to these conversations and try to write down the words that go in the blanks.

D

P: It's a really bad pain, doctor. .... here.
D: Which side?
P: .... side.
D: How long has this been going on? When did it start?
P: .... morning, doctor. I thought perhaps it was indigestion, but it's too .... for that.
D: .... Now just .... down here. That's right. Now .... exactly does it hurt? Is it here?
P: Ooh! Yes!

E

D: Good morning, ... Palmer. What's the ....?
P: Well, I've got a .... sore throat, ...
D: .... How long have you had it?
P: Oh, about .... It's .... very painful. It's difficult to ....

F

P: It's every .... about the same time, doctor. Stuffed-up nose, my .... itch, and I feel sort of .... the whole time.
D: Is it .... when you're inside or outside?
P: When I'm in the ....

G

P: I get this .... when I bend ...., doctor. Just here.
D: I see. Take your .... off.

2 Copy this list, and then close your book. Find out what each of the words or expressions means, by using a dictionary or asking your teacher. Then listen to the conversations again. Which patient has which problem?

headaches	bronchitis	back trouble
appendicitis	a pulled muscle	hay fever
tonsilitis		

3 Here are some more things the doctor said:

A Don't carry heavy things for a while.
B I think you should make an appointment at the Eye Hospital.

And here is what the patients told their families:

A He told me not to carry heavy things.
B He advised me to make an appointment at the Eye Hospital.

What do you think the doctor told the other patients? Work in groups to decide, and report to the class. You can use words from the list below, or ask your teacher for help. Begin your sentences like this:

'We think the doctor told/advised patient C ...'

to have:	an operation some physiotherapy some tests a rest an injection
to take:	some tablets some medicine some syrup some vitamins
to wear:	a bandage
to do:	some exercises

4 🔲 Pronunciation. Say these sentences. Don't separate the words.

Where does it hurt?

Only when I run.

I want you to stand up.

How often do you get them?

They stop me working.

Sometimes I can hardly see.

Do you ever get hay fever?

It's a really bad cough.

It's a really bad pain.

This side.

Just lie down here.

It's difficult to eat.

It's every year about the same time.

I get this pain.

5 Look back at the dialogues in Exercise 1 and note down five or more useful expressions to learn. Compare your list with those of the students sitting near you.

6 Choose one of these activities. Or if you have time, do them both.

A. Are you likely to have a heart attack? Work with a partner: ask each other the questions below, and note down the answers. Then your teacher will tell you how to score the questionnaire.

1. Do you usually eat very quickly?
2. Do you sometimes do more than one thing at a time – for example, work while you're eating?
3. Do you ever have trouble finding time to get your hair cut or styled?
4. Are you often in a hurry?
5. Is success in your work very important to you?
6. Do you get upset if you have to wait in a queue?
7. Is finishing a job you've started very important to you?

Now imagine you are working for an insurance company. Your job is to make up a list of about ten questions, like the one here, for people who want life insurance. You don't want to give insurance to anyone who is likely to die very soon!

B. Work in pairs. Prepare a conversation between a doctor and a patient. Use at least two of these words or expressions in the conversation. You can ask your teacher for help with other words.

often	usually	sometimes	never	always

every year/week/*etc.*   two or three times a ...
all the time   the whole time

"It's a pity you haven't got appendicitis – I'm rather good at that."

"I wish you'd called me sooner, Mrs. Moodie."

Learn/revise: appendicitis; back trouble; bronchitis; chest; (a) cold; cough; hay fever; headache; injection; insurance; muscle; operation; pain; patient; queue; success; tablet; tonsilitis; advise; bend over (bent, bent); boil; breathe; carry; hurt (hurt, hurt); itch; lie down (lay, lain); stand up (stood, stood); tell (told, told); wear (wore, worn); heavy; upset; hardly; inside; outside; always; never; often; sometimes; usually; every year/week/ *etc.*; two or three times a ...; all the time; the whole time; a pulled muscle; a sore throat; in a hurry; How often ...?

D8 ... drove off without stopping

Reading for detail; guessing meaning from context in written and recorded texts; vocabulary building and consolidation; listening for gist; listening for detail; simple report writing.

1 Read the newspaper report. Then look at the two maps and choose the map which corresponds to the report. Find on the map: a roundabout, a pedestrian crossing, a junction.

Driver forgets crashes

MOTORIST Lesley Aston doesn't remember much about her trip home from work.

But villagers at Studley, Warwicks., will never forget it.

First, her Austin 1300 rammed the back of another car waiting at a junction.

She drove off without stopping, overtook cars waiting at a pedestrian crossing and swung into a roundabout on the wrong side.

Then 20-year-old Lesley crashed head-on into a second car, swerved into a third and careered into a brick wall before coming to rest on a garage forecourt.

She later told police that she had only vague memories of what had happened, magistrates were told yesterday at Alchester, Warwicks.

Lesley, of Hewell Road, Redditch, Worcs., was fined £150 for reckless driving and failing to stop after an accident or report it.

2 Read the article again and try to guess the meaning of the following words and expressions.

trip   rammed   head-on   swerved   vague
fined   reckless   failing to stop

3 Work with another student. You have got five minutes to write down as many words and expressions as you can that have to do with driving. Examples:

steering wheel, petrol, traffic light, ...

4 Read the following account of an accident and draw what happened.

Car A tried to overtake car B approaching a road junction. Car C, which was coming in the opposite direction, swerved to avoid car A and crashed into a tree on the corner of the junction.

5 Imagine an accident – you were the only witness besides the driver(s). Or remember a real accident you have witnessed or been involved in. Write a very simple report of the accident, like the one in Exercise 4. Read it to another student: he or she must try to draw what happened.

6 🔊 Listen, and match each recording to one of the pictures. There is one extra picture.

7 🔊 Listen to parts of the recordings again. Choose a likely meaning for each of the numbered words.

First recording

1. flung
   a. couldn't   b. stayed   c. were thrown
2. scruffy
   a. rich   b. untidy   c. sleepy

Second recording

3. amber
   a. yellow   b. broken   c. fast
4. leapt
   a. jumped   b. kept   c. shouted
5. endorsed
   a. given back   b. taken off the car
   c. marked with a bad point

Third recording

6. blasting
   a. coming very loudly   b. coming very quietly
   c. falling
7. wound
   a. broke   b. thought
   c. turned a handle to move

8 Choose one of the activities.

A. Have you / a family member / a friend ever been involved in a car accident or been stopped by the police? Work in pairs or groups and tell your stories to each other. You can ask questions about your partner's story. If there is time, form new pairs and exchange stories again.

B. Turn to page 133. With a partner, choose two of the three stories. Then each of you should work on one of the stories, writing five to seven questions about it for your partner to answer. You can use dictionaries while you are writing; your partner can ask you what some words mean.

Learn/revise: accident; corner; diagram; flat; garage; jazz; junction; (driving) licence; licence number; memory; motorist; noise; pedestrian; pedestrian crossing; porter; report (*noun and verb*); roundabout; (road) sign; space; speed limit; traffic; traffic lights; trip; university; wall; approach; avoid; crash (into); draw (drew, drawn); drive (drove, driven); fail; follow; overtake (overtook, overtaken); park; realise; crazy; smart; underground (*adjective*); opposite (*adverb*); in the opposite direction; go through a red light.

Summary D

Simple Present Perfect

completion

Have you **finished** that report yet?

change

What **has happened** to that shop that used to be here?

how many times up to now?

I've played tennis six times this week.

very long or permanent states

My family **have** always **lived** in York.

Present Perfect Progressive

continuation/repetition up to now

I've been thinking about you all day.
Jane and I **have been seeing** a lot of each other lately.

duration ('how long?') up to now

Sorry I'm late – **have** you **been waiting** long?
(~~... are you waiting long?~~)

Non-progressive verbs

How long **have** you **known** Pete?
(~~... have you been knowing Pete?~~)
I've had a headache since I got up.
(~~I've been having ...~~)

Modal verbs with perfect infinitives

I stayed at home and worked. But I **could have played** football.
'I felt really ill yesterday.' 'You **should have gone** to the doctor.'
'Why did she go out?' 'It **must have been** because of the phone call.'
She **may have had** an accident.
She **can't have gone** to the cinema.

can, have to, don't have to and mustn't

You **can** kick the ball but you **mustn't** touch it.
You **have to** hit a ball over a net.
You **have to** hit a ball and run; you **can** have three tries.
You **have to** hit a ball into a small hole; you **don't have to** run.

Reporting orders and advice

The doctor **advised me to make** an appointment at the Eye Hospital.
She **told me not to carry** heavy things.

Irregular verbs in Lessons D1–D8

INFINITIVE	PAST	PAST PARTICIPLE
bend	bent	bent
break	broke	broken
choose	chose	chosen
draw	drew	drawn
drive	drove	driven
fall	fell	fallen
fight	fought	fought
hit	hit	hit
hold	held	held
hurt	hurt	hurt
keep	kept	kept
lie	lay	lain
meet	met	met
overtake	overtook	overtaken
pay	paid	paid
run	ran	run
spend	spent	spent
stand	stood	stood
steal	stole	stolen
take	took	taken
tell	told	told
throw	threw	thrown
wear	wore	worn
win	won	won

Modal verbs with perfect infinitives in sentences with if

If ... had (not) been ..., hit ..., come, etc.	... would (not) have ... might (not) have ... could (not) have	attacked ... been ... got ... etc.

If I **had** not **been** ill when I was younger, I **would have** studied physics.
If I **had gone** to university, I **might have become** a doctor.
If I **had had** more time last year, I **could have gone** to America.

Would you rather ...?

Would you rather have more or fewer brothers and sisters than you have?
Would you rather live in the same town as your parents or not?

Frequency adverbs; how often

often
usually
sometimes
never
always
ever (*usually in questions*)
every year/week/*etc*.
two or three times a ...
all the time
the whole time

Connecting words

Although there are many different kinds of families in the world, there are some things that are the same everywhere.
Not all societies have western-type marriage, **but** some kind of marriage is universal.
When a person marries, **besides** a new wife or husband, he or she gets a complete new family of in-laws.
Marriages with close relatives do not always produce healthy children, **so** all societies have rules about who can marry whom.
Each society **also** has a division of work based on age and sex.
There is a move to change this last rule **because** it can be unfair to women, **and** it will be interesting to see if it succeeds.

Prepositions of movement

down the hill   **along** the path
across the bridge   **up** the mountain
through the wood   **past** the station

Asking for and giving directions

Can you tell me the way to ...?
Take the first left.
You'll see it on your left.
Turn right at the first crossroads.
Go straight ahead for about 200 metres.
Keep straight on past the station.

Talking about illness

I've got a sore throat.
It's very painful.
It's difficult to talk.
It's a very bad cough.
It's really bad.
I get this pain when I bend over.
It's a really bad pain.
The headaches stop me driving.
How often do you get these headaches?
Are they very bad?
Do you drink?
Do you often get colds?
How long has this been going on?
How long have you had it?
When did it start?
Where exactly does it hurt?
I'll just have a look at your chest.

Vocabulary

Look through the 'Learn/revise' boxes at the ends of Lessons D1–D8.

Revision and fluency practice **D**

A choice of activities.

1 🔲 Listen to the conversation. It is about one of the things in the box. Each time the conversation stops, say what you think. Examples:

'It might be a baby.'
'It could be a fridge.'
'It can't be a piano.'
'It must be a tree.'

baby	bookcase	canary	car	dog	electric typewriter
flower	fridge	garden	house	piano	piece of beef
statue	table	tree	wardrobe		

Make up similar conversations in groups, and see if the other students can work out what you are talking about.

2 🔲 Listen to the recording two or three times, and then look at the pictures. You must make up a story which explains the sounds in the recording, and which includes the people and things in the pictures. When you are ready, tell the other students.

3 Reading report. Talk to the class about what you have been reading recently in English.

4 Memory test. Work with a partner. Both of you look very carefully at the room (and the people and things in it) for one minute. Then one of you closes his or her eyes, while the other asks questions about the room.

5 Guided tour. Prepare a 'guided tour' for a visitor to your school, your home town or some other place. Then give your talk to a group of the other students.

6 Complete the dialogue and act it out for the class.

ANN: ....
BEN: My God!
ANN: ....
BEN: ....
ANN: ....
BEN: A big red one.
ANN: ....
BEN: ....
ANN: In the car park, I think.
BEN: ....
ANN: ....
BEN: £37.50.
ANN: ....
BEN: ....
ANN: Florida.
BEN: ....
ANN: ....
BEN: As soon as possible.
ANN: ....

7 Person of the year. Work in groups of three or four. In each group, choose the man or woman of the year – the person that you think has done most for the world during the last twelve months. When you have agreed on your choice, tell the rest of the class who you have chosen and why.

8 Interview. Prepare questions for an interview with an English-speaking stranger. You must find out as much as possible about him/her, including details of his/her childhood, education, family, work, interests, and social and political attitudes. Prepare 'follow-up questions' for some of your questions. Examples:

'Do you like music?'
'Yes, I do.'
'What kind?'

'What's your job?'
'I'm a builder.'
'Do you like it?'

When you have prepared your interview, arrange for one or more English-speaking people to visit your class. (Get your teacher to help if necessary.) Interview the person/people, and write a report on what you have found out.

9 Reacting to poetry. Here are three poems about animals. How do you feel about them? (Like / dislike / no reaction / ...?) See if you can find somebody else in the class who shares your reactions.

SOFTLY
Strong and long
The tiger crouches down
Orange and black in
The green grass.
Careful little fawn how
You pass.
(*Peter Sandell*, aged 8)

MEDITATIO
When I carefully consider the curious habits of dogs
I am compelled to conclude
That man is the superior animal.

When I consider the curious habits of man
I confess, my friend, I am puzzled.
(*Ezra Pound*)

CAGED BIRD
Bars are all she knows.
But every night in her dreams
High and free she flies.
(*Evan Stabetsi*)

10 Writing poetry. The last poem in Exercise 9 is a haiku. Haikus have three lines, usually containing five, seven and five syllables respectively (though some are more free than this). See if you can complete one of the following haikus; or write one of your own.

Outside my window
Snow lies on the high branches.
....

As one gets older
People give one more respect.
....

Right at this moment
What I would most like to do
....

In a new country
....
....

When you look at me
....
....

Test D

LISTENING

1 📟 Look at the map and listen to the three sets of directions. Where does each set of directions take you to? Possibilities:

Castle
Cathays Station
Cathedral
Central Station
Hospital

National Museum
National Stadium
Queen Street Station
St David's Hall
University

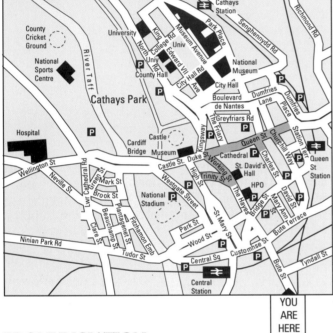

PRONUNCIATION

2 📟 Listen to the recording. Do you hear A or B?

	A	B
1.	deed	did
2.	ease	is
3.	eat	it
4.	feet	fit
5.	green	grin
6.	sheep	ship
7.	feel	fill

3 Look at these words. In each group, the underlined sounds are the same except in one word. Which word is different?

1. d<u>o</u>ne   g<u>o</u>ne   l<u>o</u>ve   s<u>o</u>n
2. g<u>o</u>t   l<u>o</u>st   h<u>o</u>liday   n<u>o</u>thing
3. h<u>air</u>   g<u>ir</u>l   w<u>or</u>k   h<u>ear</u>d
4. th<u>ere</u>   app<u>ear</u>ance   w<u>ear</u>   prep<u>are</u>
5. w<u>or</u>n   s<u>or</u>e   h<u>or</u>se   w<u>or</u>k
6. <u>ear</u>n   r<u>ear</u>   d<u>ir</u>ty   s<u>er</u>vice
7. thunde<u>r</u>storm   greengroce<u>r</u>   prefe<u>r</u>   loude<u>r</u>
8. w<u>ear</u>   p<u>ur</u>pose   em<u>er</u>gency   g<u>ir</u>l

4 Mark the main stress on these words.

assistant   condition   direction   experienced
headache   insurance   involve   operation
opposite   pedestrian   personality   police
prisoner   recover   tonsilitis   witness

GRAMMAR

5 Fill in the gaps with a structure using *must, may, should, can, could, can't, will, would, (don't) have to* or *had to*, together with the verb in brackets.

1. I don't think Agnes really wanted to see us – she said she had an appointment, but I'm sure she .... it if she really wanted to. (*change*)
2. 'Someone came to see you – a good-looking red-haired man.' 'Oh, that .... my cousin Isaac.' (*be*)
3. 'Do you know where the car keys are?' 'I'm not sure – I .... them on top of the fridge.' (*leave*)
4. I'm surprised Barbara has left – she .... her work already. (*finish*)
5. I suppose I .... my parents about my problems at school, but I didn't want to worry them. (*tell*)
6. When I was younger you .... twenty-one to vote. (*be*)
7. Americans .... a passport to go from one state of the US to another, but they .... one to go to France. (*have, have*)

6 Rewrite the sentences as in the example. Use *tell* or *advise*.

Ann: 'Take the first left.'

Ann told me to take the first left.

1. Doctor: 'Don't carry heavy things for a while.'
2. Elizabeth: 'You should get more exercise.'
3. Mark: 'I wouldn't go to Greece in August if I were you.'
4. Teacher: 'Learn the irregular verbs as soon as possible.'

LANGUAGE IN USE

7 Use each word in a question.

1. rather (*ask about preferences*)
2. the way (*ask for directions*)
3. hurt
4. problem

8 Write down five things you might say at the doctor's.

READING AND WRITING

9 Read the newspaper article and do the tasks that follow.

Fag end of the evening

From UPI in Dallas

A 35-YEAR-OLD woman who was awakened by an unknown man crawling into her bed marched him out at gunpoint, only to have him knock on her door a few moments later and ask for a light for his cigarette.

The woman told police she awoke to find a partially dressed man crawling into her bed whispering: "I want you, I love you." She responded by grabbing a small pistol from her nightstand and telling him: "I'll kill you. I want you out of my house."

The woman said she forced the man out of her apartment at gunpoint, locked the door, and called the police. But within seconds, there was a knock on the door. She opened it, its chain still in place, to find her assailant calmly asking her for a light for his cigarette. The astounded woman said she got her lighter, complied with his request, and re-locked the door.

Police arrived to see the man running from the woman's porch carrying a lighted cigarette, and arrested a 20-year-old suspect a short time later.

(from The Guardian)

Find words or expressions that mean:

1. made him walk out (*lines 1–8*)
2. by threatening him with a gun (*lines 1–8*)
3. speaking very quietly (*lines 9–18*)
4. small table next to a bed (*lines 9–18*)
5. closed with a key (*lines 19–24*)
6. surprised (*lines 24–32*)
7. did what he asked (*lines 24–32*)
8. area just outside a front door (*lines 33–38*)

Here is a summary of the article; but there are some things in it that are not true. Rewrite the summary, correcting the mistakes.

A woman woke up to find a man crawling through her window. She phoned the police, and then she made the man leave by threatening him with a knife. A few minutes later the man knocked on the door to ask to use the telephone. The police arrived, saw him running away but did not catch him.

10 Choose one of these tasks. Write 150 words or more.

1. Have you ever been a victim or a witness of a theft, a burglary, a robbery, a mugging? Write about what happened.
2. Imagine you are the woman in the story in Exercise 13. Write a letter to a close friend telling her or him what happened.
3. Have you ever been surprised when someone (or you yourself!) thought and acted quickly in a dangerous situation? Write about what happened.
4. Has anyone in your family, or any of your friends, ever done something you were proud of? Write about it.

VOCABULARY

11 Add some words and/or expressions to each list.

1. central heating, upstairs, … (*six or more words or expressions*)
2. father-in-law, grandmother, … (*ten or more*)
3. river, hill, … (*four or more*)
4. baseball bat, serve, … (*eight or more*)
5. appendicitis, injection, … (*five or more*)
6. roundabout, crash, … (*four or more*)

12 Put the right word in each blank.

1. I'm very fond .... Jill.
2. Are you .... a hurry?
3. Has John recovered .... his operation?
4. Have you ever fallen .... love .... someone who doesn't speak your language?
5. I've heard that Jo is breaking up .... Bob.
6. Veronica's mother is very proud .... her.
7. Would you like to share my lunch .... me?
8. She hit the mugger .... the head .... her briefcase.
9. Do you get on .... Alex?

13 Infinitive or -*ing* ?

1. Do your parents allow you .... with anybody you want? (*go out*)
2. Just keep .... and you'll succeed one day. (*try*)
3. The bank robber forced the customers .... on the floor. (*lie down*)
4. Do you enjoy .... languages? (*learn*)

14 Two-word expressions: match the two halves.

at	account
bank	back
car	down
full-	fever
hay	hall
lie	muscle
pay	once
pulled	park
railway	room
sitting	station
town	time

SPEAKING

15 Choose one of these tasks.

1. Describe a place you know to another student so that she/he can draw a simple sketch of it.
2. Look back at the map in Exercise 1: give another student directions to a place; see if the student can tell you where you have led him/her.

E1 Another good day

1 📼 Copy the table. Listen to the recording and circle the expressions which you hear.

TODAY	another good day not a good day sunshine rain drought
TOMORROW	it'll cloud over tomorrow evening showers today warm temperatures 36–37 maximum
SUNDAY	rather cloudy a few showers not much cooler
MONDAY	sun very hot normal temperatures

2 Look at these three ways of talking about the weather.

WITH A VERB	WITH A NOUN	WITH AN ADJECTIVE
It often **rains**.	There is often **rain**.	It is often **rainy/wet**.
It often **clouds over**.	There is often **cloud**.	It is often **cloudy**.

Now put these words into the correct columns:
blow   cold   cool   fog   foggy   hot   shine   sunshine
snow (*two places*)   sun   sunny   warm   wind   windy

Can you add the other points of the compass?

3 Read the text about the weather in East Texas. Then complete the text about the weather in Britain, using the words and expressions in the box. Finally, write a short text about the weather in your country (or another country, or an imaginary country).

THE WEATHER IN EAST TEXAS

In East Texas, in the area of the Gulf of Mexico, the climate is generally hot and often very humid. Temperatures in summer range from 30° to 40°C; 25°C is a normal winter temperature. It is sometimes cold, but only for two or three days at a time; it snows perhaps once every twenty years. It quite often rains heavily for two or three days or more, but most of the time the weather is sunny with bright blue skies. Occasionally there are droughts – periods when there is no rain for a long time. It is not usually very windy, but there are hurricanes every few years, with wind speeds reaching over 150 kilometres an hour.

THE WEATHER IN BRITAIN

In Britain, the ......1...... is very ......2......; it ......3...... a lot, but the sun often ......4...... too. ......5...... can be ......6...... cold and damp, with an average ......7...... of 5°C in the south; there is often snow. Summers can be cool or warm, but the temperature ......8...... not usually go above 30°C. It is ......9...... cloudy, and there are ......10...... grey ......11...... for days or weeks ......12....... Days are ......13...... in summer and ......14...... in winter. There is sometimes fog, especially in ......15...... and autumn, ...16...... it is not so common as foreigners think. Thunderstorms (storms with thunder and ......17......) are quite common in mountainous areas. British ......18...... never ......19...... what tomorrow's weather will be ......20.......

at a time	but	changeable	does
fairly	know	lightning	like	long
often	people	rains	shines	short
skies	sometimes	spring	temperature
weather	winters

94

4 What is the weather forecast for Western Europe? Write five or more sentences using information from the map. Example:

It will be dry and sunny in Spain.

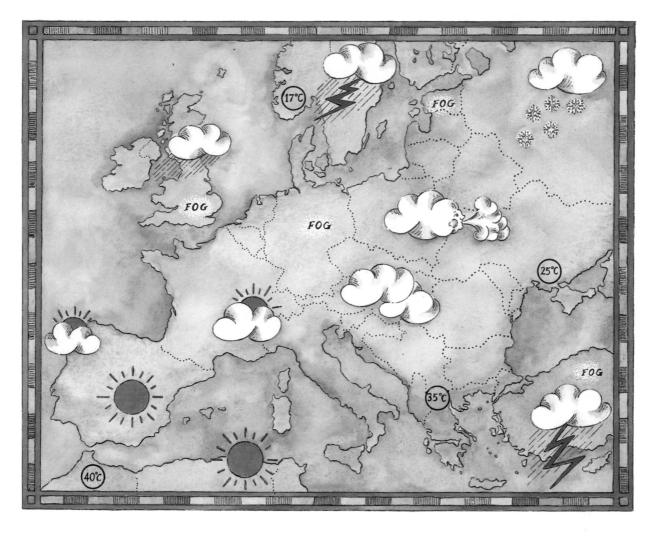

5 🔊 Pronounce these words and expressions.

hot   humid   heavy   hurricane   hour
very hot   very humid   there are hurricanes
heavy rain   it rains heavily   for hours

It'll be very hot.
It'll cloud over.
It'll rain.
It'll snow.

There'll be rain.
There'll be snow.
There'll be sunshine.
There'll be fog on high ground.

6 Prepare and give your own weather forecast for tomorrow (a good or bad one, as you like).

7 Write five sentences comparing different people's forecasts. Example:

Maria said it would be sunny tomorrow, but Paul said it would rain.

8 🔊 Listen to the song without looking at the words and write down five or more words connected with *weather* or *cars*. Then look at the words as you listen a second time. (The text is on page 133.)

Learn/revise: cloud; drought; fog; hurricane; lightning; rain (*noun and verb*); shower; sky; snow (*noun and verb*); speed; sun; sunshine; temperature; thunder; thunderstorm; weather; weather forecast; wind; spring; summer; autumn; winter; north; south; west; east; north-west; north-east; south-west; south-east; blow (blew, blown); cloud over; shine (shone, shone); average; bright; changeable; cloudy; cold; cool; damp; foggy; grey; hot; humid; maximum; normal; rainy; sunny; warm; wet; windy; fairly; heavy rain; high ground; what ... like; at a time.

E2 Focus on systems

A choice of exercises: reported speech with *would* and *had*; names of everyday objects; punctuation; spelling and pronunciation of contractions.

GRAMMAR: REPORTED SPEECH WITH *WOULD* AND *HAD*

'You **will** have a wonderful week.' My horoscope said that I **would** have a wonderful week.	'John **has** gone on a business trip.' Mary knew that John **had** gone on a business trip.

1 Here is your horoscope from the beginning of last week. Say whether it was true or not. Use *would*. Examples:

'My horoscope said I would have a wonderful week, but actually it was a terrible week.'
'My horoscope said I would make new friends, and I did.'
'My horoscope said I would get bad news on Monday, but I didn't.'

YOUR STARS THIS WEEK

ARIES (Mar 21–Apr 20)
You will have a wonderful week. Lots of money will come to you, and you will go on a long journey at the weekend. You will make exciting new friends.

Taurus (Apr 21–May 21)
There will be bad news on Monday. On Tuesday afternoon at 3.45 you will meet a tall dark stranger. This will be a good week for love, but a bad week for money.

Gemini (May 22–June 21)
You will receive an exciting offer in Wednesday's post, and on Thursday you will meet somebody who could change your life. But you will have a lot of trouble with children this week.

Cancer (June 22–July 22)
You will have a terrible week, and something very strange will happen on Thursday. You will fall out of bed on Sunday and hurt your elbow.

Leo (July 23–Aug 23)
You will get a shock on Friday, and something that you value will be stolen from you. A large animal will bring problems. There will be a lot of bills to pay.

Virgo (Aug 24–Sept 23)
You will meet an old friend that you had lost contact with, and you will quarrel violently with a member of your family. On Tuesday you will have to make an important decision.

Libra (Sept 24–Oct 23)
There will be a misunderstanding with somebody you love. If you keep your ears open you will learn an important secret. On Saturday you will break something valuable.

Scorpio (Oct 24–Nov 22)
The first part of the week will be better than the second. This will not be a good time for love, and you will not meet anybody interesting. You will make a big mistake on Thursday, and an even bigger one on Friday.

Sagittarius (Nov 23–Dec 21)
Nobody will fall in love with you this week, and you will be ill on Wednesday. A letter will bring a pleasant surprise. At the weekend, you will do something you have never done before.

Capricorn (Dec 22–Jan 20)
You will make an unexpected journey, and meet an old friend at the end of it. You will lose some money in the middle of the week. On Tuesday evening you will have a small accident – nothing serious.

Aquarius (Jan 21–Feb 18)
At last, people will realise how clever you are. You will be elected President of an important organisation. A machine will bring you unusual problems.

Pisces (Feb 19–Mar 20)
You will be very unhappy this week. You will fall into a river on Wednesday. The end of the week will be especially bad. Perhaps next week will be better. It can't be much worse.

2 🔲 Listen to the recording and try to complete some of the sentences. Example:

'Mary knew that John had gone on a business trip.'

Mary knew … had …	Mary told her mother … had …
Mary wondered if … had …	John told Joe … had …
Mary found out … had …	Joe told Mary … had …
The hotel told Mary … had …	Mary asked Joe if … had …

3 Imagine the conversation between John and Mary when John phones later on. Then write a report of it using reported speech (including structures with *would* and *had*). Example:

John rang up and said he was staying with an old friend. So Mary asked if ...

PUNCTUATION

4 Write out the letter with capitals and punctuation where necessary.

dear sue how are you these days i made a real fool of myself last week it happened like this john went off on a business trip and then i thought that hed taken my keys so i rang up his hotel im sorry the girl said but hes not here hes cancelled well i was sure hed gone off with that american woman do you remember me telling you about her last year but actually it turned out that hed met an old school friend and gone to stay with him he tried to phone me but he couldnt get through because i was telling mother all my troubles then when he got our neighbour to give me a message i wouldnt listen and shut the door in his face so when john finally rang up we had a colossal row and things are still a bit difficult sue i do feel stupid have you ever done anything like that or am i the only one give my love to fred and the kids mary

PRONUNCIATION AND SPELLING: CONTRACTIONS

5 🔲 Change the full forms to contractions and practise the pronunciation. Example:

I am   I am tired.
'*I'm*   *I'm tired.*'

I have	I have forgotten her name.
he had	He had taken my keys.
I will	I will phone you.
it will	It will rain this afternoon.
I would	I would like something to drink.
cannot	I cannot understand him.
will not	He will not be here tomorrow.
is not	The car is not ready yet.
does not	She does not work on Saturdays.
has not	The postman has not come yet.
had not	He had not taken my keys.
would not	I would not like to do her job.
could not	He could not get through.
did not	I did not believe him.

VOCABULARY: EVERYDAY OBJECTS

6 Do you know the names of all these objects?

7 Think of different uses for some of the objects, and write sentences. Examples:

A coin can be used as a screwdriver.
A bath can be used as a bed.
A brick can be used for breaking into a house.

Learn/revise: bad news; business trip; elbow; misunderstanding; organisation; river; secret; shock; stranger; cancel (cancelled); elect; find out (found, found); give sbdy a message (gave, given); have trouble with sth; lose contact with sbdy (lost, lost); make a decision (made, made); make a fool of oneself; make a mistake; make friends (with sbdy); meet (met, met); offer; quarrel (quarrelled); ring sbdy up (rang, rung); stay with sbdy; steal (stole, stolen); wonder; clever; exciting; serious; stupid; terrible; unusual; valuable; wonderful; actually; violently; *words from Exercise 6.*

E3 A dream

Listening for gist; listening for exact comprehension; discussion or writing skills work; Past Progressive tense; vocabulary; pronunciation (weak forms of words).

1 📼 You are going to hear the first part of a story. Before you listen, look at the words and expressions in the box. (They come in the story in the same order.) If there are any that you don't know, ask about them or look them up in a dictionary. What do you think happens in this part of the story? Listen to the recording and see if you are right.

by myself	moped	tent	camp sites
facilities	safer	convenient	
I camped rough	hidden	hedge	
wood	pleasant	I pitched my tent	
plastic	supper	went to sleep	

2 📼 Now listen to the second part of the recording twice. When you have done that, work in small groups and try to remember and write down what you heard as exactly as possible. The words and expressions in the box will help you (but three of them shouldn't be there).

unusual	episodes	hard to tell	1930s
World War II	on farms	barn	children
didn't last	scenes	laughing	smiling
puzzled	connect		

3 📼 Now listen to the end of the story.

98

4 🔲 Pronunciation. How are these words usually pronounced: *was, and, for, of, to, that, were, from*? Listen to the recording and see if you were right. Practise saying the sentences. Then ask other students what they were doing yesterday at a particular time.

> What were you doing at 10 o'clock yesterday evening?

> I was dancing.

> I was eating.

> I was asleep.

> I can't remember what I was doing.

Tell the class what you have found out.

> Jean was eating.

> Alex says he was asleep.

DO EITHER EXERCISE 5 OR EXERCISE 6.

5 Choose one of these questions.

– Have you ever had an experience of telepathy (knowing or dreaming what is happening to somebody else)?
– Have you ever had a dream which told you what was going to happen in the future?
– Have you ever experienced a strange coincidence?
– Or have any of these things happened to someone you know?

1. Write at least 100 words about the question you have chosen. Write on every second line of your paper. Don't spend more than ten minutes. When you have finished, exchange stories with another student. Read the other student's story and ask two or more questions about what happened.
2. Try and make your story better by doing some of the things in the box. You can look at the written version of the dream story on page 133 if you want.

> Dividing the story into paragraphs
> Using conjunctions like *and, because, but, though, when*
> Using relative pronouns like *that, which, who*
> Not making all the sentences the same length – using a variety of longer and shorter sentences

6 Choose one of the questions from Exercise 5. Work with three or four other students. Tell your story to the group. The group should choose the one or two most interesting stories to tell to another group or to the whole class.

> **Learn/revise:** camp; camp site; coincidence; dream; farm; plastic; scene; story; supper; tent; wood; the future; the 1930s; World War II; connect; go to sleep; happen; hide (hid, hidden); last; smile; travel; convenient; pleasant; safe; strange; unusual; in order; by myself.

SKILLS FOCUS
SKILLS FOCUS
SKILLS FOCUS
SKILLS FOCUS
SKILLS FOCUS
SKILLS FOCUS

E4 Nice woman, 42

Fast reading for specific information; listening for detail; asking for things when you don't know the exact words.

BILLIARD TABLES bought and sold. Mr Villis. (02805) 66 (Bucks).

GIFT CHAMPAGNE. We post a bottle with your message. From £16.50 incl. Orders or details 0642 45733

CHRISTINE'S beauty treatment and body therapy. 402 6499, 0473 4004

SMOKED SALMON
8oz sliced £7.75, 1lb sliced £13, 2lb 4oz side £18.90, 2lb 8oz side £21, 400gms offcuts £6. Prices include UK 1st class postage. Cheques with order. Cornish Smoked Fish Co. Ltd, Charlestown, St. Austell, Cornwall.

CHATEAU LATOUR, 1964. 24 bottles, £75 each. Phone (0227) 9848 evenings.

GOING INTO BUSINESS? Send £7.45 inc p&p for 'The Beginners Guide to Success in Business.' Comquip Ltd, 189 Highview, Meopham, Gravesend, Kent. (0732) 22315.

C-SCOPE METAL DETECTORS The ideal family gift to treasure from £39.99 to £449.50. Tel. Ashford (0233) 2918 today for free colour brochure.

MAKE A GUITAR 12 week courses. Details : Totnes School of Guitarmaking, Collins Rd, Totnes, Devon. 0803 65255.

HAVANA CIGARS And other fine cigars at wholesale prices. Send for list to James Jordan Ltd, Shelley Hall, Shelley, Huddersfield. Tel.: 0484 60227

400-YEAR-OLD thatched cottage between Winchester/Basingstoke: 3 dble beds, sec gdn & extras. £110,000. (0962) 88109

BEAUTIFUL farm estate, total 700 acres. Diplomats 4 bed 1832 house. £220,000 ono. 0639 73082

5 BEDROOMED HOUSE in quiet mid-Wales village. 1 acre of land, fishing and shooting available. £42,000. Tel : 059 787 687 (after 6 p.m.).

W. ANGLESEY. 2 dble beds. S/d bung. Lge with patio drs to ½-acre garden, kit/b'fast room, bathroom. Dble glaz/ins. GCH. Garage & util rm, summer hse, grn hse. Scope for extensions. £29,500 o.n.o., quick sale. Tel 040 741031.

HAVE A very happy birthday Paul.

NICE WOMAN, 42, seeks close, affectionate friendship with independentish man. Non-smoker, sense of fun, creative. Enjoys walks, talks, sensuality. Photo please. London area. Box (50) 2059. N50 3

OLGA: RUSSIAN/FRENCHWOMAN from Lille, seeks an Englishman, tall, 50s, open-minded, with whom she can have a close, but stable relationship. Box (50) 2051. N50 2

OXFORD: lively divorcee, mid forties, bored with solitude and the cat, seeks male, preferably tall, to share local pleasures and pastimes, music, the arts etc. Box (50) 2050.

VERY PERSONABLE, attractive, charming, amusing, considerate graduate, professional – 40 – own lovely coastal home, seeks lady – friendship/marriage – personality more important than age. All nationalities welcome. Box (50) 2052 N50 6

WARM, ATTRACTIVE, humorous woman, 35, lover of music , literature, cinema, theatre and leftish politics, seeks man of similar inclinations, to share it all with. London. Box (46) 1899. N49 8

SENSITIVE, TALL, caring, unattached man, 55, likes people, music, walking, seeks intelligent, helpful n/s woman, mid forties. South Essex. Box (49)2011. N49 13

SILVER CROSS detachable coach Pram (navy), shopping tray, excellent clean condition, £30; Carry Cot, £5; Baby Bath, £2.50; Atari system, joystick and paddle sticks, in good working order, needs a new mains adapter, £40; 5 Atari Cassettes, £10 each, very good condition, ideal Xmas presents. – Apply 34 Kynaston Road, Didcot, Oxon. evenings. 415702

THE TIMES (1814-1985). This Xmas give someone an original issue dated the very day they were born. £12.50 or 2 for £21. Tel 01-486 6305 or 0492 3314

PARTYMANIA, everything for your party in one "funtastic" store. – 179 Kingston Road, Oxford 513397, own parking. 376851

GIVE HER a luxurious Christmas with a special gift set of soothing bath, body and face oils. Send £9.50 to Claydon Aromatherapy, 107 Marine Parade, Worthing BN11 3QG.

LADIES NARROW SHOES. AA and narrower, sizes 2½–11½. Also wide EE. SAE Muriel Hitchcock Shoes, 3b Castle Mews, Arundel BN18 9DG.

1 Fast reading practice. Look at the small ads and see how quickly you can answer the questions.

1. What does the cheapest metal detector cost?
2. A man in South Essex is looking for a friend. How old is he?
3. Will Christine improve your mind or your body?
4. Which costs more – a 400-year-old cottage near Winchester or a 5-bedroom house in Wales?
5. Why is today a special day for Paul?
6. How much will two bottles of Château Latour 1964 cost you?
7. What town do you write to for bath, body and face oils?
8. Where can you buy things for a party?
9. How long will it take you to learn to make a guitar?
10. Does the lady who is bored with the cat prefer tall or short men?
11. How much will it cost you to give somebody a pound (1lb) of smoked salmon and a bottle of champagne (with a message)?
12. You can buy something that was produced on the day you were born. What?
13. Somebody is offering a baby bath for sale. How much for?
14. Does the nice 42-year-old woman smoke?
15. How many nationalities has Olga got?

2 Look again at the 'contact ads' (the ones in which people are advertising for friends). Write a contact ad for yourself or a friend.

3 Do you know the pronunciation, meaning and use of all of these words? Check them in a dictionary if necessary, or ask your teacher.

advertise   an advertisement   a small ad
a poster   a sale   a bargain   a gift
a catalogue   a price   choice   quality   value
free   cheap   expensive   save

4 🔊 Listen to the recording and see how many of the missing words you can fill in.

Hickman's aren't ......1...... ......2...... ......3...... you think. A Panasonic VHS video is only £......4....... If you add up the extras at other ......5......, it's ......6...... by far ......7...... Hickman's.

McIlroy's ......8...... first for choice, ...9...... and value, so make us first ......10...... ......11...... Christmas shopping. ......12...... new-look store means an even better choice of gifts for the ......13...... ......14....... Make shopping part ......15...... ......16...... pleasure ......17...... Christmas. Experience the new-look McIlroy's.

......18......, ...19......, ...20...... on Christmas shopping ......21...... Scat's Cash-and-Carry ......22...... Devizes and Salisbury. There are thousands of ......23...... for ......24...... at cash-and-carry prices all the year round.

5 Can you ask for things when you don't know the exact word? Here are some useful words and expressions.

a thing   a machine   a tool

stuff   liquid   powder   material

square   round   pointed   sharp

a point   an end   a hole   a handle

a thing with a (hole, handle, *etc.*)

a thing/tool/machine for (making ..., cutting ..., *etc.*)

a thing that you ... with/in/on/*etc.*

a thing that goes on top of / under / ...

material/liquid/powder/stuff for ...ing

How could you ask for these things if you didn't know their names?

fly-spray
'liquid for killing flies'

a typewriter
'a machine that you write with'

a fork   an umbrella   a hat   a bath   a car
beer   soap   glasses   tea   string   a hammer
shoe-polish

6 Now look at the pictures and ask for one of the things illustrated. Don't use its name (if you know it), and don't use your hands. See if the other students can say what you are asking for.

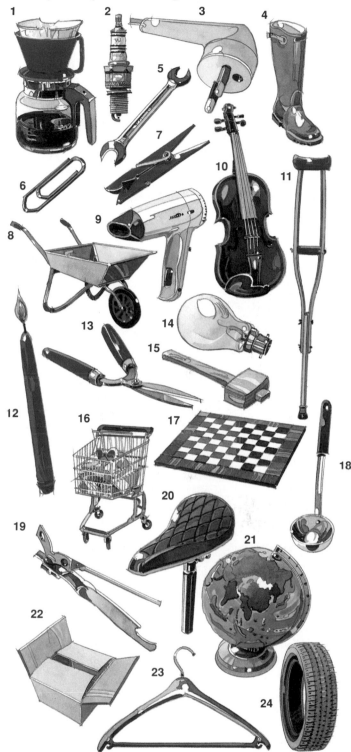

Learn/revise: advertisement; bargain; body; catalogue; choice; end; face; gift; handle; hole; liquid; machine; material; message; metal; nationality; oil; party; point; poster; powder; price; quality; sale; small ad; stuff; tool; value; advertise; be born; cost (cost, cost); improve; produce; save; bored; cheap; expensive; free; pointed; round; sharp; special; square; for sale.

E5 This is great

Formal and informal language; asking, offering and answering; grammar (verbs with two objects); reading and listening for detail; speaking practice.

1 📼 Formal and informal language. Read the dialogue and listen to the recording. Can you write down some of the differences?

HE: That's really a beautiful dress.
SHE: Thank you. I'm glad you like it.
HE: Would you like some more wine?
SHE: I beg your pardon?
HE: Would you like some more wine?
SHE: Oh, er, no thank you. But perhaps you could bring me a little orange juice?
HE: Yes, of course.

*   *   *

HE: Here you are.
SHE: Thank you.
HE: Would you like to dance?
SHE: Well, I'd love to, but I'm afraid I don't know how to tango.
HE: Actually, I think this is a waltz.
SHE: I see. I'm afraid I don't know how to waltz, either.
HE: Oh, do let me teach you. It's very easy.

2 Now can you rewrite this dialogue to make it more formal?

ALAN: This is great, Sue.
SUE: Glad you like it. It's dead easy to make. Have some more potatoes?
ALAN: Er, no, thanks. But I'd like a bit more beef.
SUE: Yes, sure. Here you are.
ALAN: Thanks.
SUE: Sauce?
ALAN: Yes, please.
SUE: And have some more wine.
ALAN: Oh, yeah. Great. Thanks. Say, how's Barry?

3 Ways of asking and offering. Match the questions and answers.

1. Excuse me. Could you help me for a minute?
2. Have you got the time?
3. Have you got a light?
4. Shall I give you a hand with the cooking?
5. Can you lend me some stamps?
6. Sprechen Sie Deutsch?
7. Could I borrow your car for half an hour?
8. Have you got change for £5?
9. Would you like to come and have a drink this evening?
10. Could I use your phone?

a. Sorry, I don't smoke.
b. I'm afraid I haven't got any.
c. Sorry, I'm using it.
d. Sorry, I'm not free. My sister's coming round.
e. Just after five.
f. I'll have a look. Just a moment.
g. Sorry, I don't understand.
h. Well, I'm in a bit of a hurry.
i. Of course. It's over there on the table.
j. That's very kind of you.

4 Grammar: verbs with two objects. Look at these sentences from the lesson.

Perhaps you could bring me a little orange juice?
I'd like a bit of that bread and cheese, if you can get me some.
Shall I give you a hand?
Can you lend me some stamps?

Bring, get, give and *lend* can be used with two objects – an indirect object
(*me* and *you* in the examples), and a direct object (*a little orange juice, some,* etc.).

A lot of other verbs can be used with two objects; for example, *buy, teach, tell,
order, send, write, offer, make, do, pass, show.*

See if you can make some examples from the table.

	me you him her us myself John	something nice Chinese anything some water a fax two photocopies a new car the house a drink a sandwich steak and chips some new pyjamas a strange letter a spoon the timetable the truth a ballpoint	. ?
Can you lend Could you bring I've just bought Can you teach She never tells I've ordered I'll send Susan has written May I offer Shall I make Can you do Could you pass Let me show His mother got			

5 Now work with as many other students as possible, making and replying to requests. Use at least four of the following beginnings: *Could you lend/tell/get/make/teach/give/show me ...?* See Exercise 3 for possible replies.

6 Work in pairs. Make up and practise a conversation including some or all of the following: a request; an offer; an invitation; a question; a disagreement; a misunderstanding. Possible situations: borrowing a car; borrowing clothes; looking for a room to rent; in a restaurant; trying to buy a computer; looking for somewhere to camp; first day in an English-speaking country. Ask the teacher for help if necessary.

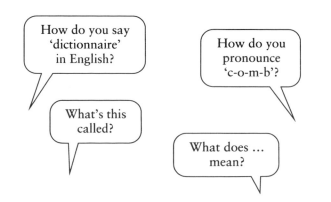

How do you say 'dictionnaire' in English?

What's this called?

How do you pronounce 'c-o-m-b'?

What does ... mean?

Learn/revise: beef; change; chips; computer; country; disagreement; dress; invitation; (a) light (for a cigarette *etc.*); misunderstanding; offer; orange juice; photocopy; pyjamas; request; restaurant; sandwich; sauce; spoon; steak; fax; timetable; (the) truth; water; borrow; bring (brought, brought); buy (bought, bought); call; camp; come round (came, come); get (got, got); help; lend (lent, lent); make (made, made); mean (meant, meant); offer; order; pass; pronounce; rent; say (said, said); send (sent, sent); show (showed, shown); teach (taught, taught); understand (understood, understood); use; write (wrote, written); glad; actually; for a minute; in a bit of a hurry; over there; How do you pronounce ...?; How do you say ... in English?; What does ... mean?; What's this called?
Formal: Do let me (teach you) ...; I beg your pardon; I'm afraid ...; I'm glad you like it; Perhaps you could bring me ...?; That's very kind of you; Yes, of course.
Informal: great; thanks; give sbdy a hand; Don't go away; Glad you like it; I wouldn't mind ... (*request*); OK; believe it or not; Say, ... (*for change of subject*); What?; Yes, sure.

103

A choice of exercises: position of adverbs; clothes and parts of the body; typical pronunciations of vowel letters.

GRAMMAR: POSITION OF ADVERBS

1 Look at the examples. Study the position of the words *always, usually, often, sometimes, occasionally, hardly ever, never*. Can you work out the rules?

She **is always** late.
Ann and Phil **are usually** at home at the weekend.
We **were very often** hungry when I was a child.
I **am never** sure what he thinks.

It **often rains** in England in summer.
My mother **sometimes loses** her temper for no reason.
I **occasionally go** to the cinema, if there's a really good film.
We **hardly ever have** lunch on Sundays.

I've **never been** to India.
You **can always ask** me for help.
She says she **will never leave** me.
I'm **quite often invited** to have dinner with the boss.
I **would never have known** if you hadn't told me.

2 Talk about the personality of somebody you know.

... is		
always	friendly.
usually	cheerful.
(very/quite) often	happy.
sometimes	unhappy.
occasionally	depressed.
hardly ever	bad-tempered.
never	worried about something.
	etc.

"*The postman's in one of his moods again, Fred.*"

3 Make sentences using *always, usually, (very/quite) often, sometimes, occasionally, hardly ever* or *never*. Example:

'*I never play the piano after midnight.*'

BEGINNINGS	ENDS
I think about life	
I go to sleep	in the bath.
I sing in a loud voice	during lessons.
I play cards	on the bus.
I write poetry	at breakfast.
I eat toast	on the roof.
I read letters	outside.
I speak English	while I'm working.
I play the piano	in the toilet.
I worry about money	in New York.
I smoke cigars	in bed.
I drink coffee	in restaurants.
I boil eggs	in shops.
I play football	after midnight.
I cry	in the police station.
I forget my name	in the river.
I wash my hands	at Christmas.
I laugh	when I'm tired.

4 Complete some of these sentences, and put in *very often, quite often, sometimes, occasionally, hardly ever* or *never*. Examples:

'*I have very often wanted to change my job.*'
'*I have never eaten snake.*'

1. I have ... wanted ...
2. I have ... eaten ...
3. I have ... played ...
4. I have ... thought ...
5. I have ... understood ...
6. I have ... studied ...
7. I have ... made ...
8. I have ... read ...

5 Look at these examples. Can you find another rule about word order?

She speaks English well.
(She speaks well English.)

I like cross-country skiing very much.
(I like very much cross country skiing.)

You must cook the meat slowly.
(You must cook slowly the meat.)

He probably has a lot of friends.
(He has probably a lot of friends.)

She carefully opened the letter.
OR She opened the letter carefully.
(She opened carefully the letter.)

6 Put the adverbs in the right places in the sentences.

1. My father plays the piano. (*very badly*)
2. I have thought of becoming a student again. (*often*)
3. My sister is happy. (*always*)
4. Small children say what they think. (*usually*)
5. We'd better clean the kitchen before your mother gets here. (*quickly*)
6. I can understand the words of songs. (*never*)
7. She likes sport. (*very much*)
8. He loses his keys. (*often*)
9. I will love you. (*always*)
10. I forget people's faces. (*never*)
11. You must tell me lies. (*never*)
12. He would like money for his birthday. (*probably*)

VOCABULARY: CLOTHES AND PARTS OF THE BODY

7 What goes where? Match the clothes and accessories with the parts of the body.

belt   blouse   boots   bracelet   brooch
contact lenses   ear-rings   glasses   glove
handbag   hat   jacket   necklace   ring
scarf   shirt   shoes   skirt   socks
T-shirt   tie   tights   trousers   watch

arm   chest   ears   eyes   face   feet
finger   hand   head   legs and feet
lower body   neck   neck and shoulders
upper body   waist   wrist

PRONUNCIATION: TYPICAL PRONUNCIATIONS OF VOWEL LETTERS

8 Look at the table. It shows the most typical pronunciations of the letters *a, e, i, o* and *u* when they are stressed. Note that a following *e* usually gives the letter a 'long' pronunciation (compare *hat* and *hate*), and that a following *r* also changes the pronunciation. Can you find more examples for each group? Can you find any common exceptions?

	short	long	before *r*	before *re*
a	/æ/ hat, matter	/eɪ/ hate, name	/ɑː/ car, start	/eə/ share, care
e	/e/ when, letter	/iː/ scene, complete	/ɜː/ serve, perfect	/ɪə/, /eə/ here, there
i	/ɪ/ sit, village	/aɪ/ fine, bite	/ɜː/ first, shirt	/aɪə/ fire, tired
o	/ɒ/ on, officer	/əʊ/ no, home	/ɔː/ sort, born	/ɔː/ more, store
u	/ʌ/ up, number	/juː/, /uː/ tune, blue	/ɜː/ turn, hurt	/jʊə/ cure, pure

Learn/revise: bad-tempered; cheerful; depressed; friendly; worried; hardly ever; occasionally; usually; *vocabulary from Exercise 7.*

E7 Every hour

1 What is your attitude to hunting animals 1) for sport 2) for their fur 3) for food?

2 Read the text and answer the questions.

Every hour, two or three kinds of animals, plants or insects die out for ever. If nothing is done about it, one million species that are alive today will have become extinct twenty years from now.

QUESTION: What is your reaction to this information?
1. You already knew.
2. You are surprised and shocked.
3. You don't believe it.
4. You are not very interested.
5. Other.

The seas are in danger. They are being filled with poison: industrial and nuclear waste, chemical fertilisers and pesticides, sewage. The Mediterranean is already nearly dead; the North Sea is following. If nothing is done about it, one day soon nothing will be able to live in the seas.

QUESTION: Which of these sources of poison is not mentioned in the text?
1. factories
2. lavatories
3. atomic power stations
4. oil tankers
5. farms

The tropical rain forests, which are the home of half the earth's living things (including many rare animals and plants), are being destroyed. If nothing is done about it, they will have nearly disappeared in twenty years. The effect on the world's climate – and on our agriculture, wood, food supplies and medicine – will be disastrous.

QUESTIONS:
1. Do you know any places where rain forests are being destroyed?
2. Do you know why the world's climate will be affected?

Fortunately, somebody is trying to do something about it. In 1961, the World Wildlife Fund was founded – a small group of people who wanted to raise money to save animals and plants from extinction. Now called the World Wide Fund for Nature, WWF is a large international organisation working to stop the destruction of the earth's natural resources. It has raised over 230 million pounds for conservation projects over the last ten years, and has created or given support to National Parks in five continents. It has helped 30 mammals and birds – including the tiger – to survive. Perhaps this is not much, but it is a start. If more people give more money – and if more governments wake up to what is happening – perhaps the World Wide Fund for Nature will be able to help us to avoid the disaster that threatens the natural world, and all of us with it.

QUESTION: Does the text say where the WWF gets its money from?

106

3 Read the texts and put in the words from the boxes. You may have to make some small changes.

OPERATION TIGER

create	left	remain	save

Seventy years ago there were 100,000 tigers in the wild. Today there are not more than 8,000 .... In 1972 the World Wildlife Fund launched 'Operation Tiger' to .... the tigers that .... Eighteen tiger reserves have been .... in India and three in Nepal.

THE LAST THIRTY ORYX

almost	hunter	natural	rare	survive
wildlife	zoo (*twice*)			

By the 1970s, ... had killed .... all of the Arabian oryx. The WWF helped to capture the last thirty .... oryx and send them to Phoenix .... in Arizona, where a herd of these .... animals has been built up. Other .... and .... parks have helped, and the oryx has been reintroduced into its .... surroundings in Oman, Jordan and Saudi Arabia.

THE LAST THOUSAND POLAR BEARS

Arctic	alive	fewer	hunting	increase
live	successfully			

Thirty years ago .... than 1,000 polar bears were left .... in the wild in Norway, Greenland and the USSR. WWF persuaded the five .... nations of Canada, the USA, Denmark (Greenland), the USSR and Norway, to agree to control .... and promote scientific study. Now the 'ice bears' are .... and breeding .... once again, and those 1,000 bears have .... their numbers to about 5,000.

THE TROPICAL FORESTS

dam	destroy	encourage	flood
in danger	international	medicine	
protect	supply		

Tropical forests have .... us with very many sorts of plants for food, ... and industry. They could probably supply many more. They also reduce .... and droughts, keep water clean, and slow down the Greenhouse Effect. But the tropical forests are being .... to make room for things like farms, ranches, mines and hydroelectric .... About 20 million hectares are lost each year – an area more than twice the size of Austria. WWF is working to .... and save the forests that are ....; to plant new trees for fuel wood and to slow down the Greenhouse Effect; and to .... governments to think about the forests and their importance when giving .... aid.

(information supplied by WWF)

4 Choose some vocabulary to learn from the texts in Exercises 2 and 3. Compare notes with other students, and talk about the reasons for your choices.

5 Work in groups of three or four. Imagine that you are the executive committee of a wildlife conservation organisation in the year 2500.

You have enough money to save several, but not all, of the following from extinction: the lion, the rabbit, the sheep, the cat, the dog, the horse, the golden eagle, the bee, the cobra, the rose. Draw up a list of priorities: three things that you will certainly save, three more that you will save if you have enough money left over, and four that you will not try to save.

Design a poster, or write a letter to be sent to all the members of your organisation, persuading people that your three priority species must be saved.

Learn/revise: animal; Arctic; climate; continent; disaster; extinct; flood; food; fur; hunter; industry; insect; lavatory; medicine; Mediterranean; organisation; place; plant; poison; tropical forest; reaction; sea; zoo; create; destroy; disappear; hunt; increase; live; remain; save; supply (sth; sbdy with sth); survive; threaten; alive; chemical; dead; international; left; living; natural; nuclear; rare; shocked; almost; fortunately; successfully; in danger.

E8 'A shock'

Speaking practice.

Work in groups of four, five or six.

Each group is to prepare, practise and perform a dramatic sketch lasting about five minutes.

The subject of the sketch is 'a shock'.

It is up to you to decide what sort of shock this is, what you do about it, what sort of person each of you is, *etc.*

Besides the shock, you must also bring into your sketch three or more of the following:

– a story
– travel
– illness
– a song
– electricity
– a suggestion
– an offer
– a meal
– a bet
– money
– love
– a little old lady
– a quick thinker
– a favour
– something very big
– something very small

Summary E

will-future

It **will be** dry and sunny.
It'**ll be** very hot.
It'**ll cloud** over.

it'll and there'll

It'll + verb

It'**ll be** very hot.
It'**ll cloud** over.
It'**ll rain**.

There'll be + noun

There'll be rain. (~~It'll be rain.~~)
There'll be snow. (~~It'll be snow.~~)
There'll be sunshine. (~~It'll be sunshine.~~)

Past Progressive tense: use and pronunciation

What **were** /wə/ you **doing** at ten o'clock last night?
I **was** /wəz/ **reading**.

Passive infinitives after modal verbs

A coin **can be used** as a screwdriver.
A bath **can be used** as a bed.

Irregular verbs in Lessons E1–E8

INFINITIVE	PAST	PAST PARTICIPLE
blow	blew	blown
bring	brought	brought
buy	bought	bought
come	came	come
cost	cost	cost
find	found	found
give	gave	given
hide	hid	hidden
lend	lent	lent
lose	lost	lost
make	made	made
mean	meant	meant
meet	met	met
ring	rang	rung
say	said	said
send	sent	sent
shine	shone	shone
show	showed	shown
steal	stole	stolen
teach	taught	taught
understand	understood	understood
write	wrote	written

Reported speech with would and had

– 'It **will** be sunny tomorrow.' 'No, it won't. It'll rain.'
  Maria **said** it **would** be sunny tomorrow, but Paul **said** it **would** rain.
– You **will** have a wonderful week.
  My horoscope **said** I **would** have a wonderful week.
– I know John **has gone** on a business trip.
  Mary **knew** John **had gone** on a business trip.
– **Has** John **gone** off with that American woman?
  Mary **wondered** if John **had gone** off …

Position of frequency adverbs

Adverbs of frequency (*always, usually, often, sometimes, occasionally, hardly ever, never*) usually go with the verb.

1. They go after am/are/is/was/were.

She **is always** late.
Ann and Phil **are usually** at home at the weekend.
We **were** very **often** hungry when I was a child.
I **am never** sure what he thinks.

2. They go before other one-part verbs.

It **often rains** in England in summer.
My mother **sometimes loses** her temper for no reason.
I **occasionally go** to the cinema, if there's a really good film.
We **hardly ever have** lunch on Sundays.

3. They go after the first part of two- or three-word verbs.

I've **never been** to India.
You **can always ask** me for help.
She says she **will never leave** me.
I'm quite **often invited** to have dinner with the boss.
I **would never have known** if you hadn't told me.

Expressing the same idea in different ways

WITH A VERB

It often **rains**. It's **snowing**. The sun **shone**.

WITH A NOUN

There is often **rain**. There will be **snow**. There was **sun(shine)**.

WITH AN ADJECTIVE

It is often **rainy/wet**. It was **sunny**.

Word order: verb, object and adverb

We do not usually put adverbs between the verb and the object.

She speaks English well.
  (She speaks well English.)
I like cross-country skiing very much.
  (I like very much cross-country skiing.)
You must cook the meat slowly.
  (You must cook slowly the meat.)
He probably has a lot of friends.
  (He has probably a lot of friends.)
She carefully opened the letter.
OR She opened the letter carefully.
  (She opened carefully the letter.)

Verbs with two objects

Many verbs can be followed by two objects. Common examples: *bring, buy, get, give, lend, make, offer, order, pass, send, show, teach, tell, write.*

Perhaps you could **bring me a little orange juice?**
Shall I **give you a hand?**
Can you **lend me some stamps?**
She wants me to **teach her French.**

Punctuation

Capital letters are used at the beginning of sentences.

It happened like this. (it happened like this)

Capital letters are used for names.

Dear Sue (Dear sue)

Capital letters are used for nationality words, including adjectives.

that American woman (that american woman)

'I' is always capitalised.

I made a real fool of myself (i made ...)

Full stops separate one sentence from another.

I made a real fool of myself last week. It happened like this.
  (I made a real fool of myself last week it happened like this)

Question marks are used instead of full stops after direct questions.

... am I the only one?

Commas are used between clauses to break up longer sentences.

Have you ever done anything like that, or am I the only one?

Commas are used to separate 'discourse markers' like *Well*.

Well, I was sure he'd gone off with that American woman.
  (Well I was sure ...)

Commas are used to separate phrases that 'interrupt' a clause.

'I'm sorry,' the girl said, 'but ...'

Commas are not used before *that*.

It turned out that he'd met an old school friend.
  (It turned out, that ...)

Brackets are used to separate less important points that interrupt the main ideas.

Well, I was sure he'd gone off with that American woman (do you remember me telling you about her last year?). But actually ...

Quotation marks are used to show that we are quoting somebody's actual words.

'I'm sorry,' the girl said ...
  (I'm sorry, the girl said ...)

Apostrophes are used in contractions.

I'm   he'd   he's   couldn't
(Im   hed   hes   couldnt)

Examples of common contractions

I'm   I've   he's (= *he is* or *he has*)
she'd (= *she had* or *she would*)   I'll   it'll
can't   won't   isn't   doesn't   hasn't
hadn't   wouldn't   couldn't   didn't

Asking for things when you don't know the exact words

a thing   a machine   a tool
stuff   liquid   powder   material

square   round   pointed   sharp

a point   an end   a hole   a handle

a thing with a (hole, handle, *etc.*)

a thing/tool/machine for (making ..., cutting ..., *etc.*)

a thing that you ... with/in/on/*etc.*

a thing that goes on top of / under / ...

material/liquid/powder/stuff for ...ing

Vocabulary

Look through the 'Learn/revise' boxes at the ends of Lessons E1–E8.

Revision and fluency practice E

A choice of activities.

1 📼 Read the text and listen to the recording. There are a large number of differences. How many can you find?

And now yesterday's weather. There may be some cloud and rain in the south-east at first tomorrow, but most of France, Belgium and northern Switzerland will have sunny periods. There may be storms, especially in the south and east, and snow is probable on low ground in northern and eastern Scotland. It will not be much colder or windier tomorrow, with temperatures ranging from 3° Celsius (27° Fahrenheit) in northern France to 9°C (48°F) in south-west England. Outlook for the weekend: it will be mainly very dry, with exceptional showers in western districts. Temperatures will be lower. There could be strong winds in southern England and Ireland, reaching gale force in some land areas.

2 📼 Listen to the recording. It is the background music from an imaginary film. Work in groups and decide what is happening in the film as the music plays.

3 Strange presents. On three separate pieces of paper, write the names of three things that would make strange birthday presents. (Examples: a baby crocodile; a chocolate clock; a bottle of sea water.) The teacher will collect the papers in, mix them up and give them out again. As soon as you get your paper, explain why the thing written on it would make a really good present for you.

4 Talk for a minute or two (to your group or the whole class) about your childhood or your family. Put in three lies, and at least one thing that is strange but true. The others have to decide which are the lies.

5 Here is the script of a game of 'Twenty Questions'. One person is thinking of a common object, and the others are trying to guess what it is. What do you think the object is?

'Is it useful?'
'Yes.'
'Can you eat it?'
'No.'
'Is it manufactured?'
'Yes.'
'Does it cost more than £5?'
'Yes.'
'Does it cost more than £100?'
'No.'
'Is it made of metal?'
'Yes, partly.'
'Is it used in an office?'
'No.'
'In a kitchen?'
'No.'
'Outside?'
'Yes.'
'Is the metal part made of iron?'
'No.'
'Steel?'
'Yes.'
'Is it a means of transport?'
'No.'
'Can you hold it in your hand?'
'Yes.'
'Has it got a point?'
'Yes.'
'Is it bigger than a lighter?'
'Yes.'
'Is part of it made of string?'
'No.'
'Is part of it made of wire?'
'No.'
'Is it used at a particular time of day?'
'No.'
'Is it waterproof?'
'Yes.'
'Is it an …?'
'Yes.'

6 Play 'Twenty Questions' yourselves in groups of four or five. Try to use words and expressions from Exercise 5.

7 Work in groups of four, five or six. Prepare and practise a sketch for the following situation. When you are ready, perform your sketch for the class.

The group is a family. (Each student in the group should play the part of one of the family members.) Father has been offered a very well-paid job abroad; he wants to accept it and take the family with him. The rest of the family disagree about whether to go or not (each person should have a good reason for staying or going). In the middle of their discussion, the postman comes with a letter for one of the family (not Father).

8 Work in pairs. Make up a conversation, lasting a maximum of 90 seconds, in which you use as many as possible of the following words.

> asleep   centimetre   end   go away   haircut
> menu   pen   purse   quick   rock   second
> sex   taste   tie   towel   zero

9 Mime a machine. See if the other students can write down the name of your machine.

10 Read the story, and list the people in order, according to whose behaviour you think was worst, whose was next worst, *etc.* Discuss your lists in groups. Useful structure: *he/she should(n't) have ...ed.*

ANNETTE AND CLIVE
Annette's boyfriend Clive went to the Far East for six months on business. Annette loved Clive desperately, and couldn't stand being away from him for so long. She wanted to go and see him, but she couldn't afford the air fare. So she telephoned Clive, asking him to come over to London for a few days to see her, but he said that he couldn't because of pressure of work. So then she went to see Ian, an old boyfriend of hers, and asked if he would lend her the money. He said he would, but only if she would go away for the weekend with him. Annette refused, and went to her father Jake. (Jake had plenty of money but didn't like Clive at all.) Jake said no. So Annette went back to Ian and agreed to his terms. They spent the weekend together, Ian lent Annette the money for the plane ticket, and on Monday she flew to see Clive.

  When Clive asked Annette how she had got the money, she told him the truth. Clive was furious and broke off their relationship. Annette flew back to London in despair. When she got home, she went to see her father and told him what had happened. Her father did not take it well. He phoned a friend of his, and the two of them went round to Ian's place and beat him up.

11 Look at the cartoons and talk about your reactions. Which ones do you find funny? Which ones don't make you laugh? Are there any that you don't understand? Discuss your reactions with other students.

"*Good morning, Mr Dolby! It's 5.15 am and this is radio station WJRM. If you name the next tune you will win a ride on an elephant and two tickets to a rock concert!*"

"*The committee on women's rights will now come to order.*"

Test E

LISTENING

1 📼 Listen and match: what will the weather be like when?

1. this morning	a. cloudy, rain
2. this afternoon	b. dry, nice
3. tonight	c. the occasional shower
4. tomorrow morning	d. showers, cloud, rain
5. tomorrow evening	e. sunny

GRAMMAR

2 Choose the right verb forms.

1. Temperatures .... a bit cooler tomorrow. (*be*)
2. There .... any rain today, but there is a possibility of some light rain tomorrow. (*not be*)
3. My horoscope said that I .... a very interesting person on Wednesday, but I didn't meet anyone at all. (*meet*)
4. I didn't know that you .... Martin. (*already meet*)
5. I tried to phone you at the office this afternoon, but they said you .... (*leave*)

3 Put each sentence into the right order.

1. a ballpoint can for lend me minute you your ?
2. and bring chips could fish some us you ?
3. he her never tells the truth .
4. holiday let me my photographs show you .
5. could me pass salt the you ?

4 Copy each sentence, adding the word or expression in brackets in the right place.

1. Jonathan is on time. (*always*)
2. Children are afraid of the dark. (*very often*)
3. I forget where I put things. (*sometimes*)
4. We invite friends to lunch on Sunday. (*hardly ever*)
5. I've been to Moscow. (*never*)
6. I can remember her husband's name. (*never*)
7. She is asked to talk to school children about being blind. (*quite often*)
8. She plays tennis. (*well*)
9. I like Josie. (*very much*)
10. You should open it. (*very carefully*)
11. You left your keys in the car. (*probably*)
12. You should tell your parents the truth. (*usually*)

LANGUAGE IN USE

5 Here is a dialogue where A (Anne) is speaking formally and B (Barry) is speaking informally. Rewrite the dialogue, so that both people speak *either* formally *or* informally.

A: That's a lovely tie.
B: Thanks.
A: Would you like another drink?
B: What?
A: Would you like another drink?
B: No, thanks. But how about some more pizza?
A: Yes, of course.
          *   *   *
A: Here you are.
B: Thanks.

VOCABULARY

6 Write the names of these.

READING

7 Answer the questions by looking at the small ads. *Don't* read all the words in all the ads.

MISCELLANEOUS FOR SALE 401

ANTIQUES, jewellery, collectables for £5 upwards, gifts for every occasion at Hardy's Antiques, 55 Oswin Road, Treeport. Open Saturdays and Sundays 11am to 4pm, weekdays 10am to 2pm except Mondays. – Tel (0235) 4182.
NEW solid pine furniture, free delivery. – Tel (0235) 8510.
SCAFFOLDING towers £120, industrial £190, immediate delivery. – Tel Lower Harborne 332.
SECTIONAL timber buildings, e.g. 12'x8' Acme with floor, £420, free catalogue. – Tel Bognor Regis 5772.
SHEDS half price, free catalogue. – Tel Bognor Regis 5772.
SWIMMING POOL, 12ft across, 3ft deep, new, guaranteed, £175. – Tel Chichester 6464.
LARGE tea chests with lids, delivered free. – Tel 317625

MISCELLANEOUS WANTED 402

OLD postcards bought and sold, Yewbarrow Postcards. – Tel Hinton Gurney 2123.
PHOTOGRAPHIC enlarger needed urgently. Prefer Apollo type but any considered. – Tel 623529.
PIANOS wanted, anything concidered. – Tel Westport 56655 or Chichester 3111.
WANTED, old furniture, bric a brac, china, curios, postcards. Houses and garages cleared. – Tel Bognor Regis 5633.

TV, VIDEO AND AUDIO 404

12" FERGUSON portable colour TV with remote control, excellent condition, £150 ono. – Tel (0235) 8869.

MUSICAL INSTRUMENTS 406

PIANOS from £350 guaranteed. Clavinovas and other digital pianos, Yamaha Keyboards, organs, guitars, sheet music and accessories. 0% interest free credit. The Music Supermarket , 71/72 Bygrave Street, Westport. – Tel 56655.

FARM & GARDEN 413

DECORATIVE bark, ideal for borders, 30 litre bags £2.50 or loose at £35 per metre, also wood chips, 60 litre bags £2.75 inc VAT, can deliver. – Tel Chesterton 683 6071.

PAVING slabs, crazy paving, sand, ballast, quick delivery. – Tel 0235 6522/7635.
TIMBER cut to your own measurements; also NPC Tagrip treatment, new sawmill operating at Irish Common, Chesterton. – Tel Chesterton 589 0766.
200 garden gnomes, free to good home. – Tel Bognor Regis 5639.
DINGWALL Supreme edge and featheredge boards for sheds. Tel Chesterton 589 0766.

PETS 415

DOG grooming, clipping, bathing and stripping of all breeds, also Cashmere baby and full-grown rabbits. – Tel Treeport 7162.
HANDSOME grey tabby cat and her ginger brother need loving home after death of owner, other cats also looking for good homes. – Tel South Coast Animal Rescue 0235 83441.
TERRIER puppies, show or pet, ready now, £120. – Tel Water Harborne 623.
COLLIE puppy, home reared, KC registered, pedigree ensured. – Tel Chesterton 776 7742.

LIVESTOCK 416

WANTED, child's first pony for eight-year-old girl, sale or hire, must be 100%, about 13/14hh, excellent and experienced home. – Tel Bognor 8858.

FURNITURE 419

ANTIQUES warehouse at Worsden, near Stowfield, 10 miles from Westport, over 1000 items of furniture. Tel (0235) 9677.
OLD and antique furniture wanted, best prices. House clearances. – Tel Bognor Regis 8080 or call at 91 Upper Parade.

SPORTING GOODS 410

GOLF CLUBS, new, complete set, 9 irons and three metal woods, one year guarantee, £129. – Tel Undersley 763.

1. What number should I phone to get my terrier bathed?
2. How much can I buy a swimming pool for?
3. What Westport number do I phone to sell a piano?
4. What Westport number do I phone to buy a piano?
5. Can you have sand delivered or do you have to go and get it?
6. How much do twelve golf clubs cost?

WRITING

8 Write the contractions for these expressions.

1. have not
2. will not
3. cannot
4. are not
5. do not
6. she is
7. she has
8. it will
9. they are
10. would not
11. I had
12. I would

9 Write this letter with correct punctuation and capital letters.

dear alice
thank you very much for a lovely time on saturday we enjoyed meeting your friends susan and carol and the food was delicious
   i have asked about the book you wanted but i dont think you can get it in this country however if you want i can write to my friend nadine in paris and i am sure she will be happy to get it for you you must meet nadine sometime anyway i am sure you two would get on really well
   well i am writing this while having my breakfast and if i dont stop now i will miss my bus thanks once again for saturday evening
love to you both
sarah

10 Write two horoscopes for tomorrow: a really good one for yourself and a really bad one for someone you don't like.

PRONUNCIATION

11 Copy the sentences and underline the stressed syllables.

1. That's a lovely tie.
2. Would you like to dance?
3. The first thing that I do when I get up is make a cup of tea.
4. I find it very difficult to get to sleep at night and to wake up in the morning.
5. Fifty years ago there were a hundred thousand tigers in the wild.

SPEAKING

12 Work with another student. Each of you must describe one or two objects in English without saying their names and without using your hands. The other must try and guess what they are.

Grammar revision section

Simple Present and Present Progressive

1 Look at the examples and think about how each tense is used.

SIMPLE PRESENT TENSE
Jan often talks to herself.
I never drink anything with my meals.
The days get longer from January to June.
We go out a lot in the summer.

PRESENT PROGRESSIVE TENSE
Look – Jan's talking to herself.
'What are you drinking?' 'Tonic water.'
The days are getting longer now.
We're going out with Annie on Tuesday.

Which tenses do we use to talk about the following?
A things that are happening now, these days
B things that are always true
C things that happen often, usually, always, never *etc*.
D things that are changing
E plans for the future

2 Write the correct verb forms.

1. 'What's that terrible noise?' 'Katy .... the violin.' (*practise*)
2. Do you know anyone who .... Russian? (*speak*)
3. I wonder if Wayne is ill – he .... thinner and thinner. (*get*)
4. Oak trees .... much more slowly than pine trees. (*grow*)
5. She can't come to the phone right now – she .... a bath. (*have*)
6. She .... to church with her brother on Sundays. (*usually go*)
7. Unemployment .... at an alarming rate. (*rise*)
8. .... you .... to the meeting next Tuesday? (*go*)
9. .... your brother ever .... at the weekends? (*work*)

3 Work in groups of four or five. One person should choose *either* a job (plumber, doctor, ...) *or* an animal to say two sentences about. The others should ask *Yes/No* questions to find out what the person or animal is. Examples:

'This person works with people. Most people don't like to visit this person.' 'Is it a doctor?' 'No.' 'A nurse?' 'No.' 'Does this person sometimes work at night?' 'Not usually.' ...

'This is an animal with a long tail. It eats meat.' 'Is it a big animal?' 'Not very big.' 'Does it live with people?' 'Yes.' ...

4 Work with a partner. Choose one of the people in the picture and say what he/she is wearing and doing. Your partner must try to guess which person you are talking about. Example:

'I'm looking at a woman. She's wearing a blue dress, and she's drinking something.' 'Is she sitting down?' ...

5 Who are these people and what are they doing? Can you write a 'riddle' like this yourself?

1. This person usually sits down and uses a machine with a screen all day. But right now she is sliding down a mountainside on two pieces of plastic. (*Answer: a computer operator who is skiing*)
2. In his job this person usually stands up, talks, listens and writes on a board. But right now he is sitting down hitting some black and white keys with his fingers.
3. On most days this person walks from house to house putting things into boxes or through holes. At the moment, though, she is standing inside a box and water is falling on her.
4. This person usually works with paints, brushes, pens, inks, paper and canvas. But right now he is pushing two wheels around by moving his legs.

Simple Past and Past Progressive

1 Look at the tables and examples and try to see how each tense is used. Can you make a rule for the Past Progressive?

SIMPLE PAST TENSE

> I left, you left, he/she left *etc.*
> did I leave? *etc.*
> I did not leave *etc.*

PAST PROGRESSIVE TENSE

> I was leaving, you were leaving *etc.*
> was I leaving? *etc.*
> I was not leaving *etc.*

Examples:
1. While I was driving to work, I heard an old friend on the radio.
2. I was trying to explain something to Mark and the phone rang.
3. When she heard the noise, she turned to see what it was.
4. What were you doing at ten o'clock last night?
5. What did you do last weekend?
6. I got a letter from Phil this morning.
7. We lived in a very small town when I was a girl.

2 Which of the two tenses do we use for these?

A a short past event
B a short event that happened before or after another event
C a shorter event which came in the middle of a longer, 'background' event
D a shorter event which interrupted a longer, 'background' event
E the 'background' situation at the moment when something happened
F the situation at a particular past moment
G a long past situation, with nothing else happening in the middle of it

3 Write the correct verb forms.

1. As usual, Roger .... while I .... to get some work done. (*phone; try*)
2. What time .... you .... up this morning? (*get*)
3. I .... Jenny while I .... up Blake Street. (*see; walk*)
4. I .... undressed when I .... a strange sound in the kitchen. (*get; hear*)
5. He .... the last twenty years of his life in Tahiti. (*spend*)
6. I .... to Chris on the phone this morning and the line suddenly .... dead. (*talk; go*)
7. Anna .... the newspaper when I .... into the office this morning. (*read; come*)

8. We .... as soon as Tom .... the tickets. (*leave; get*)
9. .... you .... the violin at about nine last night? (*play*)
10. I .... in a bank after I .... school. (*work; leave*)
11. When it .... raining we all .... into the tent. (*start; run*)

4 Say what you were doing, or what was happening, at three or more of these moments.

1. The last time your phone rang.
2. The last time you were really frightened.
3. The last time you felt very happy.
4. The last time you got really angry.
5. The last time you got very bored.

5 Write questions using two of the expressions below, or write your own question(s) with Past Progressive and Simple Past verbs. Ask some other students your questions and report the answers.

1. when you first met your best friend
2. at 11 o'clock last night
3. when you fell asleep last night
4. at 5.30 this morning
5. when you got home yesterday

6 Go and look out of the nearest window for five seconds. Then sit down and write at least three things that were happening when you looked out of the window.

7 Choose the correct caption for the cartoon.

'Come in, Ferguson. We just talked about you.'
'Come in, Ferguson. We were just talking about you.'

Present Perfect and Simple Past with time expressions

1 Look at the tables and examples. When do we use the Present Perfect with time expressions, and when do we use the Simple Past?

SIMPLE PRESENT PERFECT TENSE

> I have seen, you have seen *etc.*
> have I seen? *etc.*   I have not seen *etc.*

SIMPLE PAST TENSE

> I saw, you saw, he/she saw *etc.*
> did I see? *etc.*   I did not see *etc.*

Examples:
1. 'Have you seen Joan today?' 'Yes, I saw her at about nine, but I haven't seen her since then.'
2. I've always wanted to go to New Zealand, but I've never managed to get there.
3. I wanted to be a doctor until I was fifteen.
4. I haven't seen much of Al lately – have you?
5. We went to church every Sunday when I was a child.
6. Hannah's worked with horses all her life.
7. Benjamin's been to Africa several times this year.
8. Somebody broke into our house last night.
9. Janice went to France on holiday fifteen years ago, and she has lived there ever since.
10. I've climbed quite a lot of mountains, but I've never been up Mont Blanc.

2 Only one of these rules is true. Which one?

When we give the time of a past event:
A the Present Perfect is used when the time is finished; the Simple Past is used when it is not finished
B the Present Perfect is used when the time is not finished; the Simple Past is used when it is finished
C the Present Perfect is used for longer periods of time; the Simple Past is used for shorter periods
D the Present Perfect is used for repeated actions; the Simple Past is used for actions that are not repeated

3 Finished or unfinished time?

today	since I got up
yesterday	three years ago
this morning	for the last three years
ever	this year
never	last year
always	for the last year
when I was nine	in 1991
until I was nine	since 1991
since I was nine	recently/lately
after I got up	up to now

4 Write the correct verb forms.

1. '............... Ken .... to school at all this week?' 'He .... on Tuesday morning – that's all, I think.' (*be; come*)
2. Bridget .... in Dublin. (*always live*)
3. I .... a lovely day today – the telephone .... working at about ten, and it .... so peaceful ever since! (*have; stop; be*)
4. I .... to write to Judy yesterday. (*not manage*)
5. It certainly .... cold this winter! (*be*)
6. Karen .... an enormous amount of work last week. (*do*)
7. Isaac and Martin .... about ten years ago. (*first meet*)
8. My grandmother .... in Louisiana until she was twenty. (*live*)
9. .... you ever .... a musical instrument? (*study*)
10. I .... ill a lot last year. (*be*)
11. I .... ill for the last year. (*be*)
12. We .... each other all our lives. (*know*)
13. 'How's your new job?' 'Everything .... all right up to now.' (*be*)
14. I .... Mary recently – have you? (*not see*)

5 Work in groups and discuss the answers to these questions.

1. A woman says 'I've been in Africa for six years.' Is she in Africa when she says this?
2. A man says 'I was in Canada for three years.' Is he in Canada when he says this?
3. Somebody says 'I've worked with Sue for ten years, and I worked with Jake for twelve years.' Which one does he or she still work with?
4. Somebody says 'I did seven years' French at school.' Is he or she still doing French at school?
5. You are in America. Somebody says 'How long are you here for?' Does the person want to know when your visit started, or when it will end? How would he or she express the other meaning?

6 Write two questions: use an expression from each group. Ask other students your questions and report the answers.

First group:
When did you first ...?
How long ago ...?
When you were a child, ...?
Last year, ...?

Second group:
Have you ever ...?
Have you ... today?
What/Who ... lately?
Have you ... since ...?

7 Complete this rule:

DON'T USE THE PRESENT PERFECT WITH EXPRESSIONS OF .... TIME.

Present Perfect Progressive

1 Look at the examples. Then close your book and try to write down three of them from memory.

*Where have you been? I **have been waiting** for you since six o'clock.*
*It **has been raining** all day.*
*'You look hot.' 'Yes, **I've been running**.'*
*How long **have** you **been learning** English?*
*Who's **been sleeping** in my bed?*

2 Complete the sentences with Present Perfect Progressive verbs.

1. I .... English for three years. (*learn*)
2. She .... in the same job since 1988. (*work*)
3. It .... for the last two days. (*snow*)
4. Prices .... very fast recently. (*go up*)
5. How long .... you .... in this hotel? (*stay*)
6. 'What .... you .... all morning?' 'I .... letters.' (*do; write*)
7. 'You look tired.' 'Yes, I ....' (*work*)

3 When do we use the Present Perfect Progressive? Can you find a rule?

4 Do a small drawing to show something that you do regularly, and how long you have been doing it. Show it to another student and see if he/she can interpret your drawing. Example:

You've been playing tennis for seven years.

6 Some verbs are not used in progressive forms. Choose the correct tense (Present Perfect Simple or Progressive).

1. How long have you *known / been knowing* Alex?
2. How long have you *learnt / been learning* French?
3. How long have you *had / been having* your car?
4. Since we first met yesterday morning, I have *loved / been loving* you passionately.
5. I've *tried / been trying* to phone him all day.

7 Present Perfect or Present? Choose the right tense.

1. I *am writing / have been writing* letters for the last two hours.
2. I *am training / have been training* for a ski competition at the moment.
3. How long *are you working / have you been working* as a driver?
4. At last! *I'm waiting / I've been waiting* for you since ten o'clock.
5. *I know / I've known* her for years.
6. Why *are you looking / have you been looking* at me like that?
7. *He's / He's been* ill for a long time.
8. How long *do you have / have you had* that car?

5 Look at the pictures. What has the person been doing in each one?

He has been writing letters

119

Non-progressive verbs

1 Here are some pieces of conversation recorded at a party. Put in the right present-tense verb forms.

1. 'I .... you. You're Bill's cousin. What .... Bill .... now?' 'He .... in a circus.' (*remember; do; work*)
2. 'I .... your dress.' 'Thanks. I .... your shirt.' (*like; not like*)
3. 'Why .... you .... football boots?' 'They're not mine.' (*wear*)
4. 'It's a good party, but I .... the music.' 'I .... it's beautiful.' (*hate; think*)
5. 'You say you .... me now, but will you still love me in the morning?' 'Of course I will.' 'I .... you.' (*love; not believe*)
6. 'You have beautiful eyes.' 'You .... on my foot.' (*stand*)
7. '............... you .... some more wine?' 'No, it .... like furniture polish.' 'How .... you ....?' (*want; taste; know*)
8. 'Everything is nothing, baby. Everything is nothing.' 'I .... what you ....' 'It ....' (*not understand; mean; not matter*)
9. 'What's your name?' 'I ....' (*forget*)
10. 'I .... tired. Let's go home.' 'I .... to stay here all night.' (*get; want*)
11. 'Who .... this glass .... to?' 'I ....' 'Well, it's mine now.' (*belong; not know*)
12. 'Let me give you some advice.' 'I .... your stupid advice.' (*not need*)
13. 'I .... you're crazy.' 'I ....' 'That's because you're crazy.' 'I ....' (*think; not agree; see*)
14. 'Why .... you .... to yourself?' 'I .... my conversation more interesting than yours.' (*talk; find*)

2 Look again at Exercise 1. Make a list of the verbs that are not usually used in progressive forms.

3 Put together some of the beginnings and ends to make sensible sentences.

BEGINNINGS	ENDS
I think	'Welcome' in Welsh.
I know	any more.
I don't like	beer.
I hate	I'm right.
I don't want	in Father Christmas.
We don't need	it's Tuesday.
I remember	my first day at school.
I forget	to me.
I don't understand	washing-up liquid.
I don't believe	what you mean.
It tastes like	with everything you say.
Croeso means	you're right.
This bag doesn't belong	you.
I agree	your face.
	your name.

Since and *for*

1 Look at the examples. We use different kinds of expression after *since* and *for*. Can you make a rule?

I've lived here since 1984.
It's been raining since early this morning.
She's been ill since she came back from holiday.
I've lived here for ten years.
It's been raining for hours.
She's been ill for three months.

2 Fill in the gaps.

since yesterday = for 24 hours
for 400 years = since the 16th century
since 1977 = for ...   for ten years = since ...
since last July = ...   for the last five days = ...
since last Tuesday = ...   for the last three hours = ...
since nine o'clock = ...
since my birthday = ... the last ... days/months
all my life = ... I was born

3 Put in *since* or *for*.

1. I haven't seen Joe .... Saturday.
2. My father's worked here .... 40 years.
3. We've had the same government .... twelve years.
4. I've been looking for a job .... Easter.
5. I've had a headache .... I woke up.
6. It's been raining .... a week.
7. They've been playing cards .... 24 hours.
8. We've been painting our house .... months.

4 Write sentences with *since* and *for* for these situations.

1. Carlos works for his mother. He began doing this seven years ago.
2. Claudia began working for the World Health Organisation in 1990.
3. Jack plays the violin. He began when he was three.
4. Yasuko is taking riding lessons. She started on her last birthday.
5. Ali has a house in Marrakesh. He bought it five years ago.
6. Sergei is staying with friends in Moscow. He arrived last week.
7. Sigrid lives in Munich. She started living there five years ago.

5 Make questions beginning *How long have you lived/been/had/known ...* and ask another student. Answer questions using *since* or *for*.

Past Perfect

1 Look at the examples and try to see when we use the Past Perfect tense.

*I woke up late this morning because I **had forgotten** to set my alarm clock.*
*When I saw her I knew that we **had met** before.*
*After she **had finished** breakfast she made some phone calls.*
*I wondered why Chris **hadn't written** for so long.*
*He told me he **had** never **been** to India.*

2 Choose the best rule.

We use the Past Perfect:
A to talk about the reason why something happened
B to talk about something that happened a long time ago
C when we are already talking about the past, to go back for a moment to an earlier past time
D mainly in reported speech
E to show that a past action was completed

3 Choose the correct tense (Simple Past or Past Perfect).

1. When he .... telling the joke I realised that I .... it before. (*start; hear*)
2. When I .... at the car I could see that somebody .... into the back of it. (*look; drive*)
3. When we .... to the restaurant we .... that nobody .... to reserve a table. (*get; realise; remember*)
4. The doctor .... her and found that she .... her arm. (*examine; break*)
5. I .... abroad before, so I .... every moment of my first visit to Germany. (*not be; enjoy*)
6. We were a few minutes late, so the film .... when we .... at the cinema. (*start; arrive*)
7. When she came to England, she found that the language was quite different from the English that she .... at school. (*learn*)
8. 'Good afternoon. Can I help you?' 'Yes, I .... my watch to you for repair three weeks ago. Is it ready yet?' (*bring*)
9. I .... him twice that I .... who .... the window, but he .... me. (*tell; not know; break; not believe*)

4 Look at the examples and try to see when we use the Past Perfect Progressive. Can you make a rule?

*He was tired because he **had been looking** after the children all day.*
*When I looked out of the window I could see that it **had been raining**.*
*I suddenly realised that I **had been thinking** about Peter all afternoon.*
*When she got home she found that the children **had been playing** with her computer.*

5 Make sentences by putting together situations and reasons. Example:

'I was very hungry because I hadn't eaten for two days.'

SITUATIONS
I couldn't get a job
I couldn't get into the house
I couldn't write
I decided to have a sandwich
I didn't know what to do
I felt really stupid
I had to walk
I kept singing
I smiled at everybody in the street
I was angry
I was frightened
I was tired
I was very hungry
I was worried

REASONS
I had failed all my exams.
I had fallen in love again.
I had just won £1 million.
I had lost all my money.
I hadn't eaten for two days.
I hadn't filled in a form.
I'd been working all day.
I'd broken my pen.
I'd forgotten the name of my hotel.
I'd lost my keys.
my boss had just been very rude to me.
somebody had stolen my bike.
the last bus had gone.
the police had come for my sister.

6 Think of three things that you had never done before last weekend / your last birthday / you started school.

7 Choose the correct caption for the cartoon.

'No, he's not ours! We thought you'd brought him.'
'No, he's not ours! We had thought you brought him.'
'No, he's not ours! We thought you've brought him.'

Talking about the future

1 Write sentences to say what you are doing this evening / tomorrow / tomorrow evening / on Saturday / on Sunday / next weekend. Examples:

I'm washing my hair this evening. (I wash my hair ...)
We're seeing my parents at the weekend. (We see ...)

2 Plan what you are going to do, and when, next Saturday and Sunday. Include at least eight of the following activities (and any others that you want to add), but leave yourself some free time. Note the time of each activity.

wash your hair   play tennis   write letters
shop for clothes   see a film   go to a party
see a friend   clean the kitchen   mend clothes
practise the guitar   study English grammar
do your ironing   make a cake   wash your car
go to church   see your sister   do some gardening

3 'Telephone' another student. Try to arrange to do something together at the weekend. (Look back at your answer to Exercise 2 to see when you are free.) Use some of the expressions in the box. Example:

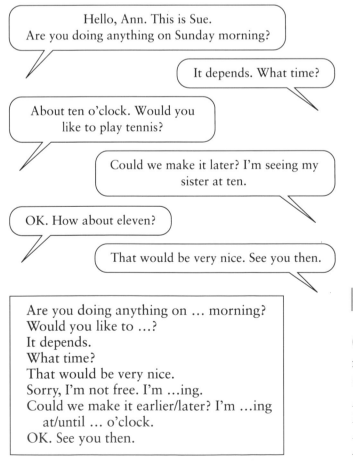

Hello, Ann. This is Sue.
Are you doing anything on Sunday morning?

It depends. What time?

About ten o'clock. Would you like to play tennis?

Could we make it later? I'm seeing my sister at ten.

OK. How about eleven?

That would be very nice. See you then.

Are you doing anything on ... morning?
Would you like to ...?
It depends.
What time?
That would be very nice.
Sorry, I'm not free. I'm ...ing.
Could we make it earlier/later? I'm ...ing at/until ... o'clock.
OK. See you then.

4 Write sentences to say what you are going to do on two or more of these occasions: next time you have a few days free; when you have finished learning English; when you leave school; during your next summer holiday; when you retire. Have you got any plans for the next year or so? Are you going to make any changes in your life? Think of something that you are never going to do again in your life.

5 Look at the pictures. What is going to happen?

6 What presents do you think people will give you next Christmas, or on your next birthday? Use *I (don't) think, I'm sure, perhaps, probably.* Examples:

I think my father will give me money.
Perhaps somebody will give me perfume.
I don't think anybody will give me a car.
Alice will give me a book. She always does.
If I'm lucky, I'll get jewellery.

7 What do you think life will be like in the year 3,000? Put *perhaps, probably (not), certainly (not)* or *not* into the sentences. Add one or more sentences of your own.

1. People will wear clothes.
2. Cars will still exist.
3. There will be a war somewhere in the world.
4. People will travel to the planets for holidays.
5. People will believe in God.
6. There will be a world government.
7. People will live longer than now.
8. Food will be very different from now.
9. Money will still exist.

PRESENT PROGRESSIVE, *GOING TO* OR *WILL*?

8 Which form would you use to talk about the following?

1. Something in the future that you think is probable.
2. Something in the future that is obviously on the way.
3. A plan to meet somebody at a particular time.
4. Your intentions for your next holiday.

9 Choose the correct forms.

1. *I'm doing / I'll do* my exams next week.
2. Have you heard? Mary *is going to have / will have* a baby.
3. I expect *I'm getting / I'll get* perfume for Christmas.
4. *Are you doing / Will you do* anything on Sunday?
5. People probably *aren't going to be / won't be* very different in the year 3,000.
6. Look at those clouds. *It's raining / It's going to rain* soon.
7. John and Sally *are going to / will* get married.
8. Look! That police car *is going to stop / will stop* outside our house.

TENSES AFTER *IF, WHEN* ETC.

10 Choose the correct forms.

1. If you (*come / will come*) round this evening I (*show / will show*) you the new clothes I've bought.
2. Perhaps I (*become / will become*) an interpreter when I (*finish / will finish*) studying English.
3. Wars (*stop / will stop*) when people (*get / will get*) more sensible.
4. If you (*go / will go*) to China next year you (*need / will need*) a visa.
5. I expect Jane (*tells / will tell*) us when she (*finds / will find*) a job.
6. It (*rains / will rain*) before we (*get / will get*) home.
7. The meeting (*starts / will start*) when everybody (*has / will have*) arrived.

Infinitives with and without *to*

1 Infinitives after auxiliary verbs. Which is correct?

1. I **will write** soon.   2. I **will to write** soon.

These verbs are followed by the infinitive without *to*, with one exception. Which is the exception?

can   could   do   may   might   must   ought
shall   should   would

2 Infinitives after ordinary verbs. Which is correct?

1. I **want go** home.   2. I **want to go** home.

What kind of infinitive comes after these?

expect   hope   manage   need   prefer   seem
start   would like

3 Put in the correct kind of infinitive.

1. I would like (*to go / go*) out tonight.
2. I hope (*to see / see*) you again soon.
3. 'That's the doorbell.' 'I'll (*to go / go*).'
4. Can you (*to lend / lend*) me some money?
5. What time do you expect (*to be / be*) home?
6. Shall I (*to carry / carry*) that bag for you?
7. We may (*to be / be*) going to Australia.
8. I didn't manage (*to do / do*) all the shopping.
9. Suddenly it started (*to rain / rain*).
10. You mustn't (*to believe / believe*) her.
11. I really ought (*to phone / phone*) my mother.
12. I don't (*to have / have*) a secretary.
13. Everybody should (*to learn / learn*) maths.
14. We need (*to talk / talk*) to Andy.
15. She seems (*to be / be*) very happy.

4 Special structures. Which is correct?

1. She doesn't even know how (*to boil / boil*) an egg.
2. 'Let's drive.' 'I would rather (*to walk / walk*).'
3. 'I don't know what (*to do / do*) this weekend.' 'Why not (*to come / come*) out with us?'
4. His parents never make him (*to study / study*).
5. Let me (*to help / help*) you.
6. You had better (*to tell / tell*) me.
7. Do you have (*to work / work*) very long hours?

5 Complete three sentences using infinitives.

1. I don't know what …
2. If you're free next weekend, why not …?
3. My parents used to make me …
4. My parents never let me …
5. In my work, I have …
6. I don't know how …
7. I don't want to learn English. I'd rather …
8. If the government want my support, they had better …

Reported speech

1 Tenses in statements and questions. Look at the examples. If the reporting verb is not past, what happens to the other verb(s)? If the reporting verb is past, what happens to the other verb(s)?

She thinks 'He's boring.'
She thinks that he's boring.

He will probably say 'I'm sure I've seen you somewhere before.'
He will probably say that he **is** sure he **has** seen her somewhere before.

He said 'I'm sure I've seen you somewhere before.'
He said (that) he **was** sure (that) he **had** seen her somewhere before.

'I **don't** remember ever meeting you,' she said.
She said (that) she **didn't** remember ever meeting him.

'I **think** we **met** on holiday,' he said.
He said he **thought** they **had met** on holiday.

He said 'I'll buy you a drink.'
He said he **would** buy her a drink.

2 Reported statements and thoughts. What did they say?

1. She said 'I'm tired.'
2. He said 'We've only just started talking.'
3. She thought 'He's really boring.'
4. She said 'It's getting late.'
5. He said 'It's still early.'
6. She said 'I started work at six o'clock.'
7. He said 'It's time to relax.'
8. She said 'I have a very busy week.'
9 He thought 'She'll be much nicer after a drink.'
10. She thought 'I made a mistake accepting his invitation.'
11. He said 'You'll feel much better after a drink.'
12. She thought 'One drink will be all right.'
13. She said 'I'll just have one before I go.'

3 Reported questions. Look at the examples. Can you make a rule about word order? When is *if/whether* used?

He said 'Where **do you live**?'
He asked her where she **lived**. (... where did she live.)

'**Have you** always **lived** in London?' he asked.
He asked her if/whether **she had** always **lived** in London.

He said 'What's **your name**?'
He asked what **her name was**.
    (... what was her name.)

He asked 'Do you like dancing?'
He asked her if/whether **she liked** dancing.

He said 'Where **did you go** to school?'
He asked her where **she had gone** to school.

4 Reported question-word questions. What did they ask?

1. He said 'What are you going to drink?'
2. She asked 'What is there?'
3. He said 'Which do you prefer – white wine, red wine or beer?'
4. She said 'What else is there?'
5. He said 'How do you feel about a small whisky?'
6. She asked 'What did you say?'
7. He said 'What do you want in your whisky?'
8. 'Why does he think I want whisky?' she wondered.

5 Reported *yes/no* questions. What did they say?

1. She said 'Can you just get me some orange juice?'
2. He said 'Can I get you a gin and tonic instead?'
3. She said 'Do you know where my coat is?'
4. He said 'Do you really want to go?'
5. She said 'Are you as stupid as you look?'
6. He said 'Did I say something to annoy you?'
7. 'Am I dreaming? Is he real?' she wondered.
8. She said 'Have you finished?'

6 Reported instructions and requests. Look at the examples. Can you make a rule?

He said 'Do have another drink.'
He invited her **to have** another drink.

She said 'Stop saying that.'
She told him **to stop** saying that.

She said 'Please don't forget my coat.'
She asked him **not to forget** her coat.

7 Reported instructions and requests. What did they say?

1. He said 'Do stay.'
2. She said 'Go and jump in the river.'
3. He said 'Don't go away.'
4. She said 'Get lost.'
5. He said 'Please give me your address.'
6. She said 'Drop dead.'
7. He said 'Don't say that.'
8. She said 'Give me my coat before I kick your teeth in.'

8 Look at the pictures. Can you suggest what the questions and answers were? Example:

Q   A

1 'He asked her what her address was.'   'She said that she lived in Paris.'

9 *Say* and *tell*. Look at the first three examples. Can you make a rule? What about the last two?

She **said** 'I want to go home.'
   (She ~~told 'I want to go home.'~~)
She **said** (to him) **that** she wanted to go home.
   (She ~~told (to him) that~~ she wanted ...)
She **told him that** she wanted to go home.
   (She ~~said him that~~ she wanted to go home.)

She **said** 'Go and jump in the river.'
She **told him to go** and jump in the river.
   (She ~~said him to go ...~~)

10 Change three of the sentences in Exercise 2, using *told* instead of *said*.

Articles

1 Look at the examples. Why is *the* used in the first three and not in the last three?

*Could you turn down **the music**? It's too loud.*
*Would you mind passing **the bread**?*
*I couldn't find **the books** you wanted.*
*Do you study **music** at school?*
*We never eat white **bread** at home.*
***Books** are very expensive.*

2 Put in *the* or – (= 'no article').

1. Why don't you like .... policemen?
2. I don't drink .... wine.
3. It's a good party, but .... music's terrible.
4. I think .... snow is the most beautiful thing in the world.
5. We couldn't play tennis yesterday because of .... rain.
6. I'll never understand .... computers.
7. Is .... money important to you?
8. I couldn't study without .... money I get from my parents.
9. Have you fed .... cats this evening?
10. People say that .... dogs are more intelligent than .... cats.

3 Look at the examples. Would any of the sentences be correct without the article *a/an*?

*My father's **a** teacher.*
*I'd like to become **an** engineer.*
*The witch turned the prince into **a** frog.*
*We converted the bedroom into **a** bathroom.*
*I used my shoe as **a** hammer.*

4 Complete some of these sentences using nouns.

1. I'd like to work as ....
2. .... is studying to become ....
3. It would be nice if I could turn myself into ....
4. I can't imagine what it would feel like to be ....
5. We ought to convert the school into ....
6. You can use a .... as a ....

5 Look at the words in the box. Eight of them cannot normally be used with *a/an*. Which are they?

> advice cold English furniture glass headache ice information light luggage news problem room table travel weather

6 Make three sentences with words from the box in Exercise 5.

125

If

1 Look at the examples and choose the correct form of the rule. Then close your book and write down the examples and the rule from memory.

*We're going swimming today **if it doesn't rain**.*
***If I have enough time tomorrow**, I'll go and see Jack.*

Rule: In *if*-clauses, we use a (*future/present/past*) tense to talk about the (*future/present/past*).

2 Put the beginnings and ends together.

BEGINNINGS
If I have enough money next year
If she passes her exams
If you don't invite Pete to the party
If we get up early enough
If you keep eating chocolate
If you don't put the meat in the fridge

ENDS
he'll be furious.
I'll travel round the world.
it will make you ill.
she's going to study medicine.
it will go bad.
we'll be able to catch the first train.

3 Put in a present tense or a *will*-future.

1. If you .... that button, a bell .... (*press; ring*)
2. If I .... time, I .... you. (*have; visit*)
3. If it ...., we .... at home. (*rain; stay*)
4. I .... you if I .... help. (*tell; need*)
5. I .... you if I .... in town. (*phone; be*)
6. If you .... that door, you .... something strange. (*open; see*)
7. I .... surprised if she .... before seven o'clock. (*be; arrive*)
8. If you .... fast, we .... time to play a game of tennis. (*eat; have*)
9. If you .... up early tomorrow, I .... you swimming. (*get; take*)
10. I .... my car if I .... to London. (*sell; move*)

4 Complete these sentences.

1. If you don't eat, you'll get …
2. If you eat too much, you …
3. If you don't have something to drink, …
4. If you drink any more beer, you'll …
5. If you don't go to bed, …
6. If you go out in the rain without an umbrella, …
7. If you go out without a coat, …
8. If you hurry, we'll be able to …

5 Look at the examples and complete the rule. Then close your book and write down one of the examples, and the rule, from memory.

*If I ever **became** rich, I **would try** to help homeless people.*
*It **would be** amazing if I **passed** my exams.*
*If I **were** you, I **would** get a haircut.*
*Everything **would be** all right if I **had** a little more money.*

Rule: When we talk about an unreal or improbable situation, we use (*a present tense / a past tense / would*) in the *if*-clause, and (*a present tense / a past tense / would*) in the rest of the sentence.

6 Choose the correct forms to complete the sentences.

1. If John (*were / would be*) here, he (*knew / would know*) what to do.
2. Do you think it (*were / would be*) a good idea if I (*phoned / would phone*) the police?
3. What (*did / would*) you do if you (*won / would win*) a million pounds?
4. If I (*had / would have*) time I (*learnt / would learn*) the piano.
5. What (*did / would*) you say if I (*asked / would ask*) you to marry me?
6. If you (*changed / would change*) your job, what (*did / would*) you do instead?
7. If today (*were / would be*) Sunday I (*were / would be*) in bed.
8. I (*went / would go*) and see Jake tomorrow if I (*knew / would know*) his address.

7 Read the sentences, and then write a similar '*if*-chain' yourself. Start: '*If I won a million dollars …*'

If I won a million dollars, I would buy a fast car.
If I bought a fast car, I would probably drive it too fast.
If I drove it too fast, perhaps I would have an accident.
If I had an accident, I would go to hospital.
If I went to hospital, perhaps I would meet a beautiful nurse and fall in love with her.
If she fell in love with me, we would get married.
If we got married, we would be very happy at the beginning.
But then perhaps I would meet somebody else.
If I met somebody else …

8 Some people were asked 'What would you do if you had plenty of time and money?' Here are pictures of some of their answers. Try to suggest what they said. Example:

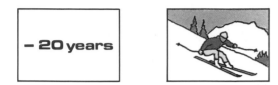

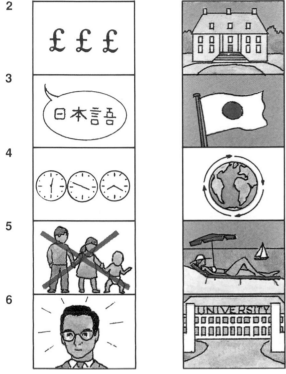

'If I were twenty years younger, I would spend all my time skiing.'

9 What would *you* do if you had plenty of money, or if you had plenty of time, or if …? Draw a pair of pictures and see if other students can put your answer into words.

10 Ordinary tenses or past + *would*? Which sentence-beginning is better?

1. a. If I become President, I will …
   b. If I became President, I would …
   Answer: *b* (because you probably won't become President)
2. a. If I feel tired tomorrow …
   b. If I felt tired tomorrow …
   Answer: *b* (you may feel tired tomorrow)
3. a. If I live to be 130, I'll …
   b. If I lived to be 130, I'd …
4. a. If I break my leg next week, I'll …
   b. If I broke my leg next week, I'd …
5. a. If wars stop, the world will be …
   b. If wars stopped, the world would be …
6. a. If it snows tomorrow, I'll …
   b. If it snowed tomorrow, I'd …
7. a. If I become rich and famous, will you …?
   b. If I became rich and famous, would you …?
8. a. If I learn to speak English perfectly, I'll …
   b. If I learnt to speak English perfectly, I'd …
9. a. If I buy a really fast car, I'll …
   b. If I bought a really fast car, I'd …
10. a. If the world ends tomorrow, I won't …
    b. If the world ended tomorrow, I wouldn't …

TALKING ABOUT THE PAST

11 Look at the examples and complete the rule. Then close your book and write down one of the examples, and the rule, from memory.

*She **would** probably **have married** John if she **had met** him earlier.*
*If you **hadn't driven** me to the station this morning I **would have missed** my train.*

Rule: When we talk about an unreal past situation, we use (*a past tense / a past perfect tense / would have* …) in the *if*-clause, and (*a past tense / a past perfect tense / would have* …) in the rest of the sentence.

12 *Would* or *had*?

1. If she'd studied harder she'd have passed her exams.
2. I'd have come to see you yesterday if I'd had time.
3. She'd have married him if he'd asked her.
4. If I'd been to university, perhaps I'd have found a better job.
5. If you'd asked me, I'd have helped you.

13 Make sentences with *if* for these situations.

1. A woman didn't lock her flat; burglars broke in.
   'If she had locked her flat, perhaps …'
2. A man drove too fast and crashed.
   'If he hadn't …'
3. A child was frightened because she was alone.
4. A man didn't understand a French film.
5. A woman didn't have time for breakfast because she got up too late.
6. A man lived by himself, and was lonely.
7. A child was cold because he wasn't wearing a coat.
8. A woman didn't go on holiday because she didn't have enough money.
9. A woman didn't get a job because her English wasn't very good.

14 Complete one or more of these sentences.

If I hadn't … yesterday, …
If Columbus hadn't …
I would have … you if …
It would have been funny if … yesterday.
If I had been able to do what I wanted when I was younger, I would(n't) have …

127

Passives

1 Look at the examples and try to fill in the blanks. Can you choose the right words to complete the rule correctly?

Active: I think somebody **will steal** their car.
Passive: I think their car **will be stolen**.

Active: Somebody **is going to steal** their car.
Passive: Their car **is going to be stolen**.

Active: Somebody **is stealing** their car.
Passive: Their car **is being stolen**.

Active: I'll be surprised if anybody **steals** their car.
Passive: I'll be surprised if their car **is stolen**.

Active: Somebody **has stolen** their car.
Passive: Their car ....

Active: Somebody .... their car.
Passive: Their car **was stolen**.

Active: When I came round the corner, somebody **was stealing** their car.
Passive: When I came round the corner, their car ....

Active: They found that somebody .... their car.
Passive: They found that their car **had been stolen**.

Rule for making passive verb forms:
1. Decide what tense you want to use.
2. Put the auxiliary verb (*be/have/do*) in that tense.
3. Add the (*infinitive / past tense / -ing form / past participle*) of the verb that you want to use.

2 Change these sentences from passive to active. Example:

'Hamlet' was written by Shakespeare. ➔ *Shakespeare wrote 'Hamlet'.*

1. This house was built by my father.
2. The cooking is usually done by Ralph.
3. The club is used by teenagers.
4. The French class will be taught by Mr Simmonds.
5. When I last saw him he was being chased by a large dog.
6. I'm being picked up by a taxi at six o'clock.

3 Change these sentences from active to passive. Example:

Somebody has broken my pen. ➔ *My pen has been broken.*

1. Somebody has invited Jane to a party.
2. Mrs Pettifer will do the cooking for us.
3. When I last saw him, a policeman was questioning him.
4. They've discovered gold in Eastern Canada.
5. Nobody ever cleans that car.
6. I could see that somebody had opened my letters.

4 Put in passive verbs.

1. Our house (*build*) in the 15th century.
2. Paper (*make*) from wood.
3. Paper (*invent*) by the Chinese.
4. German (*speak*) in several different countries.
5. This article (*write*) by a friend of mine.
6. Have you heard the news? Oil (*discover*) under the White House.
7. Your tickets (*send*) to you next week.
8. My sister's very excited: she (*invite*) to a party in New York.
9. Be careful what you say – this conversation (*record*).
10. Her new book (*publish*) next month.

5 Make five or more sentences about where things are manufactured, or where languages are spoken. Examples:

*Cars **are manufactured** in Japan.*
*German **is spoken** in Switzerland.*

6 Make two or more sentences to say where things of yours were made or bought. Examples:

*This sweater **was made** in Scotland. It **was bought** in London.*

7 Put the *-ing* form (e.g. *listening*) or the past participle (e.g. *listened*).

1. 'What is she doing?' 'She's (*listen*) to the radio.'
2. Radio 2 is (*listen*) to all over Britain.
3. When was your house (*build*)?
4. My father is (*build*) an extension at the back of his house.
5. Why are you (*watch*) that bus?
6. Last night's TV news was (*watch*) by about eight million people.
7. Storms have been (*blow*) down trees and (*damage*) people's homes in Jamaica.
8. A big tree was (*blow*) down in our garden last night.
9. The police are (*question*) some people about the damage to the shop.
10. My brother was (*question*) by the police this morning.

Comparatives and superlatives

1 Look at the following comparative adjectives. Some of them are made with *-er*, and some are made with *more*. Can you make a rule? Is the rule the same for superlatives (*oldest, most beautiful* etc.)?

more afraid   more beautiful   bigger   more boring
more careful   easier   more exact   more expensive
fatter   friendlier   happier   more intelligent
more interesting   longer   nicer   older   purer
more stupid   taller   younger

2 Do you know the comparatives and superlatives of the following words?

good   bad   far

3 Write the comparative and superlative of:

cheap   cheerful   cold   correct   dangerous
difficult   funny   hot   large   late   noisy   pretty
red   rude   sleepy   small   talkative   terrible
thin   warm   worried

4 Comparative or superlative? Look at the examples and try to make a rule.

*She's **taller** than her two sisters.*
*She's **the tallest** of the three sisters.*
*I'm **younger** than everybody else in the class.*
*I'm **the youngest** person in the class.*
*I wish we had a **faster** car – this won't go over 60 mph.*
*What's **the fastest** car in the world?*

5 Put in suitable words to complete the sentences.

1. Your TV is a lot .... than ours. (*good*)
2. This is the .... film I've ever seen. (*bad*)
3. Her accent is .... than mine. (*correct*)
4. Policemen seem to get .... every year. (*young*)
5. I'm the .... person in my family.
6. This is the .... meal I've ever eaten.
7. I have a friend who's much .... than me.
8. A friend of mine married a man who is much .... than her.
9. A friend of mine married a woman who is much .... than him.
10. Everest is the .... mountain in the world.
11. I think .... was the .... man/woman who ever lived.
12. The worst thing in the world is ....

6 Think of three people in your family or in the class. Write a sentence about each one using a superlative.

7 *As ... as.* Change the sentences as in the example.

I'm shorter than her. → *I'm not as tall as her.*

1. I'm younger than her.
2. My English is worse than hers.
3. My car's cheaper than hers.
4. My feet are smaller than hers.
5. My hair's shorter than hers.
6. My flat's smaller than hers.
7. I'm more generous than her.
8. My skin is darker than hers.

8 Think of somebody you know well. Can you think of five differences between you? Write sentences using comparatives or (*not*) *as ... as.* Think of two singers, actors, writers or sports personalities. Write two or more sentences about differences between them.

9 Choose the correct captions for the cartoons.

'You were the World's Better Baby.'
'You were the World's Best Baby.'

'The better thing about working here is going home.'
'The best thing about working here is going home.'

Additional material

Lesson A1, Exercise 6

PRIVATE DETECTIVE

He's a very small man
And his face is very thin
He wears a long grey jacket
And he's got whiskers on his chin
He keeps looking back – I keep diving into doorways
Watching every move – I still don't know his name …

He's a dangerous villain
And he's creeping like a fox
There's something in his suitcase
And now he's stepping in a phone box
He keeps looking back – I keep diving into doorways
Watching every move – but I still don't know his
    game …

Private Detective – now he's running free
Private Detective – he'll never get away from me

She's sitting in a café
And she's reaching in her bag
She's looking at a photo
And her face is very sad
She keeps looking up – I dive behind my paper
Something's gonna happen – sooner or later

Private Detective – now she's running free
Private Detective – she'll never get away from me, no,
    no, no!

She's a very smart lady
And her nails are very long
And she's talking to a stranger
And I think she's got a gun
She keeps looking up – I dive behind my paper
Something's gonna happen – sooner or later

Private Detective – now she's running free
Private Detective – she'll never get away – oh no!

Private Detective – now he's running free, no, no
Private Detective – he'll never, never, never get away
    from me!

(Steve Hall)

Lesson B1, Exercise 1

1. .... some aspirins.
2. .... corridor, ... floor.
3. .... off in the bathroom. .... covered with
   water.
4. .... accident. .... hurt. She's bleeding.
5. .... screaming .... upstairs.
6. .... burglary.
7. .... gas ....

Lesson B4, Exercises 1 and 2

Last week my next-door neighbour Steve went to a department store to buy a new suit. He chose two suits to try on and went to the changing rooms. While he was putting the first pair of trousers on, he saw a hand reach in and snatch his own trousers! He shouted, got the new trousers on and ran after the man, but didn't catch him. Now he was stuck in the department store with no trousers, no money, no credit cards and no keys. So he phoned me and I went and rescued him. We left his name, address and phone number with the department store security department.

Later that afternoon, after we managed to get a new house key made for him, he got a phone call.

'This is Mr Daley at Foley's department store,' the man said. 'We've found your wallet, and we think we've got your keys as well. Would you like to come and get them?' So I drove him back to the store.

When we got to the store nobody knew who Mr Daley was. Wondering what was happening, we drove back home. When we got there, we found that the thieves had used Steve's keys to get into his house and burgle it.

Lesson B5, Exercise 1, Dialogue 1

(The doorbell rings.)
PETER: I'll go.
ANN: OK.
       (Peter opens the door.)
PETER: Hello, hello. Nice to see you.
SUE: Hello, Peter. Are we late?
PETER: No, not at all. You're the first, actually.
JOHN: Oh, good. Who else is coming?
PETER: Come in and have a drink. Well, there's Don
       and Emma, Jo and Stephen, and my sister
       Lucy and her new boyfriend. Can't remember
       his name. Let me take your coat. You know
       Lucy, don't you?
SUE: I think we've met her once.
ANN: Hello, Sue. Hello, John. Lovely to see you. I'm
       so glad you could come. Now, what can I get
       you to drink?
SUE: What have you got?
ANN: Oh, the usual things. Sherry; gin and tonic – I
       think; vodka; I think there's some beer; a glass
       of wine …?
SUE: I'll have a gin and tonic, Ann, please.
JOHN: So will I.
SUE: Doesn't the room look nice, John? You've
       changed it round since we were here last,
       haven't you? The piano was, let me see, yes,
       the piano was over by the window, wasn't it?
PETER: That's right. And we've moved the sofa over
       there and …

Lesson B5, Exercise 5, Dialogue 2

JOHN: So you work in a pub?

LUCY: Yes, that's right.

JOHN: What's it like?

LUCY: It's nice. I like it. You meet a lot of interesting people. A lot of boring ones, too, mind you.

JOHN: I beg your pardon?

LUCY: I said, a lot of boring ones too.

JOHN: Oh, yes. I can imagine. A pub – I should think that's hard work, isn't it?

LUCY: Yes and no. It depends.

JOHN: How do you mean?

LUCY: Well, it's hard at weekends. I mean, last Saturday night, with both bars full and one barman away ill – well, my feet didn't touch the ground. But on weekdays it's usually very quiet. What about you? What do you do? You're an accountant or something, aren't you?

JOHN: I work in a bank.

LUCY: Oh yes, that's right. Ann said. That must be nice.

JOHN: It's all right.

LUCY: But you have to move round from one place to another, don't you? I mean, if you get a better job – if they make you manager or something – it'll probably be in another town, won't it?

JOHN: Yes, probably.

LUCY: I wouldn't like that. I mean, I've got lots of friends here. I wouldn't like to move somewhere else.

JOHN: Oh, we like it. We've lived here for, what, six years now. We're ready for a change.

Lesson B5, Exercise 9, Dialogue 3

DON: Have you got the salt down your end, Steve?

STEVE: What are you looking for?

DON: The salt.

STEVE: Salt. Salt. Oh, yes. Here it is. And could you pass me the mustard in exchange? This is delicious beef, Ann. Who's your butcher?

ANN: Not telling you. What are John and Lucy talking about?

JOHN: Work, I'm afraid.

SUE: I thought so. It's all John ever talks about. Work and food.

JOHN: Well, there are worse things in life. Especially if the food's like this.

ANN: Thank you, John. Would you like some more? Have another potato. Some more meat? Some beans? A carrot? A piece of bread?

JOHN: No, thanks. That was lovely, but I've had enough. Really. I'll have another glass of wine, perhaps.

EMMA: Here you are, John.
(*Crash!*)
Oh, damn! I *am* sorry, Ann. How stupid of me.

ANN: That's all right. It doesn't matter at all. Really. They're very cheap glasses.

Lesson B8, Exercise 5

DO YOU KNOW

I will snap you if you don't watch out
When you're alone or if you're in a crowd
See the action if you close one eye
Push my button when the sun is in the sky.

Do you know what it is – what it is?
Can you say what it is?
Do you know what it is – what it is?
Can you say what it is?
Tell me what it is.

Just twist my handle and flick your toe
Wind on your face just see you go
Here comes a corner so you['d] better watch out
You're feeling nervous and you['ve] gotta slow down.

Do you know …

I've got the power to save you from danger
I decide if you live or die
Pull my pin, then grip my lever
Aim me straight at the source of the fire.

Do you know …

Just punch your number, then wait for the tone
I'll take you anywhere you wanna go
I can whisper words of love in your ear
Just hold me close – I can be so sincere.

Do you know …

(Steve Hall)

Lesson C4, Exercise 1: answers

Quick-thinking van driver

A quick-thinking van driver saved 11 people trapped in a blazing house in Birkenhead early today. Mrs Anne Redman of Newbury was driving past a house in Beaufort Road when she saw the ground floor on fire. Four adults and seven children were trapped in the bedroom above. Mrs Redman backed her van across the pavement, smashed through the front fence, and drove up to the front of the house. The trapped occupants were able to jump to safety via the roof of the van.

Firemen catch a man in mid-air

Three firemen caught a man in mid-air yesterday as he leapt from a blazing house. After shouting for help, the man jumped from a top-floor window with his clothes on fire. Firemen who were fighting the fire on a balcony below heard his shouts and realised what was happening. They leaned out and grabbed him by the legs as he hurtled past. Last night 22-year-old Mr Luke Savage, of Moreton Grove, Chester, was recovering in hospital.

Policeman saves boy on motorway

Little John Parker faced death when he fell from a car as it sped down a busy motorway. He was seriously injured and lay helpless in the fast lane with traffic hurtling towards him. But a policeman had seen him fall. Police Constable Peter O'Donnell, careless of his own life, leapt from a moving patrol car. He dashed across the motorway and grabbed the five-year-old to safety from under the wheels of a vehicle that was almost upon them. Yesterday John, of The Close, Newleigh, Herts, was in hospital with head and leg injuries, but was described as 'satisfactory'.

Helicopter pilot saves swimmers
A quick-thinking helicopter pilot saved three swimmers from shark attacks yesterday. While he was flying off the Australian coast near Sydney, the pilot saw sharks approaching the swimmers. He brought his helicopter down until he was just over the water, and hovered above the sharks. After a few minutes they were frightened away, and the swimmers were able to get back safely to the beach. Swimmer Marion Jacobs said afterwards, 'He saved our lives. If he hadn't come when he did, the sharks would have had us.'

Lesson C5, Exercise 1

ASSISTANT: Good afternoon, madam. Can I help you?
CUSTOMER: Yes, I'd like to see the manager, please.
ASSISTANT: Furniture, madam? Second floor.
CUSTOMER: No, the *manager*. Ma-na-ger.
ASSISTANT: Oh, I *am* sorry. I thought you said furniture.
CUSTOMER: That's all right. But can I see the manager, please?
ASSISTANT: Well, I'm afraid she's *very* busy just now. Have you an appointment?
CUSTOMER: No, I haven't. I want to make a complaint.
ASSISTANT: A complaint. Oh, I see. Well, I'll just see if she's free.

Lesson D1, Exercise 1

Mugger meets little old lady

Jose Ramos is an experienced mugger, but he didn't know about little old English ladies. Now he does.

87-year-old Lady Vera Tucker was walking down New York's East 66th Street. She looked like an easy prey – small, grey-haired and expensively dressed, carrying a handbag over her shoulder.

Ramos came up on his bicycle and grabbed the handbag. Lady Tucker hit him on the head with her umbrella, knocking him off his bicycle, and started screaming at the top of her voice.

The unfortunate mugger tried to get back onto his bicycle and escape, but Lady Tucker kept hitting him. A lorry driver, hearing her screams, came and joined in the fight.

Holding his head, Ramos pushed the handbag at the driver and said, 'Here it is. It's over, it's over.' 'The hell it's over,' said the driver. They went on fighting, and Lady Tucker went on screaming, until a policeman arrived and took Ramos prisoner.

Lady Tucker refused medical help, saying that she felt fine. But she did allow the policeman to take her arm and escort her home.

(from *The South-Western Herald*, 28 May 1986)

Lesson D3, Exercise 8

SO NEAR YET SO FAR

Maria ......1...... on a mountainside with her mother
    and her father – she ......2...... an only child
She ......3...... so hard – in the old vineyard

Antonio ......4...... at the harbour's edge with his uncle
    and aunt ... and ......5...... his bread,
He ......6...... all day – in a rough black sea

They ......7...... at a dance in the market square
A romantic night – there ......8...... love in the air
They ......9...... each other close and he ......10...... her a ring
Both families ......11...... it ......12...... the very best thing

Maria ......13...... that the day ......14...... when she and
    Antonio ......15...... as one
They ......16...... soon – happy bride and groom

One hot summer's day on the mountainside
Maria stared as a stranger came by
In a shiny car and gold round his neck
She ......17...... the prettiest girl he'd ever ......18......

Maria ......19...... alone on the mountainside in a brand
    new dress and tears in her eyes
Now the stranger ......20...... – he ......21...... a handsome one

Antonio ......22...... on an out-of-town bus 'cause now
    his dreams ......23...... to dust
He ......24...... ......25...... away – he's just ......26...... for the city

They ......27...... at a dance in the market square
A romantic night – magic in the air
Both families ......28...... the wedding ......29...... off
So near yet so far from a perfect love.

(Steve Hall)

Lesson D5, Exercise 8

THE ISLAND

Each night I dream of a beautiful island
Surrounded by beaches and covered in flowers.
Butterflies dance through the sweet-smelling meadows
And birds sing their love songs for hours.

Crystal clear water runs down from the mountains
And flows through deep valleys as a sparkling stream.
Gentle sea breezes blow over my island
While sunshine pours over my dream.

Each night I visit the island of my dreams,
Each night I visit the island of my dreams,
I leave the real world behind,
It's somewhere deep in my mind,
Not too easy to find,
The island.

Bright orange squirrels play games in the tree tops
And chase through the branches where nightingales sing.
It looks so peaceful I wish I could take you
To where each night's the first day of spring.

Each night I visit the island of my dreams ...

(Jonathan Dykes – lyrics   Robert Campbell –music)

Lesson D8, Exercise 6

1

The time that I recall that was, er, gave me a bit of a *frisson* if you like was er, I was, er, I think I was up at university, and I was down in London at my parents' flat, and I'd been out er, moderately late, and drove er, a little Mini car back to the flat, which was in a rather smart part of London, and er, you had to park the car under the block of flats in an underground car park. And I did this one night and I noticed out of the corner of my eye that there was a car parked opposite, sort of in a right-angled road, er, facing the, the opening of the basement er, car park. And er, but I didn't pay any attention to it, I got out of the car as usual and went to see the er, night porter, and er, he saw me, recognised me, came to the door, and at that moment the doors flung open, and just like a TV, you know, TV series, er, these plainclothes people whipped out their wallets and showed, showed their er, showed their badges and said, 'Just a moment,' you know, you know, and all that sort of stuff, and you had to sort of, in there, and you thought, 'This is, this is ridiculous,' you know, 'this is r-, this is, I mean, this, this can't be serious,' but they were very serious, and they sort of almost frog-marched me to the car and asked me all these usual details, about did I know what licence number it was, how many miles I'd gone, and they took some persuading that someone looking as scruffy as I in a tiny little Mini could possibly live in such a smart block of flats.

2

The time I remember was when Piers was quite tiny and for some long-forgotten reason Peter and I were over to some friends in Burton-on-Trent, and we were in separate cars. And I was trying to follow quite closely to, behind Peter, but er, he always says I leave too much space, and so I did when he went through some traffic lights on green, and I thought, 'If I speed up a little bit I'll just get through.' And I didn't, and what I hadn't noticed was that the only other car on the road, directly behind me, was a police car, and he saw me go through the light on amber/red, I thought, but he thought it was red, so he followed us round the corner onto the bridge, overtook, stopped, and I sat tight in my car while Pete leapt out and defended me, and er, we said that we didn't want to make a noise because the baby was asleep in the back, but er, we didn't get away with it, and I did get my licence endorsed.

3

Yeah, I was driving back from France erm, years ago, and it had been a long drive, and I had had a fairly depressing experience in France, and I was driving as fast as I could through the west London suburbs to get home, and erm, I'd got this hot jazz blasting out of the erm, car cassette player at enormous volume, and erm, as I pulled up at a traffic light I saw this large white car pull up beside me, and I played back things in my mind and I realised that I had just overtaken a police car at 50 miles an hour in a 30 limit. And the policeman wound down his window, I wound down mine, and I was too perturbed to turn off the jazz. And he looked at me, and he listened to this noise coming out of the car, and he looked at me again, and he said, 'You must be bloody crazy!' And the lights changed to green and he drove off.

Lesson E1, Exercise 8

THIRTY DEGREES

It's thirty degrees in the shade
My girlfriend's spent my last dollar
I haven't seen a cloud all day
And she's run back to Minnesota.

My limousine's run clean out of gas
My radiator's dry and my tyres are flat
I'm sitting here in my ten-gallon hat
Wishing it would rain – what d'ya think of that?

It's thirty degrees in the shade
The dust is dirty where the wind blows
We're heading for a heatwave. Uh, huh
And I'm stuck here in Colorado.

My limousine's run clean out of gas
My radiator's dry and my tyres are flat
I'm sitting here in my ten-gallon hat
Wishing it would rain – what d'ya think of that?

It's hot – thirty degrees …
Thirty degrees …

Well, it's thirty degrees in the shade
My girlfriend's spent my last dollar
I haven't seen a cloud all day
And she's run back to Minnesota.

Sleep under a tree when the sun is high
It's better to walk in the desert at night.
I'll wave at the trucks and I'll hitch a ride
Got nothing to lose and I'm travelling light.

It's hot …

(Steve Hall)

Lesson E3, Exercise 5, Writing option

A few years ago I was travelling in France by myself, on a moped. I had a tent, and usually camped in the evenings: in camp sites whenever I could, both for the facilities like washing, shopping, *etc.*, and because it was a bit safer. But when I couldn't find a convenient camp site, I camped rough, trying to find places that were fairly hidden from the road. One evening like this, I found quite a nice place. It was up against a tall hedge in a little wood and couldn't be seen from the road; it was quite a pleasant spot. So I pitched my tent, covered my moped up with plastic, cooked my little supper over a camping gas fire, and got ready for bed. I read for a little while, and then went to sleep.

And I had a very unusual dream. I've never had another one like it before or since. It was in short episodes of a few minutes each, it seemed, though it's hard to tell in a dream how long things are. The people in the dream were young men and women that I had never seen and didn't know, all very happy, dressed as if it were the 1930s and 40s. Some of them were on farms; I remember a dance in a barn; some of them were walking along the streets in a small town in America. They were all Americans. Each episode had different people in it, and none of them lasted for very long. It wasn't a frightening dream at all – all the scenes were of very happy, smiling people. I woke up a bit puzzled, because it didn't seem to connect with anything that had been happening to me, and I didn't know anybody that was in the dream. It was very unusual.

I got up and fixed breakfast, packed my tent securely on the back of my moped, and set on my way. The little wood where I had slept, as I said, was up against a hedge, a very tall hedge that you couldn't see over. There was a bend in the road just at the hedge, which I hadn't been around. And when I did wheel my moped up to the road and go around the bend, I saw that just on the other side of the hedge there was a small American war cemetery from World War II – full of the graves of young men who could have lived the scenes that I had seen in my dream.

Lesson B7, Exercise 1, Dialogue 4

ANDY: I didn't like it at all.

EMMA: Oh, I thought it was lovely.

JOHN: It was rubbish. Complete rubbish. Absolute nonsense.

ANN: I didn't think much of it, I must say.

LUCY: I liked it. At the end, when she was dying, I cried. I couldn't help it. I cried and cried.

STEVE: Jo said it made her laugh.

JO: No, I didn't. Oh Steve, you are awful! Really! No, it's just that – I don't know – it didn't say anything to me.

JOHN: I'm afraid I must be very old-fashioned, but I like things to have a beginning, a middle and an end.

STEVE: Yes, so do I.

JOHN: And I don't like a lot of sex and violence.

EMMA: Oh, I love sex and violence!

ANN: More coffee, anybody?

ANDY: I don't like violence.

EMMA: But listen. Why didn't you like it? I thought it was great. Really.

ANN: So wordy. It was really really boring. They just talked and talked and talked all the time.

STEVE: I can't stand –

EMMA: No, look –

LUCY: I don't think –

DON: Three old women sitting around talking for two and a half hours. If that's what you want, you might as well go and spend the evening in the old people's home.

LUCY: It wasn't like that at all.

ANDY: Yes, it was.

LUCY: No, it wasn't.

ANDY: Yes, it was.

ANN: Who wrote it anyway?

JO: Don't know. What's his name? Fred Walker, something like that.

ANDY: Who's he?

DON: Never heard of him.

STEVE: Didn't he write ...

Lesson B7, Exercise 6, Dialogue 5

DON: Well, I'm afraid it's getting late, and we've got a long way to go.

SUE: So have we. We ought to be on our way, I suppose.

JO: Yes, we'd better be going, too. Thank you so much, Ann. We really enjoyed ourselves. Lovely food, nice people, good talk ...

ANN: Well, thank you for coming.

EMMA: You must come over to us soon. When we've finished moving. I'll give you a ring.

JOHN: Now, where's my coat?

PETER: Here it is, John.

JOHN: No, that's not mine. This is mine.

PETER: Oh, sorry. Well, whose is this, then?

ANN: Andy's, I think.

ANDY: Is it old and dirty? Yes, that's mine.

LUCY: Well, bye, Ann, bye, Peter. See you next week.

ALL: Bye, bye.

Lesson D1, Exercise 2

Little old lady in knife raid

A little grey-haired woman armed with a knife robbed an Oxfordshire shop after threatening the assistant.

The untidily dressed woman walked into The Sandwich Man shop in Parsons Street, Banbury at 9.30 at night and pulled out the bread knife from beneath her coat.

She threatened the young girl assistant and forced her to open the till before grabbing the entire day's takings.

The robbery happened on Saturday night, and police at Banbury are appealing for witnesses.

The shop owner, Mr Ken Woodd of Deddington, who also runs George's Café and Georgina's in the Covered Market, Oxford, said: 'It is unbelievable. It has never happened before in the 38 years I have been in business.'

Police took the assistant around pubs in the town after the robbery to try to find the woman, but with no luck.

Mr Woodd said the day's takings were snatched. He said it might have been as much as £180.

(from *The Oxford Mail*, 25 March 1986)

Vocabulary index

Irregular verbs: Verbs marked with an asterisk(*) are irregular. There is a complete list of the irregular verbs in *The New Cambridge English Course* at the back of the book.

Stress: In longer single words, only the main stress is normally shown (e.g. *appendicitis* /əpendɪ'saɪtəs/). This is also usually the case with fixed two-word expressions like *bank account* /'bæŋk əkaʊnt/. However, some words and expressions have variable stress; in these cases two stresses are shown (e.g. *inside* /'ɪn'saɪd/; *bad-tempered* /'bæd 'tempəd/; *lie down* /'laɪ 'daʊn/).

call: What's this called? /kɔːld/ — E5
camel /ˈkæml/ — A2
camp (noun) /kæmp/ — E3
camp (verb) /kæmp/ — E5
camp site /ˈkæmp saɪt/ — E3
camping /ˈkæmpɪŋ/ — A6
Can I use … /ˈkæn aɪ ˈjuːz/ — A7
Can you explain this word/
    expression/sentence? /ɪkˈspleɪn/ — A5
Can you remind me: why …?
    /rɪˈmaɪnd/ — A1
Can you tell me the way to …?
    /ðə ˈweɪ tə/ — D5
cancel /ˈkænsl/ — E2
capital /ˈkæpɪtl/ — C8
car park /ˈkɑː pɑːk/ — D5
card: credit card /ˈkredɪt kɑːd/ — B4
cardboard box /ˈkɑːdbɔːd ˈbɒks/ — E2
careful /ˈkeəfl/ — C1
carrot /ˈkærət/ — A2, B5
carry /ˈkæri/ — D7
cassette player /kæˈset pleɪə(r)/ — C2
cassette recorder /kæˈset rɪˈkɔːdə(r)/ — C2
catalogue /ˈkætəlɒg/ — E4
catch* /kætʃ/ — B4, B6
CD player /ˈsiː ˈdiː pleɪə(r)/ — C2
ceiling /ˈsiːlɪŋ/ — D2
cellar /ˈselə(r)/ — D2
centre /ˈsentə(r)/ — C8
champion /ˈtʃæmpɪən/ — A8
chance /tʃɑːns/ — A3
change (for £5) /tʃeɪndʒ/ — E5
change: a change /tʃeɪndʒ/ — B5
change jobs/schools etc. /tʃeɪndʒ/ — D6
change one's mind /maɪnd/ — A3
changeable /ˈtʃeɪndʒəbl/ — E1
cheap /tʃiːp/ — B5, E4
cheat /tʃiːt/ — B3
check /tʃek/ — B3, C6, D2
cheek /tʃiːk/ — A2
cheerful /ˈtʃɪəfl/ — E6
chemical /ˈkemɪkl/ — E7
cheque /tʃek/ — E2
chess /tʃes/ — A6, D6
chest /tʃest/ — D7, E6
chewing gum /ˈtʃuːɪŋ gʌm/ — C3
chin /tʃɪn/ — A2
chips (food) /tʃɪps/ — E5
choice /tʃɔɪs/ — E4
choose* /tʃuːz/ — A5, B4, D4
chop (food) /tʃɒp/ — A2
city /ˈsɪti/ — A8
clean (verb) /kliːn/ — C3, C6
clever /ˈklevə(r)/ — D4, E2
climate /ˈklaɪmət/ — E7
climbing /ˈklaɪmɪŋ/ — A6
close (adjective) /kləʊs/ — D3
close down /ˈkləʊz ˈdaʊn/ — C6
clothes dryer /ˈkləʊðz draɪə(r)/ — C2
cloud /klaʊd/ — A2, E1
cloud over /ˈklaʊd ˈəʊvə(r)/ — E1
cloudy /ˈklaʊdi/ — E1
coal miner /ˈkəʊl maɪnə(r)/ — A4
coat /kəʊt/ — B5, D1
coffee /ˈkɒfi/ — B7
coin /kɔɪn/ — E2
coincidence /kəʊˈɪnsɪdəns/ — E3
cold /kəʊld/ — E1
cold: a cold /ə ˈkəʊld/ — D7
collecting: stamp collecting
    /ˈstæmp kəˈlektɪŋ/ — A6
college /ˈkɒlɪdʒ/ — D5

comb /kəʊm/ — E2
Come in and have a drink /ˈkʌm ɪn/ — B5
come* round /ˈkʌm ˈraʊnd/ — E5
comfortable /ˈkʌmftəbl/ — C3
compact disc (CD) player
    /ˈkɒmpækt ˈdɪsk pleɪə(r)/ — C2
company /ˈkʌmpəni/ — D4
compete /kəmˈpiːt/ — A8
competent /ˈkɒmpɪtənt/ — A8
competition /kɒmpəˈtɪʃn/ — A8
competitive /kəmˈpetətɪv/ — A8
complain /kəmˈpleɪn/ — C5
complaint /kəmˈpleɪnt/ — C5
computer /kəmˈpjuːtə(r)/ — C2, E5
concert /ˈkɒnsət/ — A4
confidential /kɒnfɪˈdentʃl/ — C7
Congress /ˈkɒŋgres/ — C8
connect /kəˈnekt/ — E3
Conservatives /kənˈsɜːvətɪvz/ — C8
consider /kənˈsɪdə(r)/ — D4
consist (of) /kənˈsɪst əv/ — C8
contact (noun) /ˈkɒntækt/ — A5
contact lenses /ˈkɒntækt ˈlenzɪz/ — E6
contact: lose contact with sbdy
    /ˈluːz ˈkɒntækt/ — E2
contain /kənˈteɪn/ — B3
continent /ˈkɒntɪnənt/ — E7
continue /kənˈtɪnjuː/ — D3
convector heater /kənˈvektə ˈhiːtə(r)/ — C2
convenient /kənˈviːnɪənt/ — E3
conversation /kɒnvəˈseɪʃn/ — A5, C5
cook (verb) /kʊk/ — C6
cooker /ˈkʊkə(r)/ — C2
cooking /ˈkʊkɪŋ/ — C1
cool /kuːl/ — B8, E1
corkscrew /ˈkɔːkskruː/ — E2
corner /ˈkɔːnə(r)/ — D8
correct /kəˈrekt/ — A5
correct: Is this correct: …? /kəˈrekt/ — A5
corridor /ˈkɒrɪdɔː(r)/ — B1
cost* /kɒst/ — B8, E4
cough (noun) /kɒf/ — D7
Could I/you (possibly) …?
    /ˈkʊd … ˈpɒsəbli/ — A7
Could you do me a favour? /ˈfeɪvə(r)/ — A7
Could you lend me £10? /ˈlend/ — A7
Could you pass me … /pɑːs/ — B5
country /ˈkʌntri/ — A3, C8, E5
county /ˈkaʊnti/ — C8
cousin /ˈkʌzn/ — D3
cover (verb) /ˈkʌvə(r)/ — C3
crash (into) /kræʃ/ — D8
crazy /ˈkreɪzi/ — D8
create /kriˈeɪt/ — E7
credit card /ˈkredɪt kɑːd/ — B4
crossing: pedestrian crossing
    /pəˈdestrɪən ˈkrɒsɪŋ/ — D8
cultural /ˈkʌltʃərʊl/ — C7
culture /ˈkʌltʃə(r)/ — C7
cup: make a cup of tea /ˈkʌp əv ˈtiː/ — C1
curly /ˈkɜːli/ — A1
customer /ˈkʌstəmə(r)/ — C5
cut* /kʌt/ — B6
cut* up /ˈkʌt ˈʌp/ — C6
cycle (verb) /ˈsaɪkl/ — A7
cycling /ˈsaɪklɪŋ/ — A6
damp /dæmp/ — A6
dancing /ˈdɑːnsɪŋ/ — A6
dash (verb) /dæʃ/ — C4
daughter-in-law /ˈdɔːtər ɪn lɔː/ — D3
dead /ded/ — E7
death /deθ/ — C4

decision /dɪˈsɪʒn/ — C7
decision: make a decision
    /ˈmeɪk ə dɪˈsɪʒn/ — E2
deep /diːp/ — B8
delicious /dɪˈlɪʃəs/ — B5
Democrats /ˈdeməkræts/ — C8
demonstration /demənˈstreɪʃn/ — A5
dentist /ˈdentɪst/ — A3
department /dɪˈpɑːtmənt/ — B4
department store /dɪˈpɑːtmənt stɔː(r)/ — B4
depend: It depends /ɪt dɪˈpendz/ — B5
depressed /dɪˈprest/ — E6
description /dɪˈskrɪpʃən/ — D2
describe /dɪˈskraɪb/ — B8
desk /desk/ — B8
destroy /dɪˈstrɔɪ/ — C7, E7
diagram /ˈdaɪəgræm/ — D8
die /daɪ/ — B8
difference /ˈdɪfrəns/ — D2
difficult /ˈdɪfɪkʊlt/ — A5
dirty /ˈdɜːti/ — B7, C3
disabled /ˈdɪsˈeɪbld/ — A8
disagree /ˈdɪsəˈgriː/ — C7
disagreement /ˈdɪsəˈgriːmənt/ — E5
disappear /dɪsəˈpɪə(r)/ — E7
disaster /dɪˈzɑːstə(r)/ — E7
discover /dɪsˈkʌvə(r)/ — C6
discuss /dɪsˈkʌs/ — A5
dishwasher /ˈdɪʃwɒʃə(r)/ — C2
divide /dɪˈvaɪd/ — C8, D2
divide into /dɪˈvaɪd ɪntə/ — C8
division /dɪˈvɪʒn/ — D3
divorced /dɪˈvɔːst/ — D3
Do let me (teach you) … /ˈduː ˈlet miː/ — E5
Do you want to …? /djə ˈwɒnt tə/ — A7
Don't go away /ˈdəʊnt ˈgəʊ əˈweɪ/ — E5
door: next door /ˈnekst ˈdɔː(r)/ — B4
double /ˈdʌbl/ — A4
down (preposition) /daʊn/ — D5
draw* /drɔː/ — D8
dream (noun) /driːm/ — A4, E3
dream* /driːm/ — D3
dress /dres/ — E5
dress (= how someone is dressed)
    /dres/ — D1
dressed: get* dressed /ˈget ˈdrest/ — C1
drink: Have a drink /ˈhæv ə ˈdrɪŋk/ — B5
drink: What can I get you to drink?
    /tə ˈdrɪŋk/ — B5
drive* /draɪv/ — B1, B4, D8
driver /ˈdraɪvə(r)/ — A3
driving licence /ˈdraɪvɪŋ laɪsəns/ — B4, D8
driving: rally driving /ˈræli draɪvɪŋ/ — A6
drop /drɒp/ — B3, B6
drought /draʊt/ — E1
dry /draɪ/ — C5
dryer: clothes dryer /ˈkləʊðz draɪə(r)/ — C2
dryer: tumble dryer /ˈtʌmbl draɪə(r)/ — C2
dust (noun) /dʌst/ — C3
dustbin /ˈdʌstbɪn/ — E2
dustman /ˈdʌstmən/ — A4
each /iːtʃ/ — C8
ear /ɪə(r)/ — E6
earn* /ɜːn/ — A4
ear-ring /ˈɪərɪŋ/ — E6
east /iːst/ — D5, E1
either: You can either … or …
    /ˈaɪðə(r), ˈiːðə(r)/ — C7
elbow /ˈelbəʊ/ — E2
elect /ɪˈlekt/ — C8, E2
electric kettle /ɪˈlektrɪk ˈketl/ — C2
electric(al) /ɪˈlektrɪk(l)/ — C2

136

elephant /'elɪfənt/ — A2
else /els/ — B5
emergency /ɪ'mɜːdʒənsi/ — B1
empty (*verb, adjective*) /'empti/ — C3
end (*noun*) /end/ — B7, E4
enjoy /ɪn'dʒɔɪ/ — A8, D3, D4
enjoy …ing /ɪn'dʒɔɪ/ — D3
enjoy (your)self /ɪn'dʒɔɪ jɔː'self/ — B7
enough: I've had enough
　/aɪv 'hæd ɪ'nʌf/ — B5
envelope /'envələup/ — B8
Er, that's not quite right
　/'nɒt 'kwaɪt 'raɪt/ — A1
escape /ɪ'skeɪp/ — D1
especially /ɪ'speʃəli/ — A5
essay /'eseɪ/ — A5
eventually /ɪ'ventʃəli/ — C7
ever: hardly ever /'hɑːdli 'evə(r)/ — E6
every year/week/*etc.* /'evri 'jɪə(r)/ — D7
every (5 years) /'evri/ — C8
everyday /'evrideɪ/ — C3
exact /ɪg'zækt/ — A5
exactly: Well, I didn't exactly …
　/ɪg'zæktli/ — A1
examination /ɪgzæmɪ'neɪʃən/ — A5, C3
exception /ɪk'sepʃən/ — A3
exciting /ɪk'saɪtɪŋ/ — E2
Excuse me /ɪk'skjuːz miː/ — A7
Excuse me, I didn't mean… /miːn/ — A1
expect /ɪk'spekt/ — A3
expenses /ɪk'spensɪz/ — A4
expensive /ɪk'spensɪv/ — A7, B3, E4
expensively /ɪk'spensɪvli/ — D1
experienced /ɪk'spɪərɪənst/ — D1
expert /'ekspɜːt/ — A8
explain: Can you explain this word
　/expression/sentence? /ɪk'spleɪn/ — A5
expression: Can you explain this
　expression? /ɪk'spreʃn/ — A5
extinct /ɪk'stɪŋkt/ — E7
extra /'ekstrə/ — A4
extremely /ɪk'striːmli/ — A5, C1
eye /aɪ/ — A1, E6
face (*noun*) /feɪs/ — E4, E6
factory /'fæktri/ — A4, C1, D2
fail /feɪl/ — D8
fair (*hair*) /feə(r)/ — A1
fairly /feəli/ — E1
fall* /fɔːl/ — B1
fall* in love (with sbdy)
　/'fɔːl ɪn 'lʌv/ — C7, D4
false /fɔːls/ — D5
family /'fæməli/ — D3
famous /'feɪməs/ — A3
fancy (*verb*) /'fænsi/ — C7
farm /fɑːm/ — E3
farmer /'fɑːmə(r)/ — A3
father-in-law /'fɑːðər ɪn lɔː/ — D3
favour /'feɪvə(r)/ — A7
fax /fæks/ — E5
federal /'fedərʊl/ — C8
federation /'fedə'reɪʃn/ — C8
feed* /fiːd/ — B8
feel* /fiːl/ — A8
fetch /fetʃ/ — C1
fever: hay fever /'heɪ fiːvə(r)/ — D7
fewer /'fjuːə(r)/ — D3
fight* /faɪt/ — D1
fill /fɪl/ — C3
find* /faɪnd/ — B3, B4
find* out /'faɪnd 'aut/ — C7, E2
finger /'fɪŋgə(r)/ — E6

fire (*noun*) /faɪə(r)/ — B1
fire: on fire /ɒn 'faɪə(r)/ — C4
first floor /'fɜːst 'flɔː(r)/ — C1
first of all /'fɜːst əv 'ɔːl/ — C5
fishing /'fɪʃɪŋ/ — A6
fit (*adjective*) /fɪt/ — A8
flashlight /'flæʃlaɪt/ — C2
flat (*noun*) /flæt/ — B1, D8
flight /flaɪt/ — C3
flood /flʌd/ — E7
floor: first floor /'fɜːst 'flɔː(r)/ — C1
floor: ground floor /'graund 'flɔː(r)/ — C4
flour /'flauə(r)/ — A2
fog /fɒg/ — A2, E1
foggy /'fɒgi/ — E1
follow /'fɒləu/ — D8
fond (of sbdy) /'fɒnd əv/ — D4
food /fuːd/ — B5, E7
food mixer /'fuːd 'mɪksə(r)/ — C2
fool: make a fool of oneself
　/'meɪk ə 'fuːl əv/ — E2
foot (*feet*) /fut, fiːt/ — E6
football /'futbɔːl/ — A6
for … reason /fə(r) … 'riːzn/ — A5
for a minute /fər ə 'mɪnɪt/ — E5
for sale /fə 'seɪl/ — B3, E4
force (sbdy to do sth) /fɔːs/ — D1
forecast: weather forecast
　/'weðə 'fɔːkɑːst/ — E1
fortunately /'fɔːtʃənətli/ — E7
free (= *not busy*) /friː/ — C5
free (= *not for sale*) /friː/ — E4
free time /'friː 'taɪm/ — A3
fridge /frɪdʒ/ — C2
friend: make friends (with sbdy)
　/'meɪk 'frendz wɪð/ — E2
friendly /'frendli/ — E6
frighten /'fraɪtn/ — C4
fry /fraɪ/ — C6
full /ful/ — A4
full-time /'ful 'taɪm/ — D3
funny (= *strange*) /'fʌni/ — C5
fur /fɜː(r)/ — E7
furniture (*uncountable*) /'fɜːnɪtʃə(r)/ — C5
future: the future /ðə 'fjuːtʃə(r)/ — E3
game /geɪm/ — D6
garage /'gærɑːʒ, 'gærɪdʒ/ — D8
gardener /'gɑːdnə(r)/ — A4
gas /gæs/ — B1
general (*adjective*) /'dʒenrʊl/ — A1
generous /'dʒenərəs/ — A4, B3
German measles /'dʒɜːmən 'miːzlz/ — C3
get* (*for changes*) /get/ — C5
get* (= *arrive, receive*) /get/ — B4
get* (= *acquire*) /get/ — E5
get* dressed /'get 'drest/ — C1
get* into trouble /'get ɪntə 'trʌbl/ — C1
get* on with sbdy /'get 'ɒn wɪð/ — C1, D3
get* rid of sbdy/sth /'get 'rɪd əv/ — C1
get* up /'get 'ʌp/ — C1
gift /gɪft/ — E4
Give me … /'gɪv miː/ — A7
give* sbdy a hand /gɪv … ə 'hænd/ — E5
give* sbdy a message
　/gɪv … ə 'mesɪdʒ/ — E2
Glad you like it — E5
glad /glæd/ — E5
glad: (I'm) glad you like it
　/'glæd juː/ — E5
glad: (I'm) so glad you could come
　/'səu 'glæd/ — B5
glasses /'glɑːsɪz/ — E6

glove /glʌv/ — E6
go* straight ahead /'gəu 'streɪt ə'hed/ — D5
go* straight on /'gəu 'streɪt 'ɒn/ — D5
go* (*for sounds*) /gəu/ — C5
go* back /'gəu 'bæk/ — D6
go* out with sbdy /'gəu 'aut wɪð/ — C7
go* through a red light /'gəu 'θruː/ — D8
go* to sleep /'gəu tə 'sliːp/ — E3
goal /gəul/ — D6
gold /gəuld/ — D3
golf /gɒlf/ — D6
good-looking /'gud 'lukɪŋ/ — A1
govern /'gʌvən/ — C6, C8
government /'gʌvəmənt/ — C8
grab /græb/ — D1
grammar /'græmə(r)/ — A5
granddaughter /'grændɔːtə(r)/ — D3
grandson /'grænsʌn/ — D3
grandchild (-children)
　/'græntʃaɪld, tʃɪldrən/ — D3
grandmother /'grænmʌðə(r)/ — D3
grandfather /'grænfɑːðə(r)/ — D3
grandparent /'grænpeərənt/ — D3
great /greɪt/ — E5
green /griːn/ — A1
grey /greɪ/ — A1
grey (*weather*) /greɪ/ — E1
groom /gruːm/ — D3
ground /graund/ — B5
ground floor /'graund 'flɔː(r)/ — C4
ground: high ground /'haɪ 'graund/ — E1
grow* up /'grəu 'ʌp/ — A3, C1
guess (*verb*) /ges/ — A4, C7
guitar /gɪ'tɑː(r)/ — C3
gum: chewing gum /'tʃuːɪŋ gʌm/ — C3
hail (*noun*) /heɪl/ — A2
hair /heə(r)/ — A1
hair-dryer /'heə draɪə(r)/ — C5
hairbrush /'heəbrʌʃ/ — B8
hand /hænd/ — B4, B8, E6
hand: give sbdy a hand
　/'gɪv … ə 'hænd/ — E5
handbag /'hændbæg/ — D1, E6
handle (*noun*) /'hændl/ — E4
handsome /'hændsəm/ — A1
happen /'hæpn/ — B4, E3
hard work /'hɑːd 'wɜːk/ — B5
hard-working /'hɑːd 'wɜːkɪŋ/ — B3
hardly /'hɑːdli/ — D7
hardly ever /'hɑːdli 'evə(r)/ — E6
hat /hæt/ — E6
Have a drink /'hæv ə 'drɪŋk/ — B5
Have some … /'hæv səm/ — A7
have* trouble with sth
　/'hæv 'trʌbl wɪð/ — E2
hay fever /'heɪ fiːvə(r)/ — D7
head /hed/ — E6
head (= *boss*) /hed/ — A4, C8
head of state /'hed əv 'steɪt/ — C8
headache /'hedeɪk/ — D6, D7
health care /'helθ keə(r)/ — C8
healthy /'helθi/ — A4, D3
hear* of /'hɪər əv/ — B7
heater /'hiːtə(r)/ — C2
heavy /'hevi/ — D7
heavy rain /'hevi 'reɪn/ — E1
height /haɪt/ — A1
height: of medium height
　/əv 'miːdɪəm 'haɪt/ — A1
helicopter /'helɪkɒptə(r)/ — C4
help (*noun*) /help/ — B1, D1
help (*verb*) /help/ — E5

help: I couldn't help it /aɪ 'kʌdnt/ B7
helpless /'helpləs/ C4
Here (offering) /hɪə(r)/ A7
Here you are /'hɪə juː 'ɑː/ A7, B5
hide* /haɪd/ B3, E3
high ground /'haɪ 'graʊnd/ E1
hill /hɪl/ D5
hip /hɪp/ A2, A8
hit* /hɪt/ B6, D1, D6
hit* sbdy on (part of body) with (object) /hɪt/ D1
hobby /'hɒbi/ A8
hockey /'hɒki/ D6
hold* /həʊld/ C8, D1
hole /həʊl/ D6, E4
honest /'ɒnɪst/ B3
hoover /'huːvə(r)/ C2
hope /həʊp/ D3
horse /hɔːs/ A2
horse riding /'hɔːs raɪdɪŋ/ A6
hospital /'hɒspɪtl/ B1, D5
hot /hɒt/ E1
hotel /həʊ'tel/ B8
House of Commons /'haʊs əv 'kɒmənz/ C8
House of Lords /'haʊs əv 'lɔːdz/ C8
housework /'haʊswɜːk/ C1
How do you mean? /'haʊ djə 'miːn/ B5
How do you pronounce ...? /'prənaʊns/ A5, E5
How do you say ... in English? /'haʊ djə 'seɪ/ A5, E5
How do you spell ...? /'haʊ djə 'spel/ A5
How often ...? /'haʊ 'ɒfn/ D7
How stupid of me! /'haʊ 'stjuːpɪd/ B5
humid /'hjuːmɪd/ E1
hunt /hʌnt/ E7
hunter /'hʌntə(r)/ E7
hurricane /'hʌrɪkən/ E1
hurry: in a hurry /ɪn ə 'hʌri/ D7
hurry: in a bit of a hurry /bɪt ... 'hʌri/ E5
hurt* /hɜːt/ D7
husband /'hʌzbənd/ A3, D3
I (don't) think it's a good idea to ... /aɪ'dɪə/ C7
I (don't) think you should /ʃʊd/ C7
I beg your pardon? /'pɑːdn/ B5, E5
I can't remember - what ...? /rɪ'membə/ A1
I couldn't help it /'kʌdnt 'help/ B7
I didn't think much of it /'dɪdnt 'θɪŋk/ B7
I do apologise /ə'pɒlədʒaɪz/ C5
I don't mind /aɪ 'dəʊnt 'maɪnd/ A7
I really am very sorry /'rɪəli 'æm ... 'sɒri/ C5
I see /aɪ 'siː/ A7
I should think /aɪ ʃʊd 'θɪŋk/ B5
I thought you said ... /aɪ 'θɔːt juː 'sed/ C5
I wonder(ed) if I/you could ...? /aɪ 'wʌndəd/ A7
I would(n't) advise you to ... /aɪ 'wʊdnt əd'vaɪz/ C7
I wouldn't mind ... (request) /aɪ 'wʊdnt 'maɪnd/ E5
I'd be surprised if ... /sə'praɪzd/ C7
I'd love one/some /aɪd 'lʌv 'wʌn, 'sʌm/ A7
I'd love to /aɪd 'lʌv tuː/ A7
I'd prefer ... /aɪd prɪ'fɜː(r)/ A7
I'll bet /aɪl 'bet/ B8
I'll open it for you /aɪl 'əʊpən/ A7

I'm sorry to trouble you /'sɒri ... 'trʌbl/ A7
I'm afraid ... /aɪm ə'freɪd/ E5
I'm glad you like it /aɪm 'glæd/ E5
I'm so glad you could come /'səʊ 'glæd/ B5
I've had enough /aɪv 'hæd ɪ'nʌf/ B5
ice cream /'aɪs 'kriːm/ B8
idea: I (don't) think it's a good idea to ... /'gʊd aɪ'dɪə tə/ C7
If I were you, I'd ... /ɪf 'aɪ wə 'juː/ C7
if you prefer /ɪf juː prɪ'fɜː(r)/ C5
ill /ɪl/ D3
immediately /ɪ'miːdɪətli/ B1
important /ɪm'pɔːtənt/ A5
important: It is important to ... /ɪm'pɔːtənt tə/ C7
impress /ɪm'pres/ B3
improve /ɪm'pruːv/ E4
in a hurry /ɪn ə 'hʌri/ D7
in a bit of a hurry /'bɪt əv ə 'hʌri/ E5
in business /ɪn 'bɪznɪs/ D1
in danger /ɪn 'deɪndʒə(r)/ E7
in order /ɪn 'ɔːdə(r)/ E3
in the opposite direction /'ɒpəzɪt də'rekʃən/ D8
in-laws /'ɪn lɔːz/ D3
income /'ɪŋkʌm/ C1
increase (verb) /ɪn'kriːs/ E7
industry /'ɪndəstri/ E7
information /ɪnfə'meɪʃn/ A5
injection /ɪn'dʒekʃn/ D7
injured /'ɪndʒəd/ C4
insect /'ɪnsekt/ E7
inside /ɪn'saɪd/ D7
instead /ɪn'sted/ C5
insurance /ɪn'ʃɔːrəns/ D7
interest (on a loan) /'ɪntrəst/ D4
international /ɪntə'næʃənl/ E7
interview (verb) /'ɪntəvjuː/ C6
invent /ɪn'vent/ C6
invitation /ɪnvɪ'teɪʃn/ E5
involve /ɪn'vɒlv/ D1
iron (appliance) /aɪən/ C2
iron (verb) /aɪən/ C1
ironing /'aɪənɪŋ/ C1
Is this a (pen) or a (pencil)? /ɪz ðɪs ə/ A5
Is this correct: ...? /kə'rekt/ A5
island /'aɪlənd/ D5
It depends /ɪt dɪ'pendz/ B5
It didn't say anything to me /'seɪ 'eniθɪŋ/ B7
It doesn't matter /ɪt 'dʌznt 'mætə(r)/ B3, B5
It doesn't matter at all /ət 'ɔːl/ B5
It doesn't work /ɪt 'dʌznt 'wɜːk/ C5
It is important to ... /ɪm'pɔːtənt/ C7
It won't start /ɪt 'wəʊnt 'stɑːt/ C5
It's (not) worth ...ing /ɪts 'nɒt 'wɜːθ/ C7
It's not worth it /ɪts 'nɒt 'wɜːθ ɪt/ C7
it's over (= finished) /ɪts 'əʊvə(r)/ D1
itch /ɪtʃ/ D7
jacket /'dʒækɪt/ E6
jazz /dʒæz/ D8
job /dʒɒb/ A3, B5, C1
join /dʒɔɪn/ B8
judo /'dʒuːdəʊ/ A6
jump /dʒʌmp/ C4
junction /'dʒʌŋktʃən/ D8
keep* /kiːp/ B3, B8
keep* (...ing) /kiːp/ D1
keep* on (...ing) /'kiːp 'ɒn/ A3
keep* quiet /'kiːp 'kwaɪət/ B3

keep* straight ahead /'streɪt ə'hed/ D5
keep* straight on /'streɪt 'ɒn/ D5
kettle: electric kettle /ɪ'lektrɪk 'ketl/ C2
key /kiː/ B4
kick (verb) /kɪk/ B6, D6
kind (adjective) /kaɪnd/ B8
kind (noun) /kaɪnd/ B8
kind: That's very kind of you /'veri 'kaɪnd/ A7, E5
king /kɪŋ/ C8
knife /naɪf/ D1
knob /nɒb/ C2
Labour /'leɪbə(r)/ C8
ladder /'lædə(r)/ D6
lake /leɪk/ D5
lamp /læmp/ C2
lampshade /'læmpʃeɪd/ E2
language: foreign language /'fɒrən 'læŋgwɪdʒ/ A1
last (verb) /lɑːst/ E3
last (week, etc.) /lɑːst/ B4
later that (afternoon, day, etc.) /'leɪtə(r)/ B4
lavatory /'lævətri/ E7
law /lɔː/ C8
lead (noun) /liːd/ C2
least /liːst/ A4
leave* /liːv/ B3, B4
leave* school /'liːv 'skuːl/ A3
lecture /'lektʃə(r)/ A5
left /left/ E7
left-wing /'left 'wɪŋ/ C8
leg /leg/ B1, E6
lemon /'lemən/ A2, C3
lend* /lend/ A7, E5
lens: contact lenses /'kɒntækt 'lenzɪz/ E6
less /les/ A4, D3
less: far less /'fɑː 'les/ A4
lettuce /'letəs/ A2
level /'levl/ A4
Liberal Democrats /'lɪbərʊl 'deməkræts/ C8
licence number /'laɪsəns nʌmbə(r)/ D8
licence: driving licence /'draɪvɪŋ laɪsəns/ B4, D8
lie (noun) /laɪ/ A8
lie (not tell the truth) /laɪ/ C7
lie* (e.g. in bed) /laɪ/ B3
lie* down /'laɪ 'daʊn/ D7
lift (verb) /lɪft/ B6
light (for a cigarette etc.) /laɪt/ E5
light bulb /'laɪt 'bʌlb/ C2
lightning /'laɪtnɪŋ/ A2, E1
like: Well, you see, it's like this /'laɪk 'ðɪs/ A7
like: what ... like /'wɒt 'laɪk/ E1
limit: speed limit /'spiːd lɪmɪt/ D8
lipstick /'lɪpstɪk/ E2
liquid /'lɪkwɪd/ C3, E4
listening to music /'lɪsnɪŋ tə 'mjuːzɪk/ A6
live /lɪv/ E7
living /'lɪvɪŋ/ E7
loan /ləʊn/ D4
local /'ləʊkl/ C8
long /lɒŋ/ A1
look for /'lʊk fə(r)/ B5
lorry driver /'lɒri draɪvə(r)/ D1
lose* /luːz/ B3
lose* contact with sbdy /'luːz 'kɒntækt wɪð/ E7
love: I'd love one/some /aɪd 'lʌv 'wʌn, 'sʌm/ A7

love: I'd love to /aɪd 'lʌv tuː/	A7	
lovely /'lʌvli/	B5, B7	
Lovely to see you /'lʌvli tə 'siː juː/	B5	
lower body /'ləʊə 'bɒdi/	E6	
luck /lʌk/	D1	
machine /mə'ʃiːn/	E4	
machine: washing machine		
/'wɒʃɪŋ mə'ʃiːn/	C2	
magazine /'mægəziːn/	A3, C7	
main /meɪn/	A5	
majority /mə'dʒɒrəti/	C8	
make* /meɪk/	E5	
make* (a cup of) tea /'tiː/	C1	
make* a decision /'dɪ'sɪʒən/	E2	
make* a fool of oneself /ə 'fuːl əv/	E2	
make* a mistake /ə mɪ'steɪk/	E2	
make* friends (with sbdy)		
/'frendz wɪð/	E2	
manage (to) /'mænɪdʒ/	B4	
manager /'mænədʒə(r)/	B5, C5	
manual: technical manual		
/'teknɪkl 'mænjuːəl/	A5	
marriage /'mærɪdʒ/	D3	
married /'mærɪd/	C1, D3	
marvellous /'maːvələs/	D4	
match (= game) /mætʃ/	D6	
material /mə'tɪəriəl/	E4	
matter: It doesn't matter (at all)		
/ɪt 'dʌznt 'mætə(r)/	B5	
matter: What's the matter		
/'wɒts ðə 'mætə/	A7	
maximum /'mæksɪməm/	E1	
meal /miːl/	B3	
mean* /miːn/	E5	
mean*: How do you mean?		
/'haʊ djə 'miːn/	B5	
mean*: What does … mean?		
/'wɒt dəz … 'miːn/	E5	
measles: German measles		
/'dʒɜːmən 'miːzlz/	C3	
meat /miːt/	B5	
medicine /'medsən/	E7	
Mediterranean /ˌmedɪtə'reɪniən/	E7	
medium: of medium height		
/əv 'miːdiəm 'haɪt/	A1	
meet* /miːt/	D4, E2	
meeting /'miːtɪŋ/	A5	
member /'membə(r)/	C8	
Member of Parliament (MP)		
/'membər əv 'paːlɪmənt/	C8	
memory /'meməri/	D8	
mend /mend/	B6, C3	
message /'mesɪdʒ/	E2, E4	
metal /'metl/	B8, E4	
microphone /'maɪkrəfəʊn/	B8	
middle /'mɪdl/	B4, B7	
mind: change one's mind		
/'tʃeɪndʒ wʌnz 'maɪnd/	A3	
mind: don't mind /'dəʊnt 'maɪnd/	A3, A7	
mind: I wouldn't mind … (request)		
/aɪ 'wʊdnt 'maɪnd/	E5	
mind: Would you mind …ing?		
/'wʊd juː 'maɪnd/	A7	
mine (pronoun) /maɪn/	B7	
miner /'maɪnə(r)/	A4	
minister /'mɪnɪstə(r)/	A4, C8	
minority /maɪ'nɒrəti/	C8	
minute: for a minute /fər ə 'mɪnɪt/	E5	
mirror /'mɪrə(r)/	C3	
miss (verb) /mɪs/	D6	
mistake: make a mistake		
/'meɪk ə 'mɪsteɪk/	E2	
misunderstanding		
/'mɪsʌndə'stændɪŋ/	E2, E5	
mix up /'mɪks 'ʌp/	C3	
mixer /'mɪksə(r)/	C2	
modernise /'mɒdənaɪz/	C6	
money /'mʌni/	B4	
More (bread)? (offer) /'mɔː 'bred/	A7	
mostly /'məʊstli/	A5	
mother-in-law /'mʌðər ɪn lɔː/	D3	
motorbike /'məʊtəbaɪk/	A3	
motorist /'məʊtərɪst/	D8	
motorway /'məʊtəweɪ/	C4	
mountain /'maʊntɪn/	D5	
mouse /maʊs/	A2	
moustache /mə'staːʃ/	A2	
move (general) /muːv/	B1, D6	
move (house) /muːv/	B5, B7	
MP /'em 'piː/	C8	
mug /mʌg/	E2	
mugger /'mʌgə(r)/	D1	
muscle /'mʌsl/	D7	
muscle: a pulled muscle /'pʊld 'mʌsl/	D7	
music: listening to music		
/'lɪsənɪŋ tə 'mjuːzɪk/	A6	
mustard /'mʌstəd/	B5	
myself: by myself /baɪ maɪ'self/	E3	
nail /neɪl/	E2	
national /'næʃnl/	C8	
nationality /ˌnæʃə'næləti/	E4	
natural /'nætʃərəl/	A5, E7	
nearly /'nɪəli/	B3	
neck /nek/	D3, E6	
necklace /'nekləs/	E6	
need (verb) /niːd/	B3	
needle /'niːdl/	E2	
neighbour /'neɪbə(r)/	B4, C4	
nephew /'nevjuː/	D3	
never /'nevə(r)/	D7	
news: bad news /'bæd 'njuːz/	E2	
newspaper /'njuːspeɪpə(r)/	C3	
next door /'nekst 'dɔː(r)/	B4	
Nice to see you /'naɪs tə 'siː juː/	B5	
nice: That would be very nice		
/'veri 'naɪs/	A7	
nice: That's very nice of you		
/'ðæts 'veri 'naɪs/	A7	
niece /niːs/	D3	
nobody /'nəʊbədi/	B4	
noise /nɔɪz/	D8	
nonsense /'nɒnsəns/	B7	
normal /'nɔːml/	E1	
north /nɔːθ/	D5, E1	
north-east /'nɔːθ 'iːst/	E1	
north-west /'nɔːθ 'west/	E1	
Not at all (answer to thanks)		
/'nɒt ət 'ɒl/	A7	
note (noun) /nəʊt/	D1	
novel /'nɒvl/	A5	
novelist /'nɒvəlɪst/	D6	
nuclear /'njuːklɪə(r)/	E7	
number: wrong number		
/'rɒŋ 'nʌmbə(r)/	C6	
nurse /nɜːs/	A3, A4	
object (verb) /əb'dʒekt/	C7	
occasionally /ə'keɪʒənli/	E6	
occupied /'ɒkjuːpaɪd/	D6	
of course /əv 'kɔːs/	A7	
of course: Yes, of course		
/'jes əv 'kɔːs/	E5	
of medium height /əv 'miːdiəm 'haɪt/	A1	
offer (noun) /'ɒfə(r)/	E5	
offer (verb) /'ɒfə(r)/	A7, B3, E2, E5	
office /'ɒfɪs/	B8, D2	
officer /'ɒfɪsə(r)/	B1	
often /'ɒfn/	D7	
often: How often …? /'haʊ 'ɒfn/	D7	
Oh, thank you. Here you are.		
/'hɪə juː 'aː/	A7	
Oh, yes? /'əʊ 'jes/	A7	
oil /ɔɪl/	E4	
OK /'əʊ 'keɪ/	A7, E5	
old /əʊld/	B7	
old-fashioned /'əʊld 'fæʃənd/	B7	
on business /ɒn 'bɪznɪs/	C1	
on fire /ɒn 'faɪə(r)/	C4	
on holiday /ɒn 'hɒlədi/	D2	
on my own /ɒn maɪ 'əʊn/	C1	
on top of /ɒn 'tɒp əv/	C1	
one after another		
/'wʌn 'aːftər ə'nʌðə(r)/	D6	
operation /ˌɒpə'reɪʃn/	D7	
operator (telephone) /'ɒpəreɪtə(r)/	B1	
opinion /ə'pɪnjən/	C7	
opportunity /ˌɒpə'tjuːnəti/	D4	
opposite (adverb) /'ɒpəzɪt/	D8	
opposite: in the opposite direction		
/də'rekʃən/	D8	
orange juice /'ɒrɪndʒ 'dʒuːs/	A2, E5	
order (verb) /'ɔːdə(r)/	C5, E5	
order: in order /ɪn 'ɔːdə(r)/	E3	
ordinary /'ɔːdənri/	D1	
organisation /ˌɔːgənaɪ'zeɪʃn/	E2, E7	
organise /'ɔːgənaɪz/	C1	
out: ask sbdy out /'aːsk … 'aʊt/	C7	
out: go out with sbdy /'gəʊ 'aʊt wɪð/	C7	
outdoors /'aʊt'dɔːz/	C1	
outgoing /'aʊtgəʊɪŋ/	D4	
outside (adverb) /'aʊt'saɪd/	A8, D7	
outside (preposition) /'aʊt'saɪd/	D3	
over (preposition) /'əʊvə(r)/	C4	
over (= finished) /'əʊvə(r)/	D1	
over there /'əʊvə 'ðeə(r)/	B5, E5	
over: talk sth over /'tɔːk … 'əʊvə/	C7	
overnight /'əʊvə'naɪt/	C3	
overtake* /'əʊvə'teɪk/	D8	
overweight /'əʊvə'weɪt/	A1	
own (determiner) /əʊn/	C8	
own (verb) /əʊn/	A3	
own: on my own /'ɒn maɪ 'əʊn/	C1	
owner /'əʊnə(r)/	D1	
pack /pæk/	C3	
pain /peɪn/	D7	
painting /'peɪntɪŋ/	A6	
pair /peə/	B4	
pair of scissors /'peər əv 'sɪzəz/	E2	
pardon: I beg your pardon		
/aɪ 'beg jɔː 'paːdn/	B5, E5	
parents /'peərənts/	A3, C7	
parents-in-law /'peərənts ɪn lɔː/	D3	
park (noun) /paːk/	D5	
park (verb) /paːk/	D8	
park: car park /'kaː paːk/	D5	
parliament /'paːlɪmənt/	C8	
partly /'paːtli/	C8	
party (political) /'paːti/	C8	
party (with friends) /'paːti/	E4	
pass (= give) /'paːs/	E5	
Pass the … /'paːs ðə/	A7	
pass: Could you pass me …		
/'kʊd juː 'paːs/	B5	
past (preposition) /paːst/	D5	
path /paːθ/	D5	
patience /'peɪʃəns/	A3	
patient (noun) /'peɪʃənt/	D7	

139

pay* /peɪ/ C6
pay* back /'peɪ 'bæk/ D4
peace /piːs/ A4
pedestrian /pə'destrɪən/ D8
pedestrian crossing
  /pə'destrɪən 'krɒsɪŋ/ D8
peel /piːl/ C3
perfume /'pɜːfjuːm/ B8
Perhaps you could bring me ...?
  /pə'hæps ... 'brɪŋ miː/ E5
personal stereo /'pɜːsənl 'sterɪəʊ/ C2
personality /pɜːsə'næləti/ D4
phone (verb) /fəʊn/ B4
phone call /'fəʊn kɔːl/ B4, D2
photocopy (noun) /'fəʊtəʊkɒpi/ E5
piano: playing the piano
  /'pleɪɪŋ ðə pi'ænəʊ/ A6
pick up /'pɪk 'ʌp/ B6, C2
picnic /'pɪknɪk/ C3
piece /piːs/ B5
piece of advice /'piːs əv əd'vaɪs/ D2
piece of string /'piːs əv 'strɪŋ/ E2
pillow /'pɪləʊ/ E2
pilot /'paɪlət/ C4
pineapple /'paɪnæpl/ A2
place /pleɪs/ E7
plain /pleɪn/ A1
plan /plæn/ A5
plant /plɑːnt/ E7
plastic /'plæstɪk/ E3
play cards /'pleɪ 'kɑːdz/ B3
playing the piano /'pleɪɪŋ ðə pi'ænəʊ/ A6
pleasant /'pleznt/ E3
plug (noun) /plʌg/ C2
plug in /'plʌg 'ɪn/ C2
PM (= Prime Minister) /'piː 'em/ C8
pocket /'pɒkɪt/ B3
point (on an object) /pɔɪnt/ E4
pointed /'pɔɪntɪd/ E4
poison /'pɔɪzn/ E7
police (plural) /pə'liːs/ C8
police station /pə'liːs steɪʃn/ D5
policeman (policemen)
  /pə'liːsmən/ A4, D1, D4
policewoman (policewomen)
  /pə'liːswʊmən, wɪmɪn/ D1, D4
polish (verb) /'pɒlɪʃ/ B6
political /pə'lɪtɪkl/ C8
political party /pə'lɪtɪkl 'pɑːti/ C8
pool: swimming pool /'swɪmɪŋ 'puːl/ D5
porter /'pɔːtə(r)/ D8
possible: as ... as possible
  /əz ... əz 'pɒsəbl/ C1
possibly: Could I/you possibly ...?
  /'kʊd ... 'pɒsəbli/ A7
post office /'pəʊst ɒfɪs/ D5
poster /'pəʊstə(r)/ E4
potato /pə'teɪtəʊ/ B5
pour /pɔː(r)/ B6
powder /'paʊdə(r)/ E4
power /paʊə(r)/ A3, A4, C8
practical /'præktɪkl/ C3
precise /prɪ'saɪs/ A8
prefer: I'd prefer ... /aɪd prɪ'fɜː(r)/ A7
prefer: if you prefer /ɪf juː prɪ'fɜː/ C5
preferably /'prefrəbli/ A8
pregnant /'pregnənt/ C3
prepare /prɪ'peə/ A7, C6
President /'prezɪdənt/ C8
pretty /'prɪti/ A1
price /praɪs/ B3, E4
primary school /'praɪməri skuːl/ A3, A4

Prime Minister /'praɪm 'mɪnɪstə(r)/ C8
prisoner /'prɪznə(r)/ D1
probably /'prɒbəbli/ B5, C5
problem /'prɒbləm/ A7, C5, C7, D2
produce /prə'djuːs/ D3, E4
professional /prə'feʃənl/ A5
pronounce /prə'naʊns/ E5
pronounce: How do you pronounce ...?
  /'haʊ djə prə'naʊns/ A5, E5
pub /pʌb/ B5, D1
public transport /'pʌblɪk 'trænspɔːt/ B3
publish /'pʌblɪʃ/ C6
pull /pʊl/ B6, C4
pull down /'pʊl 'daʊn/ C6
pulled muscle /'pʊld 'mʌsl/ D7
purpose /'pɜːpəs/ A5
push /pʊʃ/ B6, D1
put* down /'pʊt 'daʊn/ B6
put* off ...ing /'pʊt 'ɒf/ C1
put* on /'pʊt 'ɒn/ B8
pyjamas /pə'dʒɑːməz/ E5
quality /'kwɒləti/ E4
quarrel (verb) /'kwɒrəl/ E2
queen /kwiːn/ C8
queue (noun) /kjuː/ D7
quick /kwɪk/ C4
quiet /kwaɪət/ B3
quite (= rather) /kwaɪt/ B7
rabbit /'ræbɪt/ A2, B8, C3
race (human type) /reɪs/ C7
railway station /'reɪlweɪ steɪʃn/ D5
rain (noun and verb) /reɪn/ E1
rainy /reɪni/ E1
rare /reə(r)/ E7
rat /ræt/ A2
rather /'rɑːðə(r)/ A3
reach /riːtʃ/ B4
reaction /ri'ækʃən/ E7
ready /'redi/ B5
real /riːl/ C8
realise /'rɪəlaɪz/ D8
really /'rɪəli/ D4
reason (for sth) /'riːzn fə/ A5
reasonable /'riːznəbl/ A4
rebuild* /'riː'bɪld/ C6
receptionist /rɪ'sepʃənɪst/ D2
record (verb) /rɪ'kɔːd/ C6
recover /rɪ'kʌvə(r)/ C4
recover (from sth) /rɪ'kʌvə frəm/ D4
red (hair) /red/ A1
refrigerator /rɪ'frɪdʒəreɪtə(r)/ C2
refund (noun) /'riːfʌnd/ C5
refuse /rɪ'fjuːz/ D1
regional /'riːdʒənl/ C8
relationship /rɪ'leɪʃənʃɪp/ C1
relative /'relətɪv/ D3
religion /rɪ'lɪdʒən/ C7
religious /rɪ'lɪdʒəs/ C7
remain /rɪ'meɪn/ E7
remember /rɪ'membə(r)/ A1
remind /rɪ'maɪnd/ A1
rent (verb) /rent/ E5
repair (verb) /rɪ'peə(r)/ C5, C6
replace /ri'pleɪs/ C5
reply (noun) /rɪ'plaɪ/ C7
report (verb) /rɪ'pɔːt/ D8
report (noun) /rɪ'pɔːt/ A5, D6, D8
Representative /'reprɪ'zentətɪv/ C8
Republicans /rɪ'pʌblɪkənz/ C8
request (noun) /rɪ'kwest/ E5
rescue /'reskjuː/ A8, B4
respect (verb) /rɪ'spekt/ C7

responsible /rɪ'spɒnsəbl/ C8
restaurant /'restrɒnt/ E5
retire /rɪ'taɪə(r)/ A3
rice /raɪs/ C3
rid: get* rid of sbdy/sth /'get 'rɪd əv/ C1
ride* /raɪd/ A8
riding: horse riding /'hɔːs 'raɪdɪŋ/ A6
right there /'raɪt 'ðeə(r)/ B1
right-wing /'raɪt 'wɪŋ/ C8
right: That's right /'ðæts 'raɪt/ B5
right: the right to do sth /ðə 'raɪt tə/ C7
ring (for finger) /rɪŋ/ C3, E6
ring (= phone call) /rɪŋ/ B7
ring* sbdy up /'rɪŋ ... 'ʌp/ E2
river /'rɪvə(r)/ D5, E2
road /rəʊd/ C8, D5
roast (verb) /rəʊst/ C6
robbery /'rɒbəri/ D1
roll (verb) /rəʊl/ B6
romantic /rəʊ'mæntɪk/ D3
roof /ruːf/ D2
round (adjective) /raʊnd/ E4
round: come round /'kʌm 'raʊnd/ E5
roundabout (road) /'raʊndəbaʊt/ D8
rub /rʌb/ C3
rubbish /'rʌbɪʃ/ B7
rugby football /'rʌgbi 'fʊtbɔːl/ A6
rule (noun) /ruːl/ A8, C7, D3, D6
ruler /ruːlə(r)/ E2
run* /rʌn/ D6
run* (sth) /rʌn/ D4
run* after /'rʌn 'ɑːftə(r)/ B4
running (sport) /'rʌnɪŋ/ A6
rush /rʌʃ/ D2
safe (adjective) /seɪf/ C3, E3
safety /'seɪfti/ C4
salary /'sæləri/ A4, C1
sale /seɪl/ E4
sale: for sale /fə 'seɪl/ E4
salt /sɔːlt, sɒlt/ B5
sandwich /'sæmwɪdʒ/ E5
sauce /sɔːs/ E5
saucepan /'sɔːspən/ C3, E2
save (from extinction) /seɪv/ E7
save (money) /seɪv/ E4
save (people) /seɪv/ C4
say* /seɪ/ E5
Say, ... (to change subject) /seɪ/ E5
say*: How do you say ... in English?
  /'haʊ djə 'seɪ/ A5, E5
say*: What do you say when ...?
  /'wɒt djə seɪ/ A5
scarf /skɑːf/ E6
scene /siːn/ E3
school leaver /'skuːl 'liːvə(r)/ D4
school: leave* school /'liːv 'skuːl/ A3
school: primary school
  /'praɪməri skuːl/ A3, A4
scissors /'sɪzəz/ E2
score /skɔː(r)/ B3
scratch /skrætʃ/ B6
scream (noun) /skriːm/ D1
scream (verb) /skriːm/ B1, D1
screwdriver /'skruːdraɪvə(r)/ E2
sea /siː/ E7
secondly /'sekəndli/ C5
secret /'siːkrɪt/ E2
security /sɪ'kjuːrəti/ B4
see*: I see /'aɪ 'siː/ A7
see*: Lovely/Nice to see you
  /'lʌvli tə 'siː juː/ B5

see*: Well, you see, it's like this /'wel, ju: 'si:/ — A7
Senate /'senət/ — C8
Senator /'senətə(r)/ — C8
send* /send/ — C6, E5
sentence /'sentəns/ — A5
sentence: Can you explain this sentence? /'kæn ju: ɪk'spleɪn/ — A5
separated /'sepəreɪtɪd/ — D3
separately /'seprətli/ — C8
serious /'sɪərɪəs/ — B3, E2
seriously /'sɪərɪəsli/ — C4, D4
serve /sɜːv/ — C6
service (e.g. fire service) /'sɜːvɪs/ — B1
sex (= male or female) /seks/ — D3
sex (= act of sex) /seks/ — B7
shake* /ʃeɪk/ — C3
Shall I ...? /'ʃæl aɪ/ — A7
share /ʃeə(r)/ — C1
share (sth with sbdy) /'ʃeə(r) ... wɪð/ — D3
sharp /ʃɑːp/ — E4
sharpen /'ʃɑːpn/ — B6
shine* /ʃaɪn/ — E1
shirt /ʃɜːt/ — E6
shock /ʃɒk/ — E2
shocked /ʃɒkt/ — E7
shoe /ʃuː/ — E6
shop assistant /'ʃɒp ə'sɪstənt/ — D1
shoplifting /'ʃɒplɪftɪŋ/ — B3
shopping /'ʃɒpɪŋ/ — C1
short (hair) /ʃɔːt/ — A1
short (person) /ʃɔːt/ — A1
short of money /'ʃɔːt əv 'mʌni/ — A7
shoulder /'ʃəʊldə(r)/ — D1, E6
shout (verb) /ʃaʊt/ — B4
show* /ʃəʊ/ — E5
shower /ʃaʊə(r)/ — E1
sign (noun) /saɪn/ — D8
sign (verb) /saɪn/ — B3
singing /'sɪŋɪŋ/ — A6
single /'sɪŋgl/ — D3
sister-in-law /'sɪstər ɪn lɔː/ — D3
site: camp site /'kæmp saɪt/ — E3
skating /'skeɪtɪŋ/ — A8
skiing /'skiːɪŋ/ — A6
skirt /skɜːt/ — E6
sky /skaɪ/ — E1
slice /slaɪs/ — B6
slightly /'slaɪtli/ — C8
slim /slɪm/ — A1
small /smɔːl/ — A1
small ad /'smɔːl æd/ — E4
smart /smɑːt/ — D8
smell* /smel/ — B8
smile (verb) /smaɪl/ — E3
smoke (noun) /sməʊk/ — B1
snake /sneɪk/ — D6
snow (noun) /snəʊ/ — A2, E1
snow (verb) /snəʊ/ — E1
so /səʊ/ — D3
sociable /'səʊʃəbl/ — B3
social /'səʊʃl/ — A5
society /sə'saɪəti/ — A4, D3
sock /sɒk/ — E6
socket /'sɒkɪt/ — C2
soldier /'səʊldʒə(r)/ — A4
sometimes /'sʌmtaɪmz/ — D7
somewhere else /'sʌmweər 'els/ — B5
son-in-law /'sʌn ɪn lɔː/ — D3
song /sɒŋ/ — A5
sore throat /'sɔː 'θrəʊt/ — D7

sorry: I'm sorry to trouble you /'sɒri ... 'trʌbl/ — A7
sorry: I really am very sorry /'rɪəli 'æm ... 'sɒri/ — C5
sort /sɔːt/ — B8
sort out /'sɔːt 'aʊt/ — C3
south /saʊθ/ — D5, E1
south-east /'saʊθ 'iːst/ — E1
south-west /'saʊθ 'west/ — E1
space /speɪs/ — D8
spade /speɪd/ — E2
speak* /spiːk/ — C6
special /'speʃl/ — E4
special: somewhere special /'sʌmweə 'speʃl/ — A1
specialist /'speʃəlɪst/ — A5
speed /spiːd/ — A5, E1
speed limit /'spiːd lɪmɪt/ — D8
spell: How do you spell ...? /'haʊ djə 'spel/ — A5
spelling /'spelɪŋ/ — A5
spend* time /'spend 'taɪm/ — D2, D3
spoil /spɔɪl/ — B8
spoon /spuːn/ — E5
spring (season) /sprɪŋ/ — E1
square (noun) /skweə(r)/ — D6
square (adjective) /skweə(r)/ — E4
squirrel /'skwɪrəl/ — A2
stain (noun) /steɪn/ — C3
stand* up /'stænd 'ʌp/ — D7
start: it won't start /ɪt 'wəʊnt 'stɑːt/ — C5
state /steɪt/ — C8
station: police station /pə'liːs steɪʃn/ — D5
station: railway station /'reɪlweɪ steɪʃn/ — D5
stay (with sbdy) /'steɪ wɪð/ — D6, E2
steak /steɪk/ — E5
steal* /stiːl/ — B1, B3, D1, E2
stereo: personal stereo /'pɜːsənl 'steriəʊ/ — C2
stick (noun) /stɪk/ — D6
stomach /'stʌmək/ — A2
store: department store /dɪ'pɑːtmənt stɔː(r)/ — B4
story /'stɔːri/ — B4, E3
straight /streɪt/ — A1
straight ahead: go*/keep*straight ahead /'streɪt ə'hed/ — D5
straight on: go*/keep* straight on /'streɪt 'ɒn/ — D5
strange /streɪndʒ/ — B3, E3
stranger /'streɪndʒə(r)/ — E2
stream /striːm/ — D5
string /strɪŋ/ — E2
stuck /stʌk/ — B4, C5
stuff /stʌf/ — B8, E4
stupid /'stjuːpɪd/ — B5, E2
stupid: How stupid of me! /'haʊ 'stjuːpɪd/ — B5
subject /'sʌbdʒɪkt/ — A5
succeed /sək'siːd/ — D3
success /sək'ses/ — D7
successfully /sək'sesfʊli/ — A8, E7
sudden /'sʌdn/ — D4
suggestion /sə'dʒestʃən/ — A5
suit (noun) /suːt/ — B4
suitable /'suːtəbl/ — A5
suitcase /'suːtkeɪs/ — B8
summer /'sʌmə(r)/ — E1
sun /sʌn/ — E1
sunny /'sʌni/ — E1
sunshine /'sʌnʃaɪn/ — A2, E1

supper /'sʌpə(r)/ — E3
supply (sth; sbdy with sth) /sə'plaɪ/ — E7
sure /ʃɔː(r)/ — B3
Sure (informal agreement) /ʃɔː(r)/ — A7
surprise: I'd be surprised if ... /sə'praɪzd/ — C7
surprised /sə'praɪzd/ — C7
survive /sə'vaɪv/ — E7
swimming /'swɪmɪŋ/ — A6
swimming pool /'swɪmɪŋ puːl/ — D5
swing* (verb) /swɪŋ/ — B6
switch (noun) /swɪtʃ/ — C2
switch (verb) /swɪtʃ/ — A8
switch off /'swɪtʃ 'ɒf/ — B6, C2
switch on /'swɪtʃ 'ɒn/ — B6, C2
T-shirt /'tiː ʃɜːt/ — E6
tablet /'tæblɪt/ — D7
take* the first left / second right / etc. /teɪk/ — D5
take* (sth) up /'teɪk ... 'ʌp/ — A8
take* part in /'teɪk 'pɑːt ɪn/ — A8
talk (sth) over /'tɔːk ... 'əʊvə(r)/ — C7
tall /tɔːl/ — A1
taste (verb) /teɪst/ — B8
tax /tæks/ — B3
tea: make (a cup of) tea /'meɪk 'tiː/ — C1
teach* /tiːtʃ/ — E5
tear* /teə(r)/ — B6
technical manual /'teknɪkl 'mænjuːəl/ — A5
tell* /tel/ — D7
tell* lies /'tel 'laɪz/ — B3
tell*: Can you tell me the way to ...? /'kæn ju: 'tel miː/ — D5
temperature /'temprɪtʃə(r)/ — E1
tend /tend/ — A4
tennis /'tenɪs/ — A6, D6
tent /tent/ — E3
terrible /'terəbl/ — B1, E2
Thank you for coming /'θæŋk juː/ — B7
Thanks /θæŋks/ — A7, E5
thanks: Yeah, thanks /'jeə 'θæŋks/ — A7
That would be very nice /naɪs/ — A7
That's all right /'ðæts 'ɔːl 'raɪt/ — A7, C5
That's right /'ðæts 'raɪt/ — B5
That's very kind of you /kaɪnd/ — A7, E5
That's very nice of you /naɪs/ — A7
That's very strange /streɪndʒ/ — C5
the (1930)s /'naɪntiːn 'θɜːtɪz/ — E3
the other night /ðɪ 'ʌðə 'naɪt/ — D4
the thing is /ðe 'θɪŋ 'ɪz/ — A7
the whole time /ðə 'həʊl 'taɪm/ — D7
theatre /'θɪətə(r)/ — D5
There's nothing wrong in ...ing /'nʌθɪŋ 'rɒŋ/ — C7
thief (thieves) /θiːf, θiːvz/ — B4
thin /θɪn/ — A1
thing /θɪŋ/ — B8
think* about sbdy/sth /'θɪŋk ə'baʊt/ — D6
thirdly /'θɜːdli/ — C5
this way (instruction) /'ðɪs 'weɪ/ — A7
threaten /'θretn/ — D1, E7
throat: a sore throat /'sɔː 'θrəʊt/ — D7
through (preposition) /θruː/ — D5
through: go through a red light /'gəʊ 'θruː/ — D8
throw* /θrəʊ/ — B6, D6
thumb /θʌm/ — A2
thunder /'θʌndə(r)/ — A2, E1
thunderstorm /'θʌndəstɔːm/ — C3, E1
ticket /'tɪkɪt/ — B3
tidy (adjective) /'taɪdi/ — C1
tidy (verb) /'taɪdi/ — B8

141

tie (noun) /taɪ/ — E6
tie (verb) /taɪ/ — B6
tight /taɪt/ — C3
tights /taɪts/ — E6
till (noun) /tɪl/ — D1
time: all the time /ˈɔːl ðə ˈtaɪm/ — D7
time: at a time /ət ə ˈtaɪm/ — E1
time: free time /ˈfriː ˈtaɪm/ — A3
time: the whole time /ðə ˈhəʊl ˈtaɪm/ — D7
times: two or three times a (year) /ˈtaɪmz ə ˈjɪə/ — D7
timetable /ˈtaɪmteɪbl/ — E5
tip (= advice) /tɪp/ — C3
tired /taɪəd/ — B8
toaster /ˈtəʊstə(r)/ — C2
toe /təʊ/ — A2
together /təˈɡeðə(r)/ — D3
tongue /tʌŋ/ — A2
tonsilitis /tɒnsəˈlaɪtəs/ — D7
tool /tuːl/ — E4
toothbrush /ˈtuːθbrʌʃ/ — E2
top: at the top of (her) voice /ˈtɒp əv ... ˈvɔɪs/ — D1
top: on top of /ɒn ˈtɒp əv/ — C1
torch /tɔːtʃ/ — B3, C2, E2
touch (verb) /tʌtʃ/ — B6, D6
tough /tʌf/ — A8, B8
towel /taʊl/ — B3, E2
town /taʊn/ — A8, B4
town hall /ˈtaʊn ˈhɔːl/ — D5
traffic /ˈtræfɪk/ — C4, D8
traffic lights /ˈtræfɪk laɪts/ — D8
training /ˈtreɪnɪŋ/ — A8
trap (verb) /træp/ — C4
travel (noun) /ˈtrævl/ — A5
travel (verb) /ˈtrævl/ — B8, D6, E3
trick (noun and verb) /trɪk/ — B4
trip /trɪp/ — D8
trip: business trip /ˈbɪznɪs trɪp/ — E2
tropical forest /ˈtrɒpɪkl ˈfɒrɪst/ — E7
trouble: back trouble /ˈbæk trʌbl/ — D7
trouble: get* into trouble /ˈɡet ɪntə ˈtrʌbl/ — C1
trouble: have* trouble with sth /ˈhæv ˈtrʌbl wɪð/ — E2
trouble: I'm sorry to trouble you /ˈsɒri tə ˈtrʌbl/ — A7
trouble: What's the trouble? /ˈwɒts ðə ˈtrʌbl/ — C5
trousers /ˈtraʊzəz/ — B4, E6
true /truː/ — D5
trust (verb) /trʌst/ — C7
truth /truːθ/ — E5
try /traɪ/ — D6
try ...ing /traɪ/ — C7
try on /ˈtraɪ ˈɒn/ — B4
tumble dryer /ˈtʌmbl draɪə(r)/ — C2
turn /tɜːn/ — B6
turn into /ˈtɜːn ˈɪntə/ — C6
turn left/right at ... /ˈtɜːn ˈleft, ˈraɪt/ — D5
turn off /ˈtɜːn ˈɒf/ — B1
turn up (= arrive) /ˈtɜːn ˈʌp/ — A8
turn up/down /tɜːn ʌp, daʊn/ — C2
TV /ˈtiː ˈviː/ — C1
twin(s) /twɪn(z)/ — B8
two or three times a (year) /ˈtaɪmz ə/ — D7
typewriter /ˈtaɪpraɪtə(r)/ — B8
umbrella /ʌmˈbrelə/ — D1, E2
uncle /ˈʌŋkl/ — D3
undecided /ˈʌndɪˈsaɪdɪd/ — D4
underground (adjective) /ˈʌndəˈɡraʊnd/ — D8

understand* /ˈʌndəˈstænd/ — E5
unemployed /ˈʌnɪmˈplɔɪd/ — C1
unexpected /ˈʌnɪkˈspektɪd/ — A3
unfair /ˈʌnˈfeə(r)/ — D3
unfortunately /ʌnˈfɔːtʃənətli/ — C3
university /ˈjuːnɪˈvɜːsəti/ — D8
unplug /ˈʌnˈplʌɡ/ — C2
unusual /ʌnˈjuːʒuːʊl/ — A8, E2, E3
up (preposition) /ʌp/ — D5
upper body /ˈʌpə ˈbɒdi/ — E6
upset /ˈʌpˈset/ — D7
upstairs /ˈʌpˈsteəz/ — B1, C1
use (verb) /juːz/ — B8, E5
use: Can I use ... /ˈkæn aɪ ˈjuːz/ — A7
useful /ˈjuːsfʊl/ — C3
useless /ˈjuːsləs/ — C5
usually /ˈjuːʒəli/ — D7, E6
vacuum cleaner /ˈvækjuːəm kliːnə(r)/ — C2
valley /ˈvæli/ — D5
valuable /ˈvæljəbl/ — B3, E2
value /ˈvæljuː/ — A4, E4
varied /ˈveərɪd/ — A3
vehicle /ˈvɪəkl/ — C4
via /ˈvaɪə/ — C4
victim /ˈvɪktɪm/ — D1
village /ˈvɪlɪdʒ/ — A3
vinegar /ˈvɪnɪɡə(r)/ — C3
violence /ˈvaɪələns/ — B7
violently /ˈvaɪələntli/ — E2
vocabulary /vəˈkæbjələri/ — A5
voice: at the top of (her) voice /ˈtɒp əv ... ˈvɔɪs/ — D1
vote /vəʊt/ — A4
wage /weɪdʒ/ — A4
waist /weɪst/ — E6
wall /wɔːl/ — D2, D8
wallet /ˈwɒlɪt/ — B3, B4
Want (a drink)? /ˈwɒnt ə ˈdrɪŋk/ — A7
want: Do you want to ...? /dju: ˈwɒnt tə/ — A7
war /wɔː(r)/ — A4
warm /wɔːm/ — B1, E1
wash (noun) /wɒʃ/ — A7
wash (verb) /wɒʃ/ — C6
washing /ˈwɒʃɪŋ/ — C1
washing machine /ˈwɒʃɪŋ məˈʃiːn/ — C2
wasp /wɒsp/ — C3
waste (time/money) /ˈweɪst ˈtaɪm, ˈmʌni/ — C1
watch /wɒtʃ/ — E6
water /ˈwɔːtə(r)/ — E5
waterfall /ˈwɔːtəfɔːl/ — D5
wavy /ˈweɪvi/ — A1
way: Can you tell me the way to ...? /ˈtel mi ðə ˈweɪ/ — D5
way: on our way /ˈɒn aʊə ˈweɪ/ — B7
way: this way /ˈðɪs ˈweɪ/ — A7
We ought to be on our way /ˈɒn aʊə ˈweɪ/ — B7
We'd better be going /wiːd ˈbetə/ — B7
We'll be right there /ˈraɪt ˈðeə/ — B1
wear* /weə(r)/ — D7
weather /ˈweðə(r)/ — E1
weather forecast /ˈweðə ˈfɔːkɑːst/ — E1
weekday /ˈwiːkdeɪ/ — B5
weight /weɪt/ — A1
Well, I didn't exactly ... /ɪɡˈzæktli/ — A1
Well, thank you very much /ˈθæŋk juː/ — A7
Well, you see, it's like this /ˈlaɪk ˈðɪs/ — A7
well-known /ˈwel ˈnəʊn/ — D2
west /west/ — D5, E1
wet /wet/ — E1

What? (= Pardon?) /wɒt/ — E5
What are these? /ˈwɒt ə ˈðiːz/ — A5
What can I get you to drink? /ˈwɒt k(ə)n aɪ/ — B5
What do you say when ...? /ˈwɒt djə ˈseɪ/ — A5
What does ... mean? /ˈwɒt dəz ... ˈmiːn/ — A5, E5
what ... like /ˈwɒt ... ˈlaɪk/ — E1
What's the matter? /ˈwɒts ðə ˈmætə(r)/ — A7
What's the English for ...? /ˈwɒts ðiː ˈɪŋɡlɪʃ fə(r)/ — A5
What's the trouble? /ˈwɒts ðə ˈtrʌbl/ — C5
What's this? /ˈwɒts ˈðɪs/ — A5
What's this called? /ˈwɒts ˈðɪs ˈkɔːld/ — E5
What's this called in English? /ˈwɒts ˈðɪs ˈkɔːld/ — A5
whether /ˈweðə(r)/ — C5
Who else? /ˈhuː ˈels/ — B5
whole: the whole time /ðə ˈhəʊl ˈtaɪm/ — D7
whose /huːz/ — B7
Why don't you ...? /ˈwaɪ ˈdəʊnt juː/ — C7
wide /waɪd/ — A5
wife (wives) /waɪf, waɪvz/ — A3, D3
win* /wɪn/ — D6
wind (noun) /wɪnd/ — A2, E1
window /ˈwɪndəʊ/ — B8
windy /ˈwɪndi/ — E1
wine /waɪn/ — B5
winter /ˈwɪntə(r)/ — E1
witness /ˈwɪtnɪs/ — D1
wonder (verb) /ˈwʌndə(r)/ — A7, B4, D2, E2
wonder: I/we wonder(ed) if I/we/you could ...? /aɪ ˈwʌndəd/ — A7
wonderful /ˈwʌndəfʊl/ — D4, E2
won't: it won't start /ɪt ˈwəʊnt ˈstɑːt/ — C5
wood (place) /wʊd/ — D5, E3
word: Can you explain this word? /ˈkæn juː ɪksˈpleɪn/ — A5
work (noun) /wɜːk/ — A4
work: it doesn't work /ɪt ˈdʌznt ˈwɜːk/ — C5
World War II /ˈwɜːld ˈwɔː ˈtuː/ — E3
worried /ˈwʌrɪd/ — A8, C7, E6
worse /wɜːs/ — B5
worth: It's (not) worth ...ing /ɪts ˈnɒt ˈwɜːθ/ — C7, D6
worth: it's not worth it /ɪts ˈnɒt ˈwɜːθ ɪt/ — C7
Would you like ...? /ˈwʊd juː ˈlaɪk/ — A7
Would you like to ... /ˈwʊd juː ˈlaɪk tə/ — A7
Would you mind ...ing /ˈwʊd juː ˈmaɪnd/ — A7
wrist /rɪst/ — B8, E6
write* /raɪt/ — E5
wrong /rɒŋ/ — B3
wrong: There's nothing wrong in ...ing /ðəz ˈnʌθɪŋ ˈrɒŋ/ — C7
wrong number /ˈrɒŋ ˈnʌmbə(r)/ — C6
Yeah, thanks /ˈjeə ˈθæŋks/ — A7
years: the (1930)s /ðə ˈnaɪntiːn ˈθɜːtɪz/ — E3
Yes, all right /ˈjes ˈɔːl ˈraɪt/ — A7
Yes, of course /ˈjes əv ˈkɔːs/ — E5
Yes, OK /ˈjes ˈəʊ ˈkeɪ/ — A7
Yes, sure /ˈjes ˈʃɔː/ — E5
You can either ... or ... /ˈaɪðə(r), ˈiːðə(r)/ — C7
You know (Lucy), don't you? /juː ˈnəʊ/ — B5
zoo /zuː/ — E7

Acknowledgements

The authors and publishers are grateful to the following copyright owners for permission to reproduce photographs, illustrations, text and music. Every endeavour has been made to contact copyright owners and apologies are expressed for any omissions.

page 20: from the *Longman Active Study Dictionary of English* edited by Della Summers. Longman 1983. page 24: Exercise 5 from *Discussions that Work* by Penny Ur, Cambridge University Press 1981. page 24: 'Buckets of Money' advertisement reproduced by permission of Glo-Leisure Ltd. page 25: "Now if the passengers ..." from *Weekend Book of Jokes 22*, reprinted by permission of Harmsworth Publications. "How to eat while reading" and "Your bath's ready, dear" reproduced by permission of *Punch*. page 27: William Davis' article reproduced by permission of *Punch*. page 29: SOS Emergency calls panel reproduced by permission of BT. page 33: "Souvenirs" and "Don't lie to me" reproduced by permission of *Punch*. page 43: 'Elephants are Different to Different People' from *The Complete Poems of Carl Sandburg*, Revised and Expanded Edition, copyright 1950 by Carl Sandburg and renewed 1978 by Margaret Sandburg, Helga Sandburg Crile and Janet Sandburg, reprinted by permission of Harcourt Brace Jovanovich, Inc. page 47: Exercise 9 from *Discussions that Work* by Penny Ur, Cambridge University Press 1981. page 49: The extract from *Family News*, by Joan Barfoot, reprinted by arrangement with The Women's Press, Macmillan of Canada and Bella Pomer Agency Inc. page 60: cartoon reproduced by permission of *Punch*. page 65: from the *Longman Active Study Dictionary of English* edited by Della Summers, Longman 1983. page 69: cartoons reproduced by permission of *Punch*. page 85: "It's a pity ..." by Gax from *Weekend Book of Jokes 21* reprinted by permission of Harmsworth Publications. "I wish you'd called me sooner" reproduced by permission of *Punch*. page 91: 'Meditatio', taken from *Collected Shorter Poems* by Ezra Pound, published by Faber & Faber Ltd; and from *Personae*, copyright 1926 by Ezra Pound. Reprinted by permission of New Directions Publishing Corporation. page 93: 'Fag end of the evening' article reproduced by permission of United Press International Ltd. page 100: magazine covers reprinted by permission of IPC Magazines Ltd. page 101: recording for Exercise 4 and page 114: recording for Exercise 1 by permission of GWR-FM Radio, a commercial radio station covering part of the South West of England. Weather report (Exercise 1) also by permission of the Met. Office, Bristol Weather Centre. page 104: "The postman's in one of his moods again" reprinted by permission of Harmsworth Publications. page 105: Exercise 7 from *A Way with Words 1* by Stuart Redman and Robert Ellis, Cambridge University Press 1989. page 114: "Today's Special", "Good morning, Mr Dolby!" and "The committee on women's rights" reproduced by permission of *Punch*. page 117: "Come in, Ferguson" reproduced by permission of *Punch*. page 121: "No, he's not ours!" reproduced by permission of *Punch*. page 129: "You were the World's Best Baby" and "The best thing about working here" reproduced by permission of *Punch*. page 134: 'Little old lady in knife raid' report from the *Oxford Mail*, by permission.

Steve Hall (music and lyrics) for *Private Detective* (Lesson A1, Exercise 6, page 7); *Do you know* (Lesson B8, Exercise 5, page 43); *So near yet so far* (Lesson D3, Exercise 8, page 77); *Thirty degrees* (Lesson E1, Exercise 8, page 95). Jonathan Dykes (lyrics) and Robert Campbell (music) for *The Island* (Lesson D5, Exercise 8, page 81).

The authors and publishers are grateful to the following illustrators and photographic sources:

Kathy Baxendale, pages 6, 31*t*, 47, 53, 86, 92. Peter Byatt, pages 42 and 43, 74, 80*t*, 83, 101. Celia Chester, pages 31*b*, 52, 59, 97. Anthony Colbert, page 54. Tony Coles (*John Hodgson*), pages 17, 28, 35, 50, 51, 75, 87. Katherine Dickinson, pages 34 and 35. David Downton, pages 39, 72 and 73, 76 and 77. Andrew Harris, page 96. Lorraine Harrison, pages 81, 94, 95. Sue Hillwood Harris, pages 62, 78. Nigel Hawtin, page 106. Kiki Lewis (*Meiklejohn*), pages 8 and 9. Edward McLachlan, pages 14, 55, 80*c*. Michael Ogden, pages 19, 61, 114. Caroline Porter, pages 108 and 109. Felicity Roma Bowers, pages 12 and 13. Chris Ryley, pages 7, 116, 119, 122, 125, 127. Peter Sutton, pages 98 and 99. Peter Tucker, page 57. Kathy Ward, pages 16, 36 and 37, 40 and 41, 102 and 103. Jack Wood, page 80*b*.

Allsport UK Ltd, page 90*l*. Animal Photography, page 90*b*. The Bettman Archive, page 64*t*. John Birdsall, page 56*tr*. Kevin Burton, page 21*b*. Andrew Campbell, page 20*c*. Central Office of Information: page 64*b*. Garrard and Co. Ltd, page 10*t*, 90*r*. Susan Griggs Agency, pages 20 and 21. The Image Bank, page 11, 56*tl*. The Image Bank / Stockphotos, page 10*b*, 90*c*. Peter Jordan / Network, page 56*br*. The Photographer's Library, page 107. Pictor International, pages 64 and 65, 106. Picturepoint-London, page 86. Popperfoto, page 56*bl*. Graham Portlock, pages 6 and 7, 15, 69, 82, 100 and 101, 108 and 109. John Ridley, pages 18, 55, 58, 59, 105. Rolls-Royce Motor Cars Ltd, page 10*c*.

Picture research by Sandie Huskinson-Rolfe (PHOTO-SEEKERS)
Photographs on pages 6 and 7, 15, 108 and 109 taken on location at the Bell School of Languages, Cambridge.

(*t* = top *b* = bottom *c* = centre *r* = right *l* = left)

Phonetic symbols

Vowels

symbol	example
/iː/	eat /iːt/
/i/	happy /'hæpi/
/ɪ/	it /ɪt/
/e/	when /wen/
/æ/	cat /kæt/
/ɑː/	hard /hɑːd/
/ɒ/	not /nɒt/
/ɔː/	sort /sɔːt/; all /ɔːl/
/ʊ/	look /lʊk/
/uː/	too /tuː/
/ʌ/	cup /kʌp/
/ɜː/	first /fɜːst/; burn /bɜːn/
/ə/	about /ə'baʊt/; mother /'mʌðə(r)/
/eɪ/	day /deɪ/
/aɪ/	my /maɪ/
/ɔɪ/	boy /bɔɪ/
/aʊ/	now /naʊ/
/əʊ/	go /gəʊ/
/ɪə/	here /hɪə(r)/
/eə/	chair /tʃeə(r)/
/ʊə/	tourist /'tʊərɪst/

Consonants

symbol	example
/p/	pen /pen/
/b/	big /bɪg/
/t/	two /tuː/
/d/	day /deɪ/
/k/	keep /kiːp/; cup /kʌp/
/g/	get /get/
/tʃ/	choose /tʃuːz/
/dʒ/	job /dʒɒb/; average /'ævrɪdʒ/
/f/	fall /fɔːl/
/v/	very /'veri/
/θ/	think /θɪŋk/
/ð/	then /ðen/
/s/	see /siː/
/z/	zoo /zuː/; is /ɪz/
/ʃ/	shop /ʃɒp/; directions /də'rekʃənz/
/ʒ/	pleasure /'pleʒə(r)/; occasionally /ə'keɪʒənli/
/h/	who /huː/; how /haʊ/
/m/	meet /miːt/
/n/	no /nəʊ/
/ŋ/	sing /sɪŋ/; drink /drɪŋk/
/l/	long /lɒŋ/
/r/	right /raɪt/
/j/	yes /jes/
/w/	will /wɪl/

Stress

Stress is shown by a mark (') in front of the stressed syllable.
mother /'mʌðə(r)/   average /'ævrɪdʒ/
about /ə'baʊt/   tonight /tə'naɪt/

Irregular verbs

Infinitive	Simple Past	Participle
be /biː/	was /wəz, wɒz/, were /wə(r), wɜː(r)/	been /bɪn, biːn/
become /bɪ'kʌm/	became /bɪ'keɪm/	become /bɪ'kʌm/
begin /bɪ'gɪn/	began /bɪ'gæn/	begun /bɪ'gʌn/
bend /bend/	bent /bent/	bent /bent/
bet /bet/	bet /bet/	bet /bet/
bite /baɪt/	bit /bɪt/	bitten /'bɪtn/
bleed /bliːd/	bled /bled/	bled /bled/
blow /bləʊ/	blew /bluː/	blown /bləʊn/
break /breɪk/	broke /brəʊk/	broken /'brəʊkn/
bring /brɪŋ/	brought /brɔːt/	brought /brɔːt/
build /bɪld/	built /bɪlt/	built /bɪlt/
burn /bɜːn/	burnt /bɜːnt/	burnt /bɜːnt/
buy /baɪ/	bought /bɔːt/	bought /bɔːt/
can /k(ə)n, kæn/	could /kʊd/	been able /bɪn 'eɪbl/
catch /kætʃ/	caught /kɔːt/	caught /kɔːt/
choose /tʃuːz/	chose /tʃəʊz/	chosen /'tʃəʊzn/
come /kʌm/	came /keɪm/	come /kʌm/
cost /kɒst/	cost /kɒst/	cost /kɒst/
cut /kʌt/	cut /kʌt/	cut /kʌt/
do /dʊ, də, duː/	did /dɪd/	done /dʌn/
draw /drɔː/	drew /druː/	drawn /drɔːn/
dream /driːm/	dreamt /dremt/	dreamt /dremt/
drink /drɪŋk/	drank /dræŋk/	drunk /drʌŋk/
drive /draɪv/	drove /drəʊv/	driven /'drɪvn/
eat /iːt/	ate /et/	eaten /'iːtn/
earn /ɜːn/	earnt /ɜːnt/	earnt /ɜːnt/
fall /fɔːl/	fell /fel/	fallen /'fɔːlən/
feed /fiːd/	fed /fed/	fed /fed/
feel /fiːl/	felt /felt/	felt /felt/
fight /faɪt/	fought /fɔːt/	fought /fɔːt/
find /faɪnd/	found /faʊnd/	found /faʊnd/
fly /flaɪ/	flew /fluː/	flown /fləʊn/
forget /fə'get/	forgot /fə'gɒt/	forgotten /fə'gɒtn/
get /get/	got /gɒt/	got /gɒt/
give /gɪv/	gave /geɪv/	given /'gɪvn/
go /gəʊ/	went /went/	gone /gɒn/, been /bɪn, biːn/
grow /grəʊ/	grew /gruː/	grown /grəʊn/
hang up /'hæŋ 'ʌp/	hung up /'hʌŋ 'ʌp/	hung up /'hʌŋ 'ʌp/
have /(h)əv, hæv/	had /(h)əd, hæd/	had /hæd/
hear /hɪə(r)/	heard /hɜːd/	heard /hɜːd/
hide /haɪd/	hid /hɪd/	hidden /'hɪdn/
hit /hɪt/	hit /hɪt/	hit /hɪt/
hold /həʊld/	held /held/	held /held/
hurt /hɜːt/	hurt /hɜːt/	hurt /hɜːt/
keep /kiːp/	kept /kept/	kept /kept/
know /nəʊ/	knew /njuː/	known /nəʊn/
lead /liːd/	led /led/	led /led/
learn /lɜːn/	learnt /lɜːnt/	learnt /lɜːnt/
leave /liːv/	left /left/	left /left/
lend /lend/	lent /lent/	lent /lent/
lie /laɪ/	lay /leɪ/	lain /leɪn/
lose /luːz/	lost /lɒst/	lost /lɒst/
make /meɪk/	made /meɪd/	made /meɪd/
mean /miːn/	meant /ment/	meant /ment/
meet /miːt/	met /met/	met /met/
must /məst, mʌst/	had to /'hæd tə/	had to /'hæd tə/
overtake /'əʊvə'teɪk/	overtook /'əʊvə'tʊk/	overtaken /'əʊvə'teɪkn/
pay /peɪ/	paid /peɪd/	paid /peɪd/
put /pʊt/	put /pʊt/	put /pʊt/
read /riːd/	read /red/	read /red/
rebuild /'riː'bɪld/	rebuilt /'riː'bɪlt/	rebuilt /'riː'bɪlt/